AGRARIAN REFORM
& PUBLIC ENTERPRISE
IN MEXICO

The Political

Economy of

Yucatán's

Henequen

Industry

AGRARIAN REFORM & PUBLIC ENTERPRISE IN MEXICO

JEFFERY BRANNON

ERIC N. BAKLANOFF

The University

of Alabama Press

WITH A FOREWORD BY

EDWARD H. MOSELEY

Copyright © 1987 by
The University of Alabama Press
Tuscaloosa, Alabama 35487

Manufactured in the United States of America

Published with the support of the Alfredo
Barrera Vasquez Institute for Yucatecan Studies,
The University of Alabama

Designed by Laury A. Egan

LIBRARY OF CONGRESS CATALOGING-IN-PUBLICATION DATA

Brannon, Jeffery.
   Agrarian reform and public enterprise in Mexico.

   Bibliography: p.
   Includes index.
   1. Henequen industry—Mexico—Yucatán—History.
2. Yucatán (Mexico)—Rural conditions.   3. Land
Reform—Mexico—Yucatán—History.   I. Baklanoff, Eric N.
II. Title
HD9156.H463M63 1987   333.3′1′7265   85–24506
ISBN 0-8173-0282-4 (alk. paper)

For Sue
　　　JTB

For Joy
　　　ENB

Contents

Tables and Illustrations

ix

Foreword

▲▲

THE MENTION of Yucatán evokes a vision of ancient Mayan ceremonial centers like Uxmal and Chichen Itzá. The region is shrouded in mystery and legend embellished even more by the propaganda of modern tourism promotions. In recent years, however, scholars in both Mexico and the United States have penetrated behind the legend with serious investigations in a number of academic disciplines that have given valuable insight into this complex and fascinating region. The work of Brannon and Baklanoff is one example of this scholarship, and it makes an important contribution to the better understanding of Yucatán and Mexico as a whole.

From about 1880 to 1917, Yucatán was the most wealthy state in the Mexican Republic. The city of Mérida was famous for its clean streets and magnificent classical buildings. Its wealth and splendor were based upon fields of henequen plants that stretched as far as the eye could see in the surrounding countryside. Haciendas were marked by the tall smokestacks of the plants that furnished steam power to run the heavy defibrating machinery, as well as by elegant country homes. In many ways, the henequen haciendas resembled the cotton plantations of our own antebellum South. Just as the latter system was based upon slave labor, Yucatecan agriculture was dependent upon peonage. John Kenneth Turner, writing in 1911, described the darker side of the institution as *"Barbarous Mexico."* More recently, the powerful murals of artist Fernando Castro Pacheco have graphically depicted the evils of the system, showing the peon being crucified on the spiny henequen plant.

Yucatán escaped the violence of the early phases of the Mexican Revolution, which erupted in 1910. But outside pressure forced the abolition of peonage, and, after 1934, Lázaro Cárdenas imposed agrarian reform on the peninsula in one fell swoop. The haciendas were broken up, and land was distributed to villagers in the *ejido* system. Traditional communal village forms were to be extended to henequen cultivation, and thus workers were to share in the production and profits. The federal government's control over the henequen industry was extended with the nationalization of the private cordage mills in the early 1960s, culminating in a public enterprise called Cordemex.

Unfortunately for the *ejidatario*, the ideals of the revolution have never been realized. The former peons have not been emancipated from the soil, but remain firmly bound by the cords of the henequen plant and the government agrarian bank. Equally as serious, the formerly prosperous cordage industry has fallen on extremely difficult times. The ejidatarios are forced to live on a shrinking governmental subsidy, and the henequen empire, once so prosperous and flourishing, has become a burden for Yucatán and for the nation.

Although this study focuses upon the henequen-based economy of Yucatán, it is a case study of an attempt to move from a commercial plantation economy to a system of community-based, government-controlled agricultural enterprise in which decisions are often made on the basis of political expediency rather than economic rationalization.

President Miguel de la Madrid is presently attempting to readjust the nation's economy to cope with its huge external debt and the inflation that threaten the political stability and social system on which the Revolutionary party is based. The fate of the henequen industry in Yucatán may well be a key in this process. The work of Brannon and Baklanoff furnishes an important background for an analysis of the grave economic crisis that Mexico faces in the 1980s.

EDWARD H. MOSELEY

Preface

▲▲▲▲▲▲▲▲▲▲▲▲▲▲▲▲▲▲▲▲▲▲▲▲▲▲▲▲▲▲▲▲▲▲▲▲▲▲▲

DURING Yucatán's Golden Age, the "henequen zone," the northwestern quadrant of the state, developed into a compact region of intense economic activity. Unlike other plantation economies in Latin America and the Caribbean, in Yucatán local entrepreneurs (instead of foreign investors) initiated, owned, and maintained control over their plantations and railroads as well as most of their public utilities. In contrast to other plantation areas, in 1910 the state had in place a machine industry that was linked to the agroindustrial henequen plantations. Local machine shops and foundries had acquired the capability to build steam engines and defibration equipment and even to improve upon their design. In the mid-1920s, a forwardly-linked, modern cordage industry was initiated in Mérida, the state's capital. The cordage factories, serving both domestic and North American markets, manufactured harvest twine, cables, ropes, and other henequen products. Among the leading national producers of hard fiber in the early 1960s—Brazil, Tanzania, the Philippines, and Mexico—only Yucatán, in Mexico, possessed a large export-oriented cordage industry.

By expropriating the family-owned plantations in the 1930s and nationalizing the private cordage mills in 1964, the Mexican government profoundly altered the henequen industry's organization and incentive structure. By 1970 two federal enterprises, the Banrural (which supervises and finances the collective *ejidos*) and Cordemex (the nationalized multiplant cordage enterprise) dominated the state's economy.

Yucatán offers social scientists an excellent regional perspective for analyzing and evaluating social reforms initiated after the Mexican Revolution. First, scholars interested in radical land-tenure changes can compare the Yucatecan experience with that of other nations which have experimented with collectivization of agriculture. Second, as a region exhibiting intense sectional

xiii

pride, it provides an appropriate setting for the study of federal-state relations. Finally, our analysis of Banrural and Cordemex will be of particular value to students of public enterprise economics.

Our interest in the theme of this book, federal intervention in Mexico's Yucatán-based henequen industry, was kindled through our association with The University of Alabama's field course entitled "Yucatán: Past and Present." Since its inception in the spring of 1972, more than four hundred students and faculty members have participated in this annual interdisciplinary Interim Program, and it has been the motivating force behind numerous scholarly publications, master's theses, and one doctoral dissertation.

In 1981 Governor Francisco Luna Kan decreed May 24–29 to be the "Week of Alabama in Yucatán," celebrating the fifty years of relationships between The University of Alabama and the people of Yucatán. This link had been initiated in the 1930s by the work of Professor Asael T. Hansen, of the university's Department of Anthropology, who contributed to the classic studies of Robert Redfield.

During our several visits to Yucatán, a number of individuals were very helpful to us: Lic. Rodolfo Ruz Menendez, director of the University of Yucatán's library; Ing. José Luis Ponce Garcia, president of the National Confederation of Industrial Chambers in Yucatán; Lic. Pedro Ignacio Manzanilla, former vice-president of Cordeleros de Mexico and erstwhile owner of Henequen Industrial, S.A.; José Martin Perez, director of industrial production for Cordemex; Srta. Ana Rosa Caracashian; Lic. Roldan Peniche Barrera; Lic. Eduardo Seijo Gutierrez; Professor Russel Ramón Vallejo Sanchez; and Francisco Anda Vela, director of the computer bank of the Centro de Investigaciones Regionales "Dr. Hideyo Noguchi."

We acknowledge a special debt of gratitude to Dr. Eduardo Tello Solís, former secretary of education and social affairs for the state of Yucatán, and Ing. Manuel Mier y Terán, previously state secretary of planning. Other individuals who helped us during the research phase of this volume include Dr. Allen Wells, of Appalachian State University; Dr. Thomas Sanders, of University Field Staff International; and Mr. William Terry, former sales representative in North America for Henequen Industrial, S.A.

We wish to thank Dr. Gilbert M. Joseph, professor of history at the University of North Carolina at Chapel Hill, who read the manuscript in its entirety, for his perceptive criticisms and valuable comments.

We are grateful to the editors of the *Journal of Developing Areas, SECOLAS Annals,* and *World Development* for their permission to publish in modified form portions of previously published articles. Thanks are extended also to The University of Alabama's Research Grants Committee for financial assistance in support of this and related research projects in Yucatán.

Dr. Ronald Hasty, dean of the School of Business Administration, and Dr. Oscar Martinez, director of the Center for Inter-American and Border Studies, both of the University of Texas at El Paso, also provided valuable financial and moral support during critical stages of manuscript preparation.

The analysis and interpretations in this book, however, are our exclusive responsibilities.

JEFFERY BRANNON
ERIC N. BAKLANOFF

AGRARIAN REFORM
& PUBLIC ENTERPRISE
IN MEXICO

1

Introduction

▲▲

AT THE TURN of the century, when President Porfirio Díaz visited Yucatán, the state had become one of the wealthiest in Mexico: "Mérida blossomed," writes Nelson Reed. "The streets were paved with macadam, had electricity to light them at night, were traversed by horse-drawn streetcars, and numbered in the scientific way—all this in advance of Mexico City."[1] In 1910, on the eve of the Mexican Revolution, Yucatán led the nation as a whole in the share of the total labor force engaged in industry—a fact especially surprising considering that the state's population represented only a small fraction of the national population.[2] Furthermore, by 1910, Yucatán had in place a modern machinery industry that was backwardly-linked to the needs of the henequen plantations,[3] the large agroindustrial estates producing harvest twine for the U.S. market.

Six decades later, in 1970, Yucatán was one of the poorest states in the Mexican union. Although it contained 1.6 percent of the national population, it contributed only 0.5 percent of Mexico's value-added by industry. The state, like other low-income areas, could be characterized as rich in population growth and poor in capital and technical resources.

Yucatán offers the social scientist an excellent regional perspective for evaluating economic and social experiments that were initiated during the Mexican Revolution. Between 1935 and 1938 President Lázaro Cárdenas (1934–40) ordered the expropriation of more than 70 percent of the state's natural-fiber-producing plantations. These expropriations were part of a broader effort he made to effect deep-seated land-tenure reform in the nation. By the close of his administration in 1940, almost 50 percent of its cropland was held in *ejidos*, which are population concentrations that possess collective or communal rights over rural property.[4]

The path that agrarian reform took in Yucatán differed significantly from that taken in most other parts of rural Mexico.

3

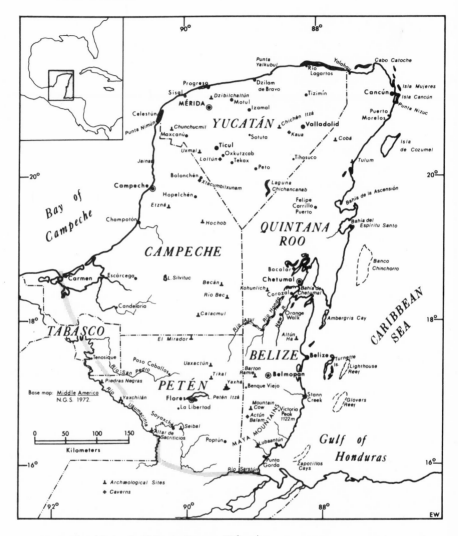

Peninsula of Yucatán. (Map by Eugene Wilson)

Cárdenas, who favored the collectivization of agriculture, chose Yucatán along with the cotton-producing La Laguna region of northern Mexico to be models of an extensive collective ejido program. Subsequent administrations, particularly those of Ávila Camacho (1940–46) and Miguel Aleman (1946–52), dismantled most of the more than five thousand collective units in favor

4

of individual production. Despite this fundamental change in the course of agricultural policy, the collective experiment in Yucatán continued to receive strong government support.

In 1964 the Mexican government increased its involvement in the henequen industry by nationalizing Yucatán's fiber-using cordage mills and placing them under the direction of a single publicly owned corporation, Cordemex. As a result of these actions and the subsequent policies that restricted the marketing freedom of the remaining private producers, the federal government by 1970 exercised almost total control over Yucatán's henequen industry, the state's premier source of both income and employment.

As the leading symbols of the federal government in Yucatán, both Cordemex and Banrural (which supervises and finances the collective ejidos) pursued policies designed to minimize social discontent and defection from the Partido Revolucionario Institucional (PRI), Mexico's dominant political party. The loss of managerial autonomy in Cordemex and Banrural associated with the primacy of political-social goals over considerations of efficiency is mirrored in their dismal operational experiences. By the latter 1970s, the henequen industry's losses were so overwhelming and production so disorganized that Cordemex and the Banrural had almost ceased performing a legitimate economic function in the state. Instead, the two public entities had become the major official disbursing agents for a massive, corrupt, and largely ad hoc social-welfare program in Yucatán.

The crisis that enveloped the henequen industry was significant in several respects. First, it marked the failure of one of the largest economic and social experiments of the Mexican Revolution. Second, the government's administration of the henequen industry offered ample evidence of the shortcomings of the institutions it created to supplant private initiative and improve rural welfare. Operating outside the discipline of the market system and without the benefit of serious efforts to coordinate production and planning, the industry drifted like a rudderless ship. The federal entities charged with administering the industry were, as Mexicans are fond of saying, "barriles sin fondo" — bottomless wells into which billions of pesos flowed with little apparent lasting benefit for the 57,000 henequen farm workers and their families.

The Mexican government's intrusion in the henequen industry

has also tended to reinforce Yucatán's traditional monocrop pattern, thereby postponing the necessary adjustment of the industry to a secular decline in the global hard fiber market that began in the early 1960s. Significantly, direct federal efforts to organize large-scale diversified agricultural projects, such as Plan Tabi, the Santa Rosa Experiment, and "Dzonot Carretero," proved to be costly failures. Finally, the course of federal involvement in Yucatán's henequen industry has had—and will continue to have—a profound impact on the development of the state economy and, to a lesser extent, on the entire Yucatán Peninsula.

The primary objective of this book is to analyze the evolution and performance of Yucatán's henequen agroindustry after the initiation of the Cárdenas land-tenure reforms. Since 1937 all phases of agricultural and industrial activity, both ejido and private, have been subject to increasing governmental control and supervision. Specifically, this study focuses on the relationship between government-induced changes in production organization and the associated incentive structure and subsequent industry performance.

The second objective of this book is to examine the impact of the changing fortunes of the henequen industry on overall regional development. Because that industry has dominated Yucatán's commercial activity and labor markets since the latter decades of the nineteenth century, the patterns and magnitude of other regional economic activity have been closely linked to the production and export of raw fiber and cordage. Importantly, the steady contraction of the world market for natural fibers and Yucatán's share of that market has prompted the federal government to initiate numerous programs to enable the state to reverse course toward a more dynamic and diversified economy. The preponderance of the federal government's role in its leading industry as well as in diversification efforts have made the state among those most heavily dependent on federal direction and resources. Thus, on another level, this volume provides a perspective on regional economic policy and state-federal relations that may contribute to a better understanding of the complex political and social dynamics of Mexican domestic economic policy.

The methodology that we employed in this investigation relies on traditional economic theory. We have tried, however, to avoid the methodological straitjacket that has limited the policy value of two previous major studies of the henequen industry by North American scholars.

During the 1950s Roland Chardon investigated the effect of land redistribution in the henequen zone on what he referred to as the "economic functional unity" of the raw fiber production unit.[5] Land redistribution left the *casco,* or hacienda core buildings, intact and in the hands of the original owner along with a maximum of three hundred hectares of land. The remainder of the fields were distributed to nearby ejidos with little regard for the effect of the geographical pattern of distribution on transportation costs or production coordination. Chardon argues that the decline in productivity and fiber quality after 1937 was primarily a result of the disruption of the economic and geographical integrity of the privately owned plantations.

When Chardon conducted his investigation, cordage production was still carried out by some fifty privately owned mills. In 1970, six years after the federal government had nationalized Yucatán's cordage mills, Carlos Tappan de Arrigunaga assessed the industry's future.[6] He found that the prospect for Yucatecan producers to profitably maintain or surpass present production levels was uncertain at best. The finding was based upon his analysis of past and projected future trends in the world demand for natural fibers and his assessment of the ability of Cordemex to compete effectively with other natural-fiber-producing nations. Tappan de Arrigunaga's findings led him to conclude that future economic transfers from the rest of Mexico to support Yucatán's henequen industry were economically unjustifiable.

Both studies are excellent technical works, but neither gives sufficient consideration to political and social variables that have had a direct and major impact on the economic performance of the industry. Tappan de Arrigunaga's conclusion, though economically sound, ignores the potential political and social implications of the withdrawal of government subsidy from an industry that, directly or indirectly, provides support for a fourth of Yucatán's population. Chardon, on the other hand, conceives the phenomenon of falling productivity to be primarily a technical problem that can be solved by instituting measures to restore the economic integrity of the production unit. His analysis fails to consider fully how changes in the organizational structure have adversely affected production incentives.

The ejidos, unlike the private plantations that dominated raw fiber production before agrarian reform, respond to the incentives and disincentives of the highly politicized federal agency—Banrural—that finances their operation, instead of world market signals. The effects of the change in incentive structure on economic efficiency have been documented in the works of Shuman, Raymond, and Rodríguez, all of whom conducted investigations of the henequen ejido.[7] A composite of their findings clearly indicates that corruption is accepted, even approved of, among henequen workers as well as agriculture bank officials and that the incentive structure of the ejido encourages workers to shirk their assigned production responsibilities.

Given the control that the federal agencies exercise over both ejido and private producers, an analysis of the economic performance of the industry must necessarily take into account the economic and noneconomic objectives of the federal government in the state. Further, it would be erroneous to consider those objectives in isolation from the larger national issues that have shaped the country's development strategy since the 1930s. Yucatán and its fiber industry have too often been viewed as a "special case" when, in fact, their status has been closely linked to and dependent upon national developmental objectives.

Post-1940 Mexican agricultural and industrial objectives have been the subject of an intense national debate since the late 1960s.[8] The debate was stimulated by the faltering growth of agricultural production and the national trauma produced by the violent confrontation at the Plaza de Tlatelolco in 1968. The basic issues, however, have their origin in the meaning of the Mexican Revolution and even more fundamentally in the definition of the nation.

The revolution was fought in part by *campesino*, or peasant, armies whose members were seeking, above all, the restitution of community lands that had been progressively appropriated by hacienda owners and speculators after the Spanish conquest. The process of privatization of rural property accelerated during the rule of President Porfirio Díaz (1876–1911); by 1910 an estimated 90 percent of Mexico's agricultural property was owned by less than 1 percent of the population, though 12 million of the country's 15 million people worked in agriculture.[9]

The Mexican Constitution of 1917 reestablished the rights of agrarian communities to the ownership and control of rural prop-

Retired henequen campesino at Hacienda Yaxcopoil. (Photo by Joel Whitman)

erty. Article 27 identifies the ejido as a legal entity and as a form of social property. The legal ownership of ejido property is vested in a population nucleus whose rights to the property are inalienable, imprescriptible, nonattachable, and nontransferable. The individual campesino who is a member of an ejido does not acquire legal title to the land he cultivates, but right of usufruct.[10] The special legal protection to which the ejido is subject resulted from the desire of the framers of the Constitution of 1917 to not only return lands that had been illegally taken from campesinos, but also to afford them security from future depredation and exploitation.

By 1940 ejidal landholding dominated the rural landscape in

Mexico, primarily because of the vigorous distribution program of President Lázaro Cárdenas. However, campesino groups were unable to control the political process after 1910 because of their inability to form a party or present a coherent program. The better organized ex-*latifundistas*, or large landholding class, continued to influence and even dominate national agricultural policy, particularly after Cárdenas.[11]

Cárdenas, unlike his predecessors, viewed the ejido as the most important and enduring production unit for the future of Mexican agriculture rather than as a transitory form that was destined to disappear with the growth of modern commercial agriculture. Beyond his aggressive expropriation of large haciendas throughout Mexico, he also committed public resources to the establishment of a collective ejido program. Cárdenas created the Banco Nacional de Crédito Ejidal (BNCE) in 1935 to give impulse to the political, social, and economic formation of the ejido system. By 1940 the BNCE had organized more than 5,000 collective ejidos, and 420,000 ejidatarios, or campesinos possessing ejido rights, were beneficiaries of bank credit.[12] According to Gustavo Esteva, only during this period could campesinos count on sufficient governmental support to confront opposing private interests in rural areas. The Cárdenas government even supplied arms to some ejidos.[13]

Cárdenas's actions underscore a view that is held by many populist and leftist critics of Mexican agricultural policy: that the campesino enjoys a historical as well as a legal right to the control and use of the nation's agricultural resources. Private, commercial production is viewed as a threat to the exercise of that right, as well as to the survival of campesino communities.

The views of Mexican populists about the conflictive relationship between campesino agriculture and capitalist production have been strongly influenced by the pioneer work of Russian economist A. V. Chayanov.[14] He observed that the Russian peasants violated many of the norms of accepted entrepreneurial behavior. Because the peasant farm unit possessed little capital and hired no wage labor, the net profit accruing to its productive activity could not be calculated. Therefore, Chayanov argued that the economic behavior of the peasant farm family in any given market situation was not dictated by the profit calculus. Rather, the degree of self-exploitation by family members was "determined by the peculiar equilibrium between family demand satisfaction and the drudgery of labor itself."[15]

Following the work of Chayanov, a substantial number of social scientists called *campesinistas* have attributed the peasant production-unit characteristics to the Mexican campesino sector.[16] Both ejido and small private campesino farms, it is argued, are family units that orient their economic activity toward sustaining and reproducing their existing conditions of life and work instead of some objective criteria of profit. The campesino mode of production exists side by side and in sharp contrast to a modern sector of Mexican agriculture made up of medium and large commercial producers that are profit oriented. When exchange takes place between the two sectors, it favors the commercial enterprises because the campesinos seek to raise their incomes to survival level without regard to the financial return on their activities. Capitalists supply certain production and consumption goods to campesinos and provide a market for their excess labor and production. They are exploited through these exchanges because of their willingness to pay above market prices for their necessities and accept below market prices for their surplus products and labor.

The writings of the campesinistas endow the Mexican campesino with almost mystical qualities. Despite what campesinistas view as the progressive deterioration of campesino communities before the onslaught of capitalist enterprise, they argue that the campesino sector is destined to persist and even grow larger. Modern agriculture and industry are unable to absorb the countryside's surplus labor. Further, "the (campesino) community appears as an indestructible force of resistance."[17]

The views of the campesinistas are not unchallenged. Other historical materialists, the so-called *descampesinistas*, follow a more traditional line of Marxist analysis and assert that capitalist penetration of the Mexican countryside has destroyed campesino forms of organization and led to the proletarianization of rural workers. Both campesinistas and descampesinistas analyze rural problems in the context of class struggle. The former group considers the campesino communities to be an anticapitalist force possessing revolutionary potential; the latter, as the source of an emerging rural proletariat.[18]

The analysis of historical materialists, which focuses on the social relations of production in the Mexican countryside, contrasts with that of another group, called structuralists. According to Alejandro Shejtman, structuralists accept the rural status quo as a given and use orthodox economic theory to formulate policies that will improve the efficiency of the nation's agriculture.[19] Structuralists differentiate among producers only with respect to size, access to resources, and the institutional arrangements that favor or impede their responses to the market. Structuralists do not distinguish between the objectives of campesino farm units and large capitalist enterprises. Both are assumed to respond rationally to market signals and to share the common objective of maximizing the return on their resources. The work of P. Lamartine Yates is representative of this view.[20]

Policy recommendations of structuralists and historical materialists reflect their divergent analytical approaches. The utopian ideal of the campesinistas is a return to a countryside of independent, self-sufficient, and democratic communities in which goods and services are produced for use rather than exchange and market transactions are minimized. Recognizing the impossibility of achieving this anarchic model of rural development,[21] they call for a strengthening of campesino units to protect them from exploitation by capital. To this end, campesinos should be given more control over public resources and their use of collective economic organization encouraged. Most critical for the survival of the campesino community and the collective ejido is a campesino political organization possessing sufficient power to demand changes in the actual structure of Mexican agriculture.[22]

Structuralists, on the other hand, favor more technical and liberal solutions to the nation's agricultural problems. Yates, for example, concludes that the resumption of adequate rates of agricultural growth will require an elimination of the institutional obstacles that insulate producers from market signals. This requires a gradual elimination of price controls as well as changes in agrarian law to allow the ejidatario to dispose of his land as he sees fit. The ultimate result of the liberalization process (which would maintain strict limits on the maximum size of agricultural units) would be an agricultural sector made up of small, but efficient, farms that produced according to the dictates of the market.[23]

Critical to our analysis of Yucatán's henequen industry are the perceptions held by both schools of thought that relate to the efficacy of the Mexican government's activist role in agriculture. Structuralists and historical materialists alike criticize the institutions and programs of the federal government and, to varying degrees, blame it for the stagnation of production and the impoverishment of the campesino population. The structuralist critique is centered around the complex of programs and laws (including agrarian reform) that restrict property rights, distort price signals, and encourage inefficiency and corruption. Historical materialists, on the other hand, focus on the contradictions between capitalist and campesino production. They allege that the government has pursued a strategy since 1940 that strengthened large commercial agriculture and debilitated the campesino units.

Arturo Warman contends that rural policies of the government have vacillated between a *política agraria* (agrarian policy) and *política agrícola* (agricultural policy). Agrarian policy is land distribution. Agricultural policy is the totality of measures that support and encourage commercial farming.[24] According to critics, agricultural policy has dominated development strategy in the countryside except during the first three years of the Cárdenas administration. Critics argue that post-Cárdenas administrations abandoned collective production, slowed the pace of land distribution, and ignored social priorities in support of a strategy of capital accumulation in agriculture that supported Mexico's industrialization model. The historical data on land redistribution, expenditures for irrigation works, and the distribution of credit lend strong support to this thesis.[25]

Collective production was promoted vigorously again in the early 1970s by the administration of Luis Echeverría Álvarez (1970–76). He averred that collectivization was the only policy that would permit Mexico to overcome the crisis in agriculture. Warman argues that the effort was a failure because it was imposed from outside and because ejidatarios resisted being organized according to profit criteria. Echeverría's notion of collectivization was to form large agroindustrial units that produced for the market and were centrally controlled. From the campesino's perspective, collectivization was a tactic to separate him from his land and use it for the benefit of others.[26]

The campesinos' modern-day aversion to collectivization is at least partially founded in past experience. Collectives have not managed to achieve economic independence because of a lack of governmental support and/or deliberate effects by officials to undermine collective autonomy. Rodolfo Stavenhagen's description of the disintegration of collective ejidos in La Laguna and Sonora during the 1940s and 1950s is graphic evidence of how agricultural policy turned away from Cárdenas's concept of collectivization.[27] Those collective ejidos, including the ones involved in henequen production, that did survive became what Peter Singelmann calls controlled collectives—enterprises "completely dependent on outside institutional (government) supports which the members have to accept under imposed, not negotiated conditions."[28]

Efforts at collectivizing production and further agrarian reform came to a halt under President José López Portillo (1976–82). Historical materialists point out that his now-defunct Mexican Food System (SAM), in conjunction with the Ley de Fomento Agrario (which permitted joint agricultural ventures between ejidos and private commercial farms), offered merely a technical solution. And the solution was designed to permit the further penetration of international capital, debilitate the campesino sector, and "get the job done."[29]

The federal government's interest in the ejidos has responded to political as well as economic interests. Agrarian reform did not create an independent Mexican peasantry. Instead, beginning with Cárdenas, the ejidos' economic dependence on the federal government was converted into political support for the dominant party and the state. Two of the major instruments he created to bind the campesinos to the state were the Confederación Nacional del Campesino (CNC) and the BNCE.

The CNC, which all ejidatarios must join, is one of the three sectors of the PRI. Requests for land as well as other campesino demands must be channeled through the CNC. Its national directors are appointed by the president and answer directly to the chief executive, instead of rank-and-file members. Grass roots officials are also appointed from above and they exercise political control over their constituency. The officials are themselves controlled by a complex network of relationships that are based upon personal loyalties and the granting of individual favors and benefits.[30] The BNCE, which was merged in 1974 with two other agricultural banks to become the Banrural, became the major source of official agricultural credit for the campesino sector. Today, along with the CNC and the Banrural, more than a hundred other federal organizations operate in the countryside and exercise some degree of political control.

However, the relationship between the state and the campesinos is not totally one-sided. Politicians still give lip service to agrarian reform. Land redistribution was the most visible outcome of the Mexican Revolution. As such, it lends support to the PRI's claim to be the party of revolution. The government, therefore, cannot renounce campesino agriculture because of the potential political consequences. Esteva characterizes the government's dilemma as one in which it must keep the campesinos close enough to prevent them from becoming independent while keeping them sufficiently distant to avoid being forced to yield to their historical demands.[31]

The highly political relationship between the government and campesino sector has produced corruption and inefficiency in the delivery of technical and credit services by federal agencies. The relationship between Banrural and the campesino sector has been compared to the institution of debt servitude that existed in Mexico before the revolution.[32] According to leftist critics of national agricultural policy, the economic dependency of the campesino on the state has permitted the government to subordinate the goal of social justice to other criteria, specifically those of a capitalist development model.[33]

The ejidatarios of Yucatán's henequen zone, as we show in chapters 2 and 3, are many generations removed from the idealized conditions of the natural economy of the campesino. The term "rural proletariat" is a more accurate description of the thousands of workers who have labored in the henequen fields since large commercial plantations began to be organized during the last half of the nineteenth century.[34]

The characteristics of agricultural production in Yucatán's henequen zone represented an exception to the general pattern of production in prerevolutionary Mexico, which centered on the hacienda[35] and the cultivation of traditional grain crops for subsistence. After 1940 collective production continued on the henequen ejidos, even though nationally it was abandoned in favor of individual exploitation. Further, though the federal government slashed credit and technical assistance to the nation's ejidos between 1940 and 1970, Yucatán's henequen ejidos continued to be one of the major clients of the BNCE.

On the surface, the evolutionary pattern of the henequen industry, both before and after the revolution, suggests that perhaps it should be considered as a case apart and outside the logic of the Mexican agricultural development model. This is not the case, however. The federal government's relationship with the industry was consistent with its policy of favoring and providing support to commercial agriculture. Although the scale of fiber production never again reached the levels achieved during the First World War, the industry's export income has continued to yield a substantial hard-currency income in support of Mexico's industrialization drive. Further, the government did not permit the henequen ejidos to achieve any measure of economic independence, despite the demonstrated capacity of the activity to support profitable production during much of the post-World War II period. Henequen workers became employees of the Mexican state. Their unequal relationship with the government has been one of subordination and political manipulation and their level of economic well-being is below that of the mass of Mexican campesinos, who were neglected in favor of commercial producers.

The nationalization of the private, fiber-using cordage mills is a further indication of Yucatán's place in mainstream agricultural policy. During the early 1960s, the government, through the BNCE, began to stimulate agroindustrialization in the countryside. These efforts were intensified during the renewed collectivization efforts of the Echeverría administration. The president himself was a frequent visitor to the state, perhaps to study the Yucatán prototype because it was among the oldest collective agroindustrial activities in the nation.

If the involvement of the federal government in Yucatán is considered to be consistent with the general agricultural policy objectives after 1940, the performance of the henequen industry under government control may offer some indication as to why that policy is deemed to be a failure by critics. One important finding of our study is that initial government attempts to rationalize henequen and cordage production along commercial lines ultimately came into conflict with the more fundamental public goal of manipulating the work force for political advantage. The outward manifestations of this conflict are the perverse set of economic incentives that were established with the primary objectives of influencing the political behavior of the campesinos and advancing the self-interests of industry and government officials.

Ironically, the political status quo in Yucatán is still a tenuous one for the PRI, despite the precedence the government has accorded to political objectives over economic ones. Yucatecans blame the government and its agents, not the producers or the world market, for the sorry state of their once-proud henequen industry.

2

Yucatán: Cultural Geography and Early History

▲▲

YUCATÁN today is one of the three Mexican states that make up, along with the former British possession of Belize, the Yucatán Peninsula. The state contains a surface area of 43,379 square kilometers, and in 1980 its population was estimated to be 1,000,000 people.[1] Until 1852 the peninsula was a single political unit whose administrative center was Mérida, the present capital of the state of Yucatán. Internal disputes and a devastating civil war led to the separation of the land areas of the present-day states of Campeche and Quintana Roo from the jurisdiction of Mérida.

THE PHYSICAL AND CULTURAL ENVIRONMENT

In contrast to much of the rest of Mexico, the land surface of Yucatán is practically flat. The only major relief feature is in the southern part of the state. A low range of hills known as the Puuc, or Sierrita de Ticul, extends 120 kilometers from just south of Maxcanu, in the southeastern part of the state, to Tzucacab, which is near the border of Quintana Roo.

Yucatán is located in a tropical zone and, like most such regions, has distinguishable wet and dry seasons. The wet season normally extends from May through early October, and the dry season runs through the winter months. Seasonal variation in rainfall favors a one-crop-a-year agricultural cycle. Conditions would permit two or three crops per year if alternative sources of water were available.[2] Rainfall averages a thousand millimeters annually except in coastal areas. This amount of rainfall is adequate for growing purposes, but farming is hampered by the erratic annual pattern of precipitation[3] and by lack of surface water.[4]

Vegetation and soil conditions are not uniform throughout the state because of geological variations and differences in rainfall. The soil in the northwestern quarter, the henequen zone, is extemely thin and rocky; large areas consist of little more than exposed limestone caprock. Vegetation, though abundant, is of the scrub variety because of the area's soil and precipitation characteristics and land-clearing practices. The henequen zone, where Mérida is located, has been the most heavily populated and cultivated part of the state since the colonial period. In the eastern half of Yucatán, the soil is somewhat deeper and is minimally suitable for the production of a wider variety of agricultural products. During the last two decades, the east has become the major cattle-producing region in the peninsula.

The best soils and climatic conditions for agricultural production are in the Sierra region, the southeastern quarter of the state. Unlike the situation in the other subregions of Yucatán, modern mechanized production is possible in this area, though past efforts to exploit these lands commercially have been sporadic. Most campesinos in Yucatán still rely on the primitive, though proven, methods of slash-and-burn agriculture that were used by their Maya ancestors to cultivate the major food staple, corn.

The meagerness of the natural resources is also evident in the lack of mineral and forest wealth. Yucatán apparently does not possess any exploitable metallic ore deposits. Pémex, the government-owned and -controlled petroleum monopoly, has discovered petroleum off its coast, but similar exploitation in other parts of Mexico has not produced significant increases in local income and employment. Ironically, the surface rock outcroppings that hinder intensive agricultural production have become increasingly valuable as a source of building materials. This quarrying activity and the mining of salt on the northern coast, an endeavor that predates the Spanish conquest, are the only extractive industries in the state worthy of mention.

Centuries of slash-and-burn agriculture and the extensive cultivation of henequen all but eliminated market-quality stands of timber in most parts of the state. Large stands of cedar and mahogany were common in the less-populated southern and eastern parts during the earlier decades of this century, but imprudent commercial exploitation and clearing operations by cattle raisers have reduced their numbers so drastically that the state produces only 10 percent of local lumber consumption.[5]

The poverty of their resource base has limited Yucatecans' economic and social contact with the rest of Mexico. Despite the ferocity of the struggles that attended the conquest of the peninsula by the Spanish in the sixteenth century, little was known or written about the region until an American, John Stephens, published accounts of his extensive travels there during the late 1830s and 1840s.[6] However, Yucatán's development was also strongly influenced by the physical isolation of the peninsula. Anthropologist Robert Redfield observed in the early 1940s that "in everything but literal truth it (Yucatán) is an island . . . inaccessible except by boat or airplane."[7]

The major cause of the geographical isolation is the large expanse of swamp and jungle located in the depression between the state of Chiapas and the Yucatán Peninsula. The barrier was so formidable that rail and highway links between Mérida and central Mexico were not completed until 1950 and 1961, respectively. Before 1950 people and commodities were transported overland from Chiapas to the Yucatán Peninsula on narrow, unpaved cart paths.[8] Because of the difficulties of travel, scarcely two decades ago fewer than 4,500 people entered the state annually by rail, bus, and automobile.[9]

Until the 1960s the ports were the main link to Mexico and the rest of the world. Shipping activity is limited, however, by the lack of good harbors along the state's 379-kilometer Gulf coastline. Only small ships can dock in Progreso, Yucatán's major port, even though the main pier extends 2.4 kilometers into the Gulf of Mexico. Before the completion of pier facilities at Progreso during the latter part of the nineteenth century, ships were forced to anchor as far as 5 kilometers off the coast and use small boats to load or discharge cargo and passengers. This procedure was rendered highly dangerous by violent and unpredictable *nortes*, or strong windstorms.

The difficulties of sea travel to and from Yucatán were compounded by geography. Service between Progreso and major external markets has always been poor because the peninsula is located outside major shipping lanes. During the latter part of the nineteenth century and the first half of this century, service was so irregular that the government needed to subsidize privately owned lines directly or provide shipping services itself.[10]

The most valuable resource that the Spanish found when they invaded and conquered the peninsula in the sixteenth century was human labor. Although in a state of decline, a relatively advanced agriculturally based society still thrived in the peninsula. The Maya, estimated to have numbered around 240,000 in 1549,[11] were gradually reduced to a state of dependence by Spanish settlers. Rendered captive by the strict enforcement of debt peonage laws after 1860, the indigenous population in the henequen zone became the primary source of labor for the large henequen haciendas.

The mixing of the Spanish and Maya people and cultures, the limited immigration of Europeans and other racial stocks, and the geographical isolation of Yucatán created a people who are culturally distinct from populations in other parts of Mexico. The Maya heritage is still strongly evident in the state today, particularly outside Mérida. Maya is spoken by about half of the population and is the primary language in most of the numerous small villages that dot the rural areas. Cultural and language differences have undoubtedly contributed to the feeling of "separateness" that many Yucatecans, even today, exhibit in their relationships with the rest of the nation.

EARLY ECONOMIC AND POLITICAL DEVELOPMENT

The Colonial Economy

The province of Yucatán at the beginning of the nineteenth century included within its boundaries the present states of Yucatán, Campeche, and Quintana Roo. Two cities, Mérida and Campeche, were the major centers of Spanish-Creole population and influence.

Mérida had traditionally dominated the province because of its status as the legitimate seat of both secular and clerical power. The city's location also favored its rise to prominence. Situated in the northwestern corner of the peninsula, where groundwater is accessible, it became the focal point of Spanish settlement in Yucatán. Despite the relatively poor soils and erratic precipitation in the northwestern region, a significant proportion of the province's population was clustered within a radius of eighty kilometers around Mérida. In this area, economic activity was organized around the dominant economic institution: the hacienda.

The hacienda system in Yucatán developed later than in most of the rest of Latin America. However, by 1800 the institution was firmly in place in the henequen zone.[12] Activity was organized around the production of cattle and corn. Surplus beef and grain were sold in local markets, and beef by-products, such as hides, were exported to Caribbean markets. However, the need to maintain the haciendas' resident populations and the primitive state of the region's roads caused production activity to be oriented toward self-sufficiency.

Initially, the land-extensive production on the haciendas required relatively small quantities of full-time labor. A few resident workers, the majority being *vaqueros*, or cowboys, carried out the daily chores on the estates. Most of the labor requirements of corn production were filled by a class of workers known as *luneros*. They were granted access to hacienda water and a place to grow corn in exchange for working one day a week on the hacienda.[13] As corn production increased after 1750, the luneros became more dependent upon the haciendas because of the scarcity of corn-growing land in the northwest. By 1800 the majority of the campesinos living within eighty kilometers of Mérida were resident workers on haciendas.[14]

Typically, the hacienda in Latin America evolved in an economic environment characterized by capital scarcity and limited markets. Within these limitations, the *hacendado*, or hacienda owner, sought a small, secure return by producing cash crops for a stable local market. Noneconomic considerations conflicted with the efficient management of the hacienda's resources. Property ownership enhanced the social prestige of the hacendado and his family. He, therefore, sought secure investments, which channeled capital away from other types of commercial activity on the hacienda.[15]

Beyond the eighty-kilometer radius of Mérida, the hacienda system was less pervasive. There, the indigenous Maya village was the dominant unit and the system of economic life was much the same as it had been before the conquest.[16] Typically, the agricultural cycle began in the late summer and early fall, when a section of land that had lain fallow for fifteen to twenty-five years was selected and cleared. The cleared brush was then piled and left to dry until the early spring; before the onset of the first spring rains, it was burned. This not only retarded the growth of weeds and insects, but also left a residue of ashes that enriched the thin, rocky soil. After the first spring rains, corn was sown in the patches of soil that could be found interspersed in the rocky limestone surface. Harvest began in the late summer and often continued into the winter, depending upon the variety of corn. Beans, tomatoes, and chilies were, as a general rule, planted among the corn to provide a supplement to the basic corn diet. Once cleared, a *milpa*, or cornfield, could normally be used for only two or three years. Productivity normally fell rapidly after the first year. Thus, the population in this region was semi-nomadic.

Just as self-sufficiency was characteristic of the hacienda, so it was for the whole province in colonial Yucatán. Outside of a few articles produced for export, each region within the province produced only what could be consumed within the region.[17] Intraregional trade was severely limited by the primitive state of transportation and communication. Howard Cline estimated that by the end of the colonial period in 1821 only 105 kilometers of passable cart roads existed in Yucatán. They were located in its northwestern part and linked Mérida with nearby villages and cattle haciendas.[18]

The structure of the colonial economy was also influenced by factors external to Yucatán. Spain's mercantilist policies placed severe restrictions on the types of economic activities that could be profitably undertaken. Yucatecans were permitted to export small amounts of woven cotton, beef, beeswax, hides, salt, and dyewood, but most exports were tightly controlled by Spain until the latter decades of the eighteenth century, when King Charles III opened the markets of Mexico to the rest of the world.

Spain's trade policies slowed the growth of both internal and external commercial activity. Governmental efforts to improve internal transportation were sporadic until the end of the eighteenth century. Authorities had little inclination (probably because of the restrictions of the Crown) and less in the way of funds to promote the construction of roads. Those that did exist were not maintained by the provincial government, but were the charge of individual Indian villages, which were responsible for providing the necessary labor.[19]

In contrast to Mérida's agricultural orientation, Campeche, a port city 150 kilometers south of the capital city, achieved importance as a center of trade, particularly in salt and wood products, during the colonial period. Until 1811 it was the only authorized international port in the peninsula. By building strong trade ties with the Mexican Gulf ports, commercial interests in Campeche came to dominate the trade of the province and, increasingly, to challenge the preeminence of Mérida.[20]

The primitive transportation system in the province retarded the growth of common political and economic interests between the two cities. Campeche's elite, because of the orientation of their trade, identified their interest with Mexico. Mérida's contact with Mexico, in view of the city's relative isolation and the orientation of its external trade, was much more limited during the colonial period. As a result, its citizens tended to identify their economic interests less with Mexico and more with present and potential trading partners in the Caribbean and the United States. The growing rivalry between the two cities intensified in 1811, when the port of Sisal, which is located only fifty-two kilometers from Mérida, was reopened as an international port. Sisal's commerce quickly came to rival that of Campeche. By 1845 Sisal was shipping cargoes twice the value of those being shipped by Campeche.[21] Intraregional rivalry and conflict between Campeche and Mérida would finally result in the political fragmentation of Yucatán during the last half of the nineteenth century.

The Economy after Independence

The political and economic interests of the Mérida elite were mutually reinforcing after Mexican independence in 1821. They observed that an expansion of commercial activity would be necessary if the state were to become economically self-sufficient. Self-sufficiency would in turn enhance prospects for political autonomy.[22]

Yucatán joined the Mexican Republic in 1821 though it had taken virtually no active role in the struggle for independence against Spain. At the time of independence, the majority of the active political elements in Mérida was strongly in favor of a federalist form of government, which would give them a semi-autonomous status within the republic. Yucatán had not been governed by the viceroy of New Spain during the colonial period and *Meridianos* wanted to maintain the tradition of separate administration. This placed Mérida in direct conflict with Campeche, which favored close ties with the capital. The ensuing conflict between the two cities mirrored the larger Federalist-

Centralist controversies that wracked Mexico until the 1870s. The struggle over autonomy was the source of occasional violent clashes between the two cities, and, on more than one occasion, military skirmishes between the forces of Mérida and the federal government.

During much of the early nineteenth century, Yucatán had been taxed by Mexico as if it were a foreign country. Merchants were forced to pay discriminatory duty on their exports.[23] Yucatán's strong states'-rights position after independence further strained relations with Mexico City. In 1838 the federal government levied taxes on Yucatecan commodities and drafted its citizens for the war effort against the rebellious state of Texas. The state legislature reacted to these levies by declaring Yucatán to be independent and entering into a defensive alliance with what had then become the Republic of Texas. Between 1839 and 1846 local Yucatecan forces twice repelled invading Mexican forces. The most effective sanctions that the nation imposed during this period were economic ones. The conflict severely disrupted the state's trade with Mexican ports, which worsened relations between political elements in Mérida and Campeche.

Although Yucatán formally rejoined the Mexican nation in 1846, the reunion was a fragile one. The state declared itself to be neutral in the war between the United States and Mexico. A short time later, official envoys actually proposed to Secretary of State James Buchanan that the United States annex Yucatán.

The recent American and French experiences encouraged the Yucatecan elite to tinker with existing social and political institutions. In 1825 state legislators approved a constitution that went so far as to grant civil rights to domestic servants. In reality, this progressive movement effected little true change within the realm of economic activity. An inexpensive and captive supply of Indian labor was the major resource of the enterprising hacendado. As commercial agricultural production expanded in the nineteenth century, restrictions on the freedom of the indigenous masses were tightened rather than relaxed.

In contrast to the turmoil that characterized both Yucatán's internal political affairs and its relationship with Mexico, the state's economy made impressive gains between 1821 and 1847. The relaxation of trade restrictions in New Spain that followed the Bourbon reforms of the 1770s had demonstrated the benefits of economic liberalism to Yucatecans.[24] After independence, feudal attitudes toward commerce in the state seemed to disintegrate more rapidly than in other parts of Mexico.[25]

The initial impact of independence on Yucatán's economy was negative. Without the protection of the Spanish Crown, many of the state's traditional export commodities fared poorly against competition in Gulf of Mexico and Caribbean markets.[26] Trade was disrupted further by the renewal of conflict between Spain and Mexico in 1823. Cotton cloth production for internal consumption also reflected the effects of trade liberalization as local producers were unable to compete with cheaper imports. However, cotton continued to be a significant crop in the region until the mid-nineteenth century primarily because of the efforts of an enterprising Valladolíd businessman who established a textile factory in the region in the 1830s. Although he could not compete in the internal market with the cheaper cloth from British Honduras, he was able to sell to markets outside Yucatán. This unusual enterprise, which flourished until 1845, supported 117 local native families directly and many Maya cotton growers indirectly.[27]

Yucatecan producers began to explore the commercial possibilities of several nontraditional cash crops, including silkworms. After a period of experimentation, investor interest finally settled on sugar and henequen. Sugarcane production was an almost immediate commercial success. By 1845 the value of raw sugar and liquor manufactured from sugar had risen to 1,660,413 pesos, or 59.1 percent of the value of commercial production.[28] The majority of the sugar produced was consumed internally, though during the 1830s and 1840s exports became increasingly important to the industry.

Before independence, little sugarcane was grown in Yucatán because of the restrictions imposed by the Spanish government on the production and commercialization of sugarcane products. It was widely recognized, however, that the Sierra region, in the southern part of the state, possessed soil and climate conditions that were well suited to the large-scale production of cane. Exploitation of these lands began in earnest soon after independence because of the disruption of trade relations with Spanish Cuba. Rising sugar prices and the loss of the major market for Yucatecan cattle stimulated the initial growth of sugar haciendas around Peto and Tekax. Sugar prices were so favorable until 1840 that a sugar hacendado could recover his initial investment with one good harvest.[29] As the sugar boom continued, entrepreneurs began to cultivate lands to the east and west of those towns along what was regarded as the frontier of the state.

Unlike the situation in the populated northwestern portion of Yucatán, where the pattern of landholding was relatively set, the southern and eastern parts contained large areas of unclaimed land. The availability of these lands and the increased commercial activity in the sugar-growing region attracted not only Creoles, but also ambitious *mestizos,* or people of mixed European and Indian stock, who enjoyed little opportunity for upward mobility in the settled and more traditional northwest. The broader opportunities for acquiring land on the frontier caused the fertile lands in the Sierra region to be occupied and cultivated by a relatively larger number of proprietors than in the northwest, where landholding patterns had evolved from the *encomienda,*[30] or the privilege granted by the Crown to collect tribute from villages in specific areas.

The legislature actively supported the growth of the sugar industry. Between 1821 and 1846 more than seven hundred kilometers of new roads were constructed throughout the state, including ones that connected Mérida with major population centers, such as Peto and Tizimín, in the sugar-producing regions.[31] Sugar growers were also aided by the liberal tax policies applied to sugar and sugar derivatives and through the sale of public lands at low prices.[32] The combination of high prices and government aid accelerated the flow of local capital and population into the sugar-growing areas.

The government also took steps to alleviate the labor shortage that confronted sugar producers. The Maya who lived in the frontier region were unaccustomed to the work cycle of the sugar hacienda. Arnold Strickon refers to this group as "Free Maya" in order to contrast them with the "Hacienda Maya" of the northwest.[33] Sugar production required large quantities of reliable labor, particularly at harvest time. This work cycle conflicted with that of slash-and-burn corn production, which had been practiced by the Free Maya in the region for centuries. The state government coerced the participation of the Indians in the hacienda labor force by allowing the transfer of their land to sugar hacendados and by strengthening the existing system of debt peonage.[34]

The population and the food production of the Sierra region increased markedly during the twenty-five years following independence. Before the sugar boom, the southern part of the state had been a thinly populated frontier area. By 1847 it contained 200,000 people, or a third of the state's population, and produced two-thirds of Yucatán's basic food staple, corn.[35] On the eve of the Caste War, the south had begun to rival Mérida as the center of commercial activity and was regarded as the key to the state's future prosperity and growth.

Although henequen production did not increase as dramatically as that of sugar, major steps were taken to initiate its exploitation during the first few decades of the nineteenth century. The virtues of the indigenous plant were well known before independence, but the Indians were the only ones who exploited it commercially. The Maya cut leaves from henequen plants growing wild in the country and used the fiber to elaborate small quantities of hammocks, fish nets, coarse sacks, and ropes. After Mexican independence, the growth of world shipping caused a steady increase in the demand for ship riggings and other articles manufactured from henequen fiber. Hacienda owners around Mérida, attracted by the increasingly profitable prices for henequen products, began to cultivate the spiny plant as a supplementary source of income.

The hacienda system as it existed in the northwestern portion of the state was critical to the beginning of successful commercial exploitation of henequen in Yucatán.[36] Henequen production is relatively labor-intensive. As previously mentioned, the haciendas around Mérida, in contrast to those in the rest of the state, already possessed both resident work forces and access to markets.

The henequen plant also thrived in the rocky, soil-poor northwestern part of Yucatán. Requiring little moisture and flourishing where other crops could not be grown successfully, it was compatible with the traditional crops grown on the hacienda. Several varieties of henequen, which is a member of the *agave* family, are native to the peninsula. The most common type, *agave fourcroydes*, came to dominate commercial plantings in the northwest even though another variety, *agave sisalana*, is superior in some uses.

Despite the steadily increasing external demand for articles elaborated from henequen fiber and entreaties by the state government to increase fiber production, planting increased slowly after independence. Hacendados initially planted henequen merely to supplement the income from their estates. Shortages of capital and labor as well as the absence of an adequate technology for separating the fiber from the leaves of the plant were formidable obstacles to the expansion of production.

The leaves of the henequen plant cannot usually be harvested until it is five to seven years old. During this period, labor must be available to weed the fields at least twice a year. After the plant begins producing, the field needs to be weeded at least once a year. Labor is also needed to clear and plant new fields (the average life cycle of the henequen plant is twenty years). The harvesting of the leaves takes place year-round and requires that a reliable and relatively large labor force be available. Because of the characteristics of the life cycle of the plant, the grower must make a substantial investment in a new field well before realizing any significant income flows. Local capital sources in early nineteenth-century Yucatán simply did not allow for the rapid conversion to large-scale production. Adequate supplies of capital would not begin flowing into the state until the 1860s, when financial sources in the United States began to profit from investment in henequen production.

The only technologies available to henequen producers for removing the fiber from the leaves were primitive manual techniques employed by the Maya. The pulp of the leaf had to be scraped away from the fiber using hand tools. As a result, a larger labor force was needed to remove the fiber than to cultivate the fields. After independence, the state government worked hand in hand with interested hacendados to encourage the invention of a mechanical rasper that would reduce the labor requirements for large-scale production. The government offered patent rights and cash premiums to the individual who could build and demonstrate the reliability of a mechanical rasper. Most of the aspirants prior to 1850 were foreigners and none of their machines was both efficient as well as simple and reliable enough to be operated by untrained Indian labor.[37] The technological breakthrough, and the potential for the rapid expansion of production, would not come until the late 1850s, when inventive Yucatecans would set their minds to the task.

The state worked closely with the hacienda owners to augment and regularize the labor supply. As stated earlier, legislation strengthened debt peonage laws and, just before the Caste War, approved the forced movement of labor.[38] By the mid-1840s the incipient industry was one of the state's leading employers and accounted for more than 13 percent of exports.[39]

Despite the commercial successes with sugar and henequen, the economy of Yucatán on the eve of the disastrous Caste War remained devoted to subsistence production. Because of the obstacles to the expansion of henequen production as well as the primitive nature of the transportation infrastructure, diversification of the haciendas around Mérida proceeded slowly. Of the total land under cultivation, 94.8 percent was sowed in corn, the basic food staple of the population; 2.9 percent in henequen and tobacco; and less than 2 percent in sugarcane.[40]

THE CASTE WAR

Commercial henequen production began near Mérida and was readily adaptable to the established hacienda system. The increase in sugar production, however, was accomplished by bringing previously unexploited and sparsely populated frontier lands under cultivation. Indians on the frontiers found themselves and their traditional milpa increasingly conscripted by aggressive sugar hacendados. Faced with the alternatives of submitting to commercial hacienda discipline, fleeing the land, or fighting, the Indians chose to fight. From 1847 to 1852 widespread conflict devastated much of the peninsula. At one point in 1848, the defenses of Mérida and Campeche were all that stood between the insurgents and complete domination of the peninsula. By 1852 Yucatán had lost half its population and effective control over four-fifths of its territory.[41] Although Indians fought on both sides, the Caste War took on the aspect of a race war between the whites and the indigenous Maya.

Mexican military help during this crucial period was not forthcoming. This reflected the central government's weakness and its reaction to the positions Yucatán had taken in the wars with Texas and the United States. So critical was the situation in 1848 that the governor of Yucatán offered complete "domination and sovereignty" of the state to the first among Spain, Great Britain, or the United States who would render "powerful and effective help" to the state's beleaguered Creoles.[42] The federal government and several nations finally did assist Yucatán. By 1855, though the Indians had not been defeated, the Creoles were again in firm control of the major population centers and had turned their thoughts to rebuilding.

The political and economic consequences of the conflict were severe for Yucatán. The war exacerbated the old conflict between Mérida and Campeche. Campeche declared itself to be an independent entity in 1858 and laid claim to more than a third of the territory of the state. The war-weary Meridianos were unable to prevent the secession, and, supported by the government in Mexico City, Campeche became a separate state. Despite this setback, regional pride continued to assert itself in Yucatán's relations with the central government. In 1863 Yucatecan militia tried gamely, though unsuccessfully, to resist the troops of Archduke Maximilian who were sent to bring Yucatán into the newly created Mexican Empire.

The Caste War canceled many of the economic gains that Yucatán had made since independence. The sugar-producing regions in its southern and southeastern parts, where the fighting had been most intense, sustained the most damage. Sugar mills were destroyed, cane fields burned, and thriving population centers deserted. The devastating effects of the bloody and prolonged conflict were not limited to the sugar industry. Yucatán's 1,388 haciendas are estimated to have owned as many as 1,000,000 head of cattle in 1846. To feed their soldiers, both armies slaughtered the animals by the thousands. In 1862, seven years after the fighting had ended in most areas, a partial agricultural census reported that fewer than 100,000 head of cattle remained in the state.[43] Cattle haciendas throughout the province were completely abandoned, and many remained so until the latter decades of the century. The incipient henequen industry was also affected. The total area sowed is estimated to have fallen by almost 50 percent from 1844 to 1860.[44] Many of the fields, however, were near Mérida and remained unharmed. Production and export of henequen continued throughout the war despite a severe shortage of field labor.[45]

As in most civil wars, the damage inflicted by the contending armies on the population was severe. Deaths, emigration, and the loss of land area to Campeche reduced the population of Yucatán by a half—from 504,635 inhabitants in 1845 to 248,156 in 1862.[46] The population did not achieve pre-Caste War levels again until 1950. The distribution of population was noticeably altered in favor of the central and northwestern zones. By 1883 only 15.1 percent of the much-reduced population lived in the sugar-growing regions, while the proportion of the total population living in Mérida and surrounding towns increased to 50 percent.[47] Although the state government tried repeatedly to repopulate the frontier areas after 1858, few people were willing to relocate there from the less-fertile northwest and risk attack from the large force of hostile Indians that had retreated into the forests just south of the sugar-growing region.

Conditions in Yucatán after 1855 did not favor a resumption of pre-Caste War patterns of economic activity. Instead, the inhospitable soil and climate of the northwestern corner of the state and rising fiber prices quickly convinced landowners that profitable alternatives to the increased production of henequen were few.

After the Caste War, only about a fifth of the state was judged to be secure enough from rebel action to pursue normal agricultural activities. This area included Mérida and a few surrounding *municipios*, or townships.[48] The curtailment of raw fiber supply during the Caste War in conjunction with increasing demand caused prices to quadruple between the mid-1850s and 1867.[49] Owners of haciendas in the secure zone around Mérida responded to the price increases by steadily expanding their plantings of henequen. Fortunately, the plant, unlike other agricultural commodities, thrived in the rocky soil of the northwestern part of the state.

The progressive conversion of the corn and cattle haciendas around Mérida into henequen plantations was aided by other factors as well. Large numbers of Maya fled to the northwest to escape the death and destruction of the Caste War. The influx of refugees and soldiers provided hacienda owners with an abundant source of captive labor. The increase in the supply of labor was crucial to efforts to expand because the cultivation of the plant and the processing of the leaves were more labor-intensive than traditional crops.

Yucatecans were also quite familiar with the technical aspects of henequen production. After the first henequen plantation was established in 1830, a number of investigations were undertaken to determine the best methods to cultivate the plant on a large scale. Supported by the embattled state government, research efforts were intensified after the war.[50] By 1860 the major obstacles to large-scale production, though not overcome, were well known. The coincidence of the traumatic dislocations of the Caste War with the increased interest in the commercial possibilities of henequen prompted a well-known Yucatecan historian to suggest that the war was responsible for the expansion of production after 1860.[51] This seems to be an oversimplification. In the absence of the conflict, the high prices of the last three decades of the nineteenth century would have stimulated increased plantings of henequen. Yucatecans possessed adequate technology, favorable growing conditions, a resident labor force, and close proximity to United States markets. The major significance of the war was that it created a set of conditions that caused the landed elite to concentrate their productive energies almost single-mindedly on henequen.

Yucatán, as a consequence of this concentration, lost a significant opportunity to diversify economically. The continued exploitation of the frontier lands could have provided the flexibility and the impetus for a much-needed diversification of the agricultural economy, which as early as 1900 had begun to experience the negative effects of the monocultural approach.

3

The Development and Decline
of the Plantation Economy

▲▲▲

During the final decades of the nineteenth century, Yucatán's economy became increasingly transformed through its integration into a larger world economy in which the demand for raw materials was growing rapidly. The state's production and exports of henequen fiber expanded dramatically after 1880 and reached historic peaks during World War I. Two major demand factors—the invention by Cyrus McCormick of a twine-binding reaper in 1878 and the rapid expansion of American grain production—provided the continuing stimulus to Yucatán's preeminent export industry. By 1910 henequen fiber headed the list of Mexico's nonmetallic exports, and Yucatán's landed elite had achieved a level of prosperity rivaled by few of their counterparts in other Mexican states.

Henequen prosperity radically changed the market orientation, organization, and technology of the subsistence-oriented haciendas in Yucatán. By the turn of the century, according to Roland Chardon, the corn-and-cattle hacienda in the henequen zone had become

a plantation in the classical sense: a large-scale agricultural industrial producer of one main crop destined for a distant foreign industrial market. Its capital investment in lands and buildings, while low on a world scale, was substantially higher than that of other farms. Furthermore, the henequen hacienda maintained a substantial resident population, which provided most of the labor required; nearby *pueblos* supplied additional casual labor whenever necessary, with workers either commuting to the fields or temporarily residing on the hacienda. In addition, the henequen hacienda usually provided most of the services necessary in an agricultural community: health care, burial, and a local store for provisions. Even though he usually lived in Mérida, the hacendado assumed these responsibilities and also maintained law and order through his foremen.[1]

Yucatán's Golden Age was short-lived, lasting only to the end of the First World War. On the eve of President Lázaro Cárdenas's famous land expropriation decree in 1937, the highly specialized economy was tottering on the edge of ruin. Beset by competition as well as world depression and fearing radical changes in land tenure, the henequen hacendados produced less than half the volume of fiber they had produced in 1916. Land reform sharpened the crisis. The newly formed ejidos were not given the equipment needed to process the henequen leaves, nor did their members possess the skills to manage the plantations. Because production could not take place without these crucial inputs, the henequen ejidos were dependent from the beginning on the federal government for financial and administrative aid.

The first part of this chapter traces the development and decline of the henequen monoculture and analyzes the impact of export-led growth on the structure of the state economy. The latter part of the chapter focuses on the initial impact of agrarian reform in Yucatán and the factors that led to the active involvement of the Mexican federal government in henequen fiber production.

The Rise of the Henequen Monoculture in Yucatán

Howard Cline has argued that after independence the Yucatecan elite was unlike their counterparts in other parts of Mexico in that they possessed a spirit of enterprise and a desire for economic progress.[2] Events after the Caste War add support to his thesis. Private and public interests worked feverishly to stimulate the production of henequen. Legislation was passed in 1850 that provided tax exemptions for producers and established cash incentives to encourage the industrialization and export of the fiber.[3]

The most imposing technical obstacle to large-scale production was surmounted in the late 1850s, when two Yucatecans, Manuel Cecilio Vallamor and Eleuterio Antonio Solís, invented a ma-

36

chine that separated the raw fiber from the leaves. Before the invention of the mechanical rasper, or *desfibradora,* ten man-days were required to process the two thousand leaves, or *pencas,* that one man could cut in a single day.[4] The first desfibradoras were constructed of wood and required a fairly sizable labor force to operate. These manually operated machines utilized blades mounted on a rotating flywheel to strip the pulp from the fiber. The early versions could process a hundred leaves per hour.[5] After 1860 steam power was gradually adapted to the machines. Technical improvements by local mechanics also enhanced their speed, safety, and reliability. By the last decade of the nineteenth century, thirteen hundred steam-powered desfibradoras were in use in Yucatán, some of which were capable of processing twenty thousand leaves per hour.

The capital requirements for converting a subsistence hacienda into a large-scale henequen plantation were heavy.[6] The hacendado needed to purchase rasping and packing equipment as well as build sheds to house the machinery. Narrow-gauge Decauville railroad lines had to be laid throughout the hacienda to transport the harvested leaves from the field to the processing plant and to move the baled raw fiber to the nearest railhead. Further costs were incurred to maintain newly planted fields until they began to produce, usually four to seven years after planting. An outlay of about $130,000 was needed to finance the initial investment in building and equipment and to maintain the fields on an average-size hacienda for seven years.[7] The typical henequen hacienda in late-nineteenth-century Yucatán contained 1,000–2,000 hectares.

To circumvent the restrictions of the capital-scarce environment of postwar Yucatán, an enterprising Yucatecan businessman set up local credit facilities through a New York correspondent, Thebaud Brothers. This firm also sold machinery that could not be acquired in Yucatán to the hacendados.[8] After 1860 this indirect method of financing production—North American cordage brokers and manufacturers working through "independent" local export agents—became the predominant mechanism for channeling foreign capital to the henequen industry. These credit arrangements also established the commercial and financial mechanisms through which North American interests would come to exert influence over Yucatecan producers. By pledging future fiber production to local export houses, hacendados obtained the credit they needed to expand their haciendas.

Even so, the transition from corn and cattle to henequen was a gradual one. Most landowners continued to plow their profits back into expanded plantings until about 1910.[9]

Yucatecans also worked persistently to lower internal and external transportation costs. Local investors combined their efforts and funds with those of the state government to build modern transportation facilities in Yucatán during the last three decades of the nineteenth century. Progreso, a new port that is closer to Mérida than the port of Sisal, was opened in 1871. To insure that regular service would be established among Progreso, Veracruz, and New York, the federal government paid a subsidy to a U.S. steamship company.[10] Rail transportation replaced the system of primitive cart roads around Mérida. By 1890 Yucatán possessed the most extensive rail system of any state in Mexico.[11] In addition to more than 800 kilometers of standard-gauge track, it consisted of over 1,600 kilometers of intermediate gauge and Decauville track in service.[12] These rail lines were located within the northwestern quadrant of the state, or henequen zone, and significantly lowered the cost of moving fiber from the haciendas to Mérida and Progreso.

The feverish efforts of Yucatecans to lower production costs and expand henequen production after the Caste War created supply conditions favorable to the growth of a modern, export-oriented agroindustry. However, the rapid expansion of the henequen industry during the latter part of the nineteenth century was attributable to external factors over which local producers had little control.

The twine-binding harvester, which uses natural-fiber twine to tie wheat as it is harvested, was invented in 1878. The doubling of American wheat exports between 1880 and 1885 and the subsequent adaptation of the harvester to other grain crops substantially increased the external demand for agricultural-grade twine. After 1880 United States agriculture consumed 90 percent of Yucatán's fiber production. These events exerted an immediate impact on the state because it was one of the two major suppliers of commercial-quality fibers.[13] Exports of raw fiber and manufactured articles from Yucatán, which had risen steadily from 202 tons in 1860 to 9,444 tons in 1879, were averaging more than 100,000 tons annually by 1910.[14] Yucatecans recognized the dangers of binding themselves to a single market. To encourage the diversification of markets, the state legislature offered to pay a premium on henequen fiber shipped to Europe.[15] These efforts failed, however, and Yucatecan hacendados remained firmly tied to a few large U.S. buyers.

Political changes in Mexico created a favorable internal environment for the rapid expansion of fiber production. President Porfirio Díaz, who ruled from 1876 to 1910, brought peace and stability to the nation. His political and economic policies also created an environment that favored its economic growth. During the Díaz era, the country acquired the beginnings of an industrial base and a national transportation system.

The internal peace that Díaz imposed upon Mexico extended to Yucatán, where internal politics had been tumultuous during the 1850s and 1860s. Henequen hacendados took advantage of the liberalism of the period to obtain favorable land and labor legislation. The Díaz administration's liberal interpretation of the *Ley Lerdo*[16] enabled the hacendados to acquire land that previously had been held in common by the indigenous Maya. A. J. Graham Knox notes that, "Between 1856 and 1910 at least sixty-six Indian communities in the state had their village lands, amounting to some 134,000 *hectareas*, alienated by the expanding *haciendas*. As a result, many of the previously independent Mayan villagers had little choice but to move to the estates and accept employment offered by the henequen hacendados."[17]

The expansion in production was contingent upon the availability of large quantities of cheap labor. The state's debt peonage laws were strengthened to insure hacendados an adequate supply of labor. Government officials and hacienda owners rigorously enforced these laws, and the hacienda labor force quadrupled between 1880 and 1900, increasing from 20,767 to 80,216.[18] Even these measures proved to be insufficient. The state's low rate of population growth and the rapid increase in henequen production combined to produce a chronic shortage of agricultural labor. To augment the local supply of labor, state and federally sponsored immigration began during the 1880s and continued into the early decades of the twentieth century. An estimated 15,000 laborers were brought to Yucatán during this period,[19] some voluntarily and others, like the rebellious Yaqui Indians of northern Mexico, in chains.

Despite occasional periods of low prices, henequen production was highly profitable for the small, privileged class that controlled its production and export. The elite who made up this class numbered about three hundred families. An even smaller group, perhaps twenty to thirty families, through ownership of distribution and marketing mechanisms as well as land, controlled up to 90 percent of total fiber production. These families owned the largest henequen haciendas as well as a large share of the business establishments and urban real estate in Mérida.[20]

By 1910 the few families that made up the *casta divina*, or divine caste, were extremely wealthy and far removed from the rigors and privation their fathers and grandfathers had faced in building prosperity out of the ashes of the Caste War. Large portions of their wealth were spent on expensive imported consumer goods from Europe and ornate mansions in Mérida. Their children were sent to the United States or to Europe to be educated. All significant economic, political, and social activity in Yucatán was initiated by and centered around this small group. The elevated status of the casta divina contrasted sharply with that of dozens of small planters who struggled just to continue producing and whose interests were more often than not subordinated to those of the elite class. Mérida, which by 1910 was the residence of 80,000 of the state's 340,000 population,[21] assumed a facade of modernity.

In contrast, most of the state's population still labored under what David Franz describes as a "massive burden of ignorance and rusticity." Illiteracy reached 85 percent in the rural areas of the state and 41 percent in Mérida. The populations of only seven towns exceeded four thousand, and most people lived in isolated hamlets of less than five hundred.[22]

THE END OF THE GOLDEN AGE

The high prices and large profits that characterized the henequen boom set economic and political forces in motion that eventually undermined Yucatán's prosperity. Fiber producers found themselves vulnerable to the price-fixing efforts of large American buyers and, more importantly, to competition from other hard-fiber-producing nations.

In contrast to most other plantation economies in the Americas, Yucatecans maintained control over the land, physical capital, and local transportation infrastructure that were essential to the production of henequen fiber. José Luis Sierra V. states that the absence of direct foreign investment in Yucatán when it was so prevalent in the rest of Mexico was a consequence of the high social cost of a foreign owner maintaining the conditions of labor exploitation on the henequen hacienda.[23] This is a plausible explanation, particularly in light of the mechanism that U.S. capitalists soon were able to establish to exercise indirect control over production. Foreign, particularly U.S., capital was critical in the financing of production and processing equipment during the latter part of the nineteenth century. Technicians from the United States also participated actively in the operation of the state's railroads and other public services.[24] The preponderant role of foreign capital in the growth of the henequen industry has led historians Gilbert Joseph and Allen Wells to conclude that the industry was "penetrated and controlled indirectly" by U.S. cordage interests.[25]

The hundreds of henequen haciendas delivered their fiber to local import-export houses to liquidate loans, purchase equipment, and import consumer goods. The import-export houses, in turn, sold the fiber to a few American buyers, the most prominent among them being International Harvester and Peabody and Company. These marketing and financing arrangements as well as the competitve structure of the market encouraged American buyers to attempt to manipulate the price of raw fiber.

In 1902 International Harvester Company (IHC) was formed, under the leadership of Cyrus McCormick, owner of McCormick Harvesting Machine Company, by a merger of five of the largest harvesting-machine companies in North America. By 1911 IHC, which also manufactured harvest twine, had captured almost two-thirds of the U.S. binder-twine market.[26] Because more than 90 percent of Yucatecan henequen was exported to the United States, the formation of IHC significantly reduced the competition for raw fiber. Further, in 1902 IHC signed a secret agreement with a prominent Yucatecan export house, Molina y Compañía, which agreed to purchase raw fiber at prices dictated by IHC. This agreement was supplemented by an informal agreement between IHC and Peabody and Company under which IHC enjoyed the right to determine the nature of Peabody's transactions in the Yucatán fiber market.[27]

Joseph and Wells argue that those agreements, in conjunction with the financial support given to Molina y Compañía by IHC that allowed the export house to expand its control over the local market, were primarily responsible for the steady decline in raw fiber prices between 1902 and 1911. International Harvester, thus, stands accused by Joseph and Wells of creating an informal empire in Yucatán during that period and thereby stifling the region's prospects for long-term economic growth. The historians' thesis has been challenged by the authors of this volume and other scholars who argue that external economic conditions immediately before and during the period better explain the decline in prices.[28]

The efforts of henequen producers to counter the American oligopsony were frustrated by the inability of the numerous growers to act in concert and their failure to raise sufficient financial capital to valorize raw-fiber supplies.[29] Finally, in 1915, General Salvador Alvarado, who had been appointed governor of the state by Mexican President Venustiano Carranza, temporarily broke the oligopsony. By seizing control of the state railroad system, he induced 90 percent of the hacendados to sell their fiber to a state agency, Comisión Reguladora del Mercado de Henequen (Reguladora).[30] This act set the stage for a confrontation between the United States and Yucatán during World War I. Stockpiling efforts by the United States government and the successful Yucatecan monopoly caused prices to rise sharply from $.0559 a pound in 1916 to more than $.14 a pound in 1918.[31] The value of Yucatán's total fiber sales between November 1915 and November 1918 exceeded 190 million.[32] Despite the economic measures applied by the United States government to counter the monopoly, supplemented with vigorous protests to the Mexican government, Reguladora continued to function until 1921.

The prosperity of the World War I period was short-lived. Competition from other hard-fiber-producing nations rapidly eroded Yucatán's dominant position in the world market after 1920. Before the Spanish-American War, only abaca, a hard fiber produced in the Philippines, competed with henequen in United States markets. The war so severely disrupted the supply of abaca that by 1900 Yucatán had an almost total monopoly on world hard fiber production. As late as 1920, only 14,000 tons of fiber were produced outside Mexico. The competitive situation changed radically after 1920 as plantings of sisal increased greatly in Java and Africa in response to high wartime profits and prices.[33] Lower labor costs in these areas permitted sisal to be highly competitive with henequen. By 1927 Asian and African nations accounted for almost 50 percent of world hard fiber production.[34]

During this critical period, Yucatán's competitive position vis-à-vis the new producers worsened because hacendados attempted to maintain prices at near World War I levels. Prices fell immediately after the war because the United States had stockpiled raw fiber during the conflict. In 1925 President Calles, reacting to the petitions of the distressed planters, ordered the formation of Henequeneros de Yucatán Cooperativa Limitada, whose function was to establish an orderly market and restore high prices. Henequeneros' pricing policies accelerated Yucatán's market-share losses. Within a decade after the organization was formed, the state was producing only 14 percent of the world's hard fibers and the local industry had virtually collapsed.[35]

The Great Depression and the invention of the combine, which did not use twine, contributed to the industry's woes during the 1930s. Raw fiber prices, which had plummeted to $.065 a pound in 1919, remained at $.06 a pound or less during all but four of the next twenty-three years. Production fell drastically and exports reached an all-time low in 1940, when they were less than a fourth of the 201,990 tons shipped in 1916.[36] The decrease in output created widespread unemployment and unrest among the henequen workers. Most of the thirty thousand to thirty-five thousand of them worked only one or two days a week. Field wages, which reached a high of twenty to twenty-five pesos a week during the boom period, fell to five pesos or less.[37]

GROWTH AND DIVERSIFICATION OF THE MONOCROP ECONOMY

By the first decade of the twentieth century, the economic well-being of Yucatán was solidly linked to the fortunes of a single industry. Just before the Caste War, less than 3 percent of the cultivated land in Yucatán was sown in henequen, and exports of this commodity represented about 16 percent of the total value of goods shipped out of the state.[38] By 1910 almost 200,000 hectares, or more than 70 percent of all cultivated land, was sown in henequen, and the value of nonhenequen exports had fallen to less than 5 percent of total exports.[39] Because raw fiber production attracted the majority of the state's capital and work force, increasing quantities of corn, beef, and vegetables as well as other staples needed to be imported after 1900. Although the large inflows of export income during the Golden Age did not spark the diversification of the regional economy during the early twentieth century, significant preconditions were established for the later emergence of industry. By the 1960s Yucatán would possess the world's largest and most modern cordage industry.

The monocrop orientation of Yucatán's economic evolution during the last decades of the nineteenth century was probably unavoidable. Most regional economists deem it unlikely that the expansion of primary production will support rapid and diversified development except under the most favorable conditions. Douglass North and the so-called staple theorists have presented evidence that primary production led rather than inhibited growth in parts of Canada and the United States. Similar conditions are usually absent in underdeveloped nations today and were certainly not present in nineteenth-century Yucatán.[40]

The success of export-led growth and development in North's model is dependent upon the existence of "spill-over," or linkage, effects from initial export activities. Backward linkages exist if the expansion of an export industry causes firms that supply materials to the export industry to locate in the region or to increase their existing production. The export industry generates forward linkages if the expansion of its production causes other firms to increase production or locate locally so they can use the export industry's products as inputs.

Linkage effects are relatively weak in underdeveloped nations, where, typically, subsistence agriculture is still important and interdependence among economic activities is low. Production for export is likely to be dominated by the exploitation of agricultural products and minerals, activities that present few opportunities for the formation of the types of backward and forward linkages that directly stimulate significant new private or public investment.[41] If the export industry does generate strong linkage effects, the question still remains as to whether or not they will be fully exploited. The underdeveloped region may lack an adequate transportation system. More important, outside investors may be unaware of the investment opportunities in the region.[42]

The industry with the strongest forward linkage to raw fiber production, the manufacture of cordage, contracted rather than expanded during the period of henequen prosperity. Before the

44

Caste War, a number of "cord lofts" in Mérida manufactured ropes, cables, and bagging. After the conflict, manufactured goods continued to account for the majority of Yucatán's henequen exports until 1878 and the opening of the U.S. agricultural market.[43] After that date, Yucatecan growers began to send their raw fiber to the United States, and the industry languished. The local mills that continued to operate were unable to penetrate U.S. markets and declined rapidly in importance. A serious effort, backed by the state government and McCormick Harvesting Machine Company, was made by prominent Yucatecans to revive the moribund industry in 1897. McCormick Harvesting Machine Company, which operated no binder twine-producing factories, apparently viewed the project as a means of obtaining a reliable supply of harvest twine. National Cordage Company was attempting to monopolize harvest-twine production in the 1890s.[44] The new cordage mill, La Industrial, S.A., was capitalized initially at 800,000 pesos. It operated sporadically until 1907 when, like its predecessors, it succumbed to outside competitive forces.

On the surface, the failure of La Industrial and the earlier mills is somewhat puzzling. Because the elaboration of harvest twine is not a weight-adding process, American mills enjoyed little or no advantage over Yucatecan producers because of their closer proximity to the final consumers. Keith Hartman speculates that a cordage industry may have failed to develop because of a lack of unity among the Yucatecan elite. "Considering the grasp held by Yucatecans on the American fiber market, nothing seems odder than the lack of cordage mills in Mérida; a combined effort by hacendados could have easily forced the United States to take finished Mexican twine as well as raw Mexican fiber."[45]

Hartman's analysis discounts the difficulties inherent in the task of uniting several hundred producers in a common cause. He also ignores the activities of McCormick Harvesting Machine Company and its successor, IHC. McCormick Harvesting Machine Company rapidly lost interest in La Industrial and by 1900 was manufacturing binder twine in the United States. After the formation of IHC in 1902, the new firm augmented its production capacity by purchasing a number of existing mills. Later, during the regime of General Salvador Alvarado, IHC and the U.S. Food Administration actually blocked efforts by Yucatecans to establish a cordage mill in Argentina.[46] Also, apparently little interest in cordage manufacture existed among potential investors, the henequen hacendados, who were content to restrict their role to the production of raw fiber.

Production costs may have also been relatively higher in Yucatán than in the United States. Free labor was extremely scarce during the years in which raw fiber production was expanding. During periods of rapidly rising raw fiber prices, cordage mill owners were often forced to suspend production because of their inability to absorb the increased raw-material costs and still sell the finished goods at a profit.

The effect of backward linkages on the local economy was more substantial. The backwardly-linked industries that did develop, however, were so closely tied to raw fiber production that they exerted little independent impact on the state economy. By 1900 Yucatecans had built an impressive railroad system throughout the henequen zone. Yet, inasmuch as few if any other activities could produce a return comparable to that being earned on henequen, the railroads did little to stimulate new industry.

Yucatán did create an extensive machine industry, which was unusual for a predominantly agrarian economy.[47] The expansion of the henequen production required hacendados to make relatively large investments in equipment to process and pack raw fiber. At first, rasping equipment and steam power plants were imported from the United States. By the beginning of the twentieth century, however, many fine machine shops in Mérida were specializing in the repair and construction of steam power plants, desfibradoras, packing machines, and sugar mills.[48] The fact that much of the equipment used today was constructed in Yucatán during that period testifies to the quality of the workmanship of those early shops.

Because the machine shops, like the railroads, depended heavily on the henequen industry, they declined in importance as a source of local income and employment after 1920. However, the skills accumulated by local entrepreneurs and labor were a critical element in the reemergence of a cordage industry in Yucatán in the mid-1920s. Local machine shops and foundries, though unable to produce the most advanced equipment used in cordage production, were able to manufacture the replacement parts and less complicated machinery for the mills.[49]

Apart from efforts by the henequen oligarchy to establish local banks, little other new activity resulted directly from the expansion of henequen production during the last two decades of the nineteenth century.[50] Nonhenequen-related activities were overshadowed by those that were linked to the production and export of raw fiber. The structure of local labor and capital markets and taxes predisposed the investor toward henequen-related activities. The impact of the considerable export income on investment was also dampened by discriminatory tax laws[51] as well as the structure of local labor and capital markets.

Characteristically, a plantation system produces a highly unequal distribution of income because the majority of the labor force receives subsistence wages. In view of the low purchasing power of most of the population, little incentive exists for local investment in facilities to produce goods for mass consumption. The possibilities of expanding both export and locally oriented activities may be further reduced by income leakages if the small landowning elite import large quantities of luxury goods or remit profits and interest abroad. On the other hand, if the optimum size is the smaller family-type farm, the final demand stimulus to investment will be stronger because a more equitable distribution of income will result and, consequently, a larger market for mass consumption goods and services. In addition, less of the income generated from export sales will flow back to developed areas in the form of remittances since the owner of the family-type holding normally will not have access to significant sources of external financing.[52]

Although it is generally conceded that the henequen workers' standard of living was higher than that of most of their counterparts in many other parts of Mexico, their wages seldom rose much above the subsistence level.[53] Certainly, the hacienda population, which accounted for more than half the population of the state, never constituted a mass market for anything more than foodstuffs and a few other basic necessities, much of which needed to be imported by the first decade of the twentieth century.

The small henequen elite used much of their newfound wealth to imitate the fashion of the upper classes in France and other European countries, where they frequently traveled. Large quantities of luxury clothing, jewelry, and furniture were imported from Europe and the United States. Agents of major jewelers in

Paris, Madrid, London, and Mexico City visited Mérida regularly to exhibit their latest creations to the rich, who competed among themselves in a dazzling display of conspicuous consumption.

The rigid economic and social structure of Yucatecan society during the period of henequen prosperity also limited the potential for diversified growth. The henequen workers, who occupied the lowest stratum of Yucatecan society, lacked virtually any upward mobility or opportunity for education. Prevented by law from leaving the hacienda to seek other employment unless his debt to the owner was repaid, the campesino spent his working life in the henequen fields or performing menial tasks. Then, as today, the tasks involved in the production of henequen fiber required almost no skill. Workers, therefore, did not acquire skills that were transferable to other sectors of the economy.

The work regimen of the hacienda, the oppressive climate, and the limits on social and economic mobility deprived Yucatán of the stimulus that mass immigration often provides to a developing area. Few ambitious and skilled immigrants were attracted during the henequen boom. In 1900 only 2,500 residents were listed as foreign-born.[54] Many workers were either imported against their will—for example, the rebellious Yaquis of Sonora—or under labor contracts and left the state at their first opportunity. The Christian Lebanese and Spaniards who immigrated made contributions to local commerce and later to the growth of a modern cordage industry in Yucatán that were disproportionate to their numbers.[55]

Finally, the frequent fluctuations in the price of raw fiber caused local investors to adopt a "boom or bust" philosophy that impeded sound investment practices. When henequen prices were rising, speculation was rife in those activities which stood to gain the most from the increase: henequen lands and the railroads. The overvaluation of stocks as well as real estate and the abuse of credit that accompanied these periods of furious speculation undermined the soundness of the already vulnerable monocrop economy; falling raw fiber prices were inevitably accompanied by a rash of bankruptcies and business failures.[56]

In addition to the factors mentioned above that limited diversified growth around the initial export base, investment in local industry was hampered by the lack of access to external markets. The benefits that might have accrued to potential export industries from the improvements in internal transportation effected after 1880 were negligible compared to the imposing external transportation problems they confronted. Overland access to Mexican and Central American markets was blocked by dense tropical forests. Progreso, the state's only suitable port, did not lie on major trade routes. Under these circumstances, the growth of local industries was limited by the small local market, whose potential in turn was constrained by excessive dependence on henequen exports and the highly unequal distribution of income.

REVOLUTION AND REFORM

In the midst of the deepening crisis of the 1930s, President Lázaro Cárdenas instituted radical land-tenure reform in Yucatán's henequen zone. His action culminated more than two decades of largely frustrated attempts by postrevolutionary administrations to effect meaningful economic and political reform in the state.

Yucatán, isolated geographically and firmly under the political control of the henequen elite, experienced little turmoil or bloodshed during the early years of the Mexican Revolution. Before 1915 local political leaders were able to accommodate themselves to the succession of military governors who were imposed by the various claimants to power in Mexico City. The governors, in turn, did little to alter the economic and political status quo in the state.

In 1915 the first real threat to the continued dominance of the henequen elite was rebuffed when Yucatecan separatists overthrew reform-minded Governor de los Santos, who had been appointed by President Carranza. Ironically, this rebellious act brought a man to the state who, in his revolutionary zeal, devoted himself to bringing about fundamental changes in its political and economic system. Carranza sent General Salvador Alvarado to reconquer Yucatán. The latter arrived with seven thousand troops and a variety of military equipment, including airplanes. Quickly and with little bloodshed, he reestablished the federal military presence.

A self-acknowledged reformer, Alvarado issued an avalanche of legislation covering all aspects of economic, social, and political life during his three years as governor. Politically, he sought to weaken the power of the elite by allowing the middle class and the newly organized labor unions to participate in state politics while excluding the most powerful of the old order.[57] The power of the elite was further reduced by his successful efforts to make Reguladora the sole buyer and seller of henequen fiber in the state.

Some land was distributed to landless campesinos by Alvarado, but the henequen haciendas were hardly affected. The general's reform program did not include a radical restructuring of the agricultural sector. Instead, he wanted to transform the henequen haciendas into *pequeñas propiedades,* or private small holdings. This would have entailed some reduction in the size of the largest haciendas. However, his intention was to stabilize and modernize the industry, not to disrupt the existing production organization. Although he favored an independent agricultural work force as well as decent wages and working conditions, he opposed the massive expropriation of henequen properties for the benefit of the workers.[58]

From 1922 to 1924 the best known of Yucatán's native sons, Marxist Governor Felipe Carrillo Puerto, would attempt to weaken the power of the elite even further by identifying his administration with the welfare of the rural masses through the formation of peasant leagues and the initiation of some meaningful land reform. He did envision the eventual expropriation of the henequen haciendas and the formation of workers' collectives to exploit the land. His strategy was a gradualist one, however, that was abruptly halted by his assassination in 1924.[59] Some writers have hypothesized that he was killed by hacendados who opposed his reform program, but this has not been substantiated.

Both Alvarado and Carrillo Puerto recognized that the hacendados' control over the campesinos would need to be broken to govern the state effectively and make it an integral part of the evolving Mexican nation. They knew this change could be accomplished only by a restructuring of the pattern of land ownership in the henequen zone.[60] Their failure to take this step represents, in part, the conservative turn that the Mexican Revolution took after 1915. More directly, it indicates that both, despite their philosophical differences, realized that the achievement of their respective social visions depended upon the continued health of the economy, which, in turn, was almost totally dependent on income from henequen. Neither was willing to risk the potential economic chaos that might envelop the state if the henequen plantations were delivered to the overwhelmingly illiterate and unskilled campesinos who labored on them. As a consequence, fourteen years of revolutionary leadership produced little real economic change in the state.

From 1915 to 1933 a total of 390,798 hectares, or 20 percent of all cropland in Yucatán, was distributed to 22,114 ejidatarios.[61] Less than a third of this total was suitable for normal agriculture, and the vast majority of the land was located outside the henequen zone.[62]

In 1935 President Lázaro Cárdenas, who knew little about either Yucatán or henequen, quickened the pace of agrarian reform in the state by delivering almost a fourth of all henequen lands to ejidos. The newly created ejidos were formed into forty-eight credit societies that were to be financed by a federal agriculture bank, Banco Nacional de Crédito Agrícola. The hacendados resisted the expropriation immediately by refusing to process ejido leaves. Cárdenas responded to this by declaring the rent of the processing equipment as well as the cultivation and exploitation of henequen to be public utilities and by sending in federal troops to enforce the order.

That year and the following one was a period of tremendous chaos. Only 15.3 percent of all henequen lands were cultivated because of the unsettling effect of the expropriation and the low world market prices for fiber.[63] The ejidos fared no better than private producers. Many ejidatarios were actually worse off than before the reform because the capital used to finance the ejidos was raised through a tax on their production. Fearing further expropriations, the hacendados proposed an alternative to further radical reform.[64] When Cárdenas rejected their plan, many of them overcut their plants in order to gain a quick return on their investment and at the same time to leave the ejidos with unprofitable fields.[65]

Cárdenas favored the collectivization of Mexican agriculture. Yucatán was chosen, along with the cotton-producing La Laguna region of northern Mexico, to be a model for his collective ejido program. The Mexican president dramatized the importance of the reorganization of agriculture in Yucatán by traveling to Mérida in 1937 to announce further sweeping reform. He was accompanied by the contingent of engineers, surveyors, and government officials who were needed to carry out the expropriations. The essence of his decree on August 8 of that year was as follows: (1) all privately held henequen land was to be expropriated, except for 150 hectares (later amended to 300 hectares) per individual, which included the processing equipment; (2) processing equipment would be acquired for use by the ejidos; (3) ejidos would receive 4 hectares of land per ejidatario; (4) ejidos would cultivate their henequen lands collectively; and (5) financing would be provided to the ejidos by a federal bank. In accordance with Cárdenas's decree, approximately 80,000 hectares of land sown in henequen were delivered to the ejidatarios in 1937. Ejidos found themselves in possession of 105,569 hectares, or 61 percent of all land sown in henequen, and that held by private producers dropped from 151,003 hectares in 1936 to 66,213 hectares the following year.[66]

Cárdenas' agrarian reform program in Yucatán and the rest of Mexico not only fulfilled his promise to achieve social justice for the nation's campesinos; it was also a highly successful political strategy. Two political ends were served that hastened the political integration of the country and consolidated the power of its political elite. In the first place, land reform had universal appeal among the landless rural masses. The ejidatarios have proven to be a durable base of support for the dominant political party, the Partido Revolucionario Institucional (PRI). Rather than allowing these peasants to become an independent political force after liberating them from their debilitating dependence upon Mexico's landowners, Cárdenas organized them into a labor federation, the Confederación Nacional del Campesino (CNC), linked directly to the Partido Nacional Revolucionario, PRI's predecessor. Since 1938 this large group of campesinos has become increasingly dependent upon the subsidies and credits of various agencies of the federal government and is, in fact, its local political extension in many Mexican states. Second, land reform diminished the political influence of the large landowners (both native and foreign) in the country. The economic, political, and social status of this group was largely dependent upon its ability to exploit and control the large rural labor force. Radical land reform weakened the local political power of this landowning elite and thereby accelerated the political integration of the nation after the mid-1930s.

AGRARIAN REFORM AND ITS AFTERMATH

From its inception, the massive reorganization of Yucatán's henequen industry was a fiasco. Conditions became so chaotic in the henequen zone that some groups of ejidatarios mutinied and demanded a return to the old system.[67] Finally, in February 1938, barely six months after Cárdenas's momentous decree, the federal government, unable to cope with the problems that land reform had introduced and hard put to continue subsidizing the henequen ejidos, turned control of the industry over to the state government.

In their determination to reap the political and social benefits of land reform and wrest control of the henequen industry from the hacendado class, Cárdenas and his followers did not consider carefully the economic consequences of land redistribution in Yucatán.[68] The hundreds of haciendas were surveyed and their lands distributed to ejidos within two weeks after Cárdenas made the expropriation announcement. The number of ejidos in the henequen zone was increased from 53 to 276. A new federal credit agency, the Banco Nacional de Crédito Ejidal (BNCE), was to aid in the transition. Its function during the transition period was to render technical, administrative, and financial assistance to the ejidos until such a time as the collective units were on a firm financial footing. The federal government, in effect, replaced the hacendado.

Problems arose immediately because of the haphazard way in which land had been redistributed. Because the ex-hacendados were allowed to keep the processing equipment along with 300 hectares of land, the ejidos did not receive the equipment necessary to process their leaves. Further, their fields were not always contiguous or even within reasonable walking distance of the ejidatarios' villages. Worse yet, only a small number of the 276 ejidos possessed lands that were properly proportioned between fields in the productive stage and fields in the nonproductive stage of the henequen plant's extended growth cycle. Some ejidos, for example, received few or no exploitable fields and therefore could not generate an income sufficient to support their members.[69]

Possessing neither processing equipment, money capital, nor administrative expertise, the ejidos were, from the beginning, completely dependent upon the federal government. In 1937 Cárdenas had ordered the hacendados to rent the necessary processing equipment to the new ejidos. The state government was late in executing this part of the decree. When Governor Canto Echeverría did comply, he delivered fewer units than had been stipulated, an indication that friction was rising between the state and federal governments. The hacendados, who were receiving virtually worthless bonds for compensation, attempted to resist the order by appealing to the courts and by sabotaging the equipment.[70] The organizational problems and delaying tactics disastrously affected productivity[71] and the status of the credits that had been advanced to the ejidos. The majority of the new ejidos generated losses rather than profits. Therefore, instead of progressing toward a firm financial footing, they simply fell deeper in debt to the BNCE. Unemployment also continued to be a problem and to contribute to unrest among the ejidatarios because land reform did not reduce the labor surplus in the henequen zone.

The inability of the BNCE to cope with the problems of the new collectives caused Cárdenas to try an alternative solution in 1938. What he decided to do, in effect, was to eliminate federal control over the ejidos and return jurisdiction to the state. Undoubtedly, one of the major factors in his decision was the increasing financial drain that ejido operations were inflicting upon the fiscally strapped federal government. The BNCE advanced 16 million pesos to the collectives and recovered only 9 million.[72] With the assent of Cárdenas in 1938, the bank turned the administration of the ejidos over to the governor of the state, who placed it under the aegis of a reorganized Henequeneros de Yucatán.

Henequeneros was charged with the following responsibilities: (1) oversee production and sale of fiber; (2) oversee the industrialization of raw fiber; and (3) provide social services for the ejidatarios in the henequen zone. The organization's initial capital was 10 million pesos. Any producer who would agree to sell all his fiber to the state agency could be a member. The governor was the president of the directing body of the agency, whose members included representatives from both private and ejido producers. The federal government was also represented, but, from the beginning, control of the organization and administration of the industry were in the hands of Yucatecans.[73]

One of the first actions of the agency was to correct the worst mistakes that had been made during the hasty redistribution. First, ejidatario wages were standardized throughout the zone. This eliminated the income disparities among ejidos that had resulted from the initial distribution. Second, competent technical personnel were assigned to plan and oversee ejido production. Despite the changes, Henequeneros experienced difficulties at first because of continuing friction between the hacendados and ejidos over possession of processing equipment and because of the continued depressed state of the world market for henequen.

The entry of the United States into World War II proved to be the salvation of both Henequeneros and the henequen industry. In 1941 the United States, cut off from other sources of hard fiber, contracted to purchase 1.25 million bales from Henequeneros at nine cents a pound. The prospects of prosperity brought a temporary solution to the problem of who should possess the processing equipment. All equipment was returned to the previous owners to allow completion of the contract; ejidos were "relieved" of the responsibilities of processing. In accordance with this division of labor, ejidos received 48 percent of the price paid by Henequeneros for raw fiber, and the owners of the processing equipment were paid 52 percent.[74]

Critics of this period claim that the ex-hacendados, now pequeños propietarios, took advantage of the new state organization to regain control of the industry and recover the wealth they had lost during the expropriations and more. One author cites income-distribution data for the period as evidence of the corrupt nature of Henequeneros during World War II. In 1946, for example, the organization paid 23,000 ejidatarios 42,256,299 pesos, and half that sum was allotted to 250 pequeños propietarios. Further, during the period in which the state agency controlled production, distribution of income to the different producing sectors was as follows: ejidos produced 70 percent of the fiber and received 20 percent of its value; pequeños propietarios produced 20 percent and received 36 percent of its value; *parcelarios* (small private producers) produced 10 percent and received 2 percent of its value. The 42 percent that remained was absorbed for the administration of Henequeneros, which made it a practice to purchase raw fiber from members at less than world market prices.[75]

Right after World War II, the industry fell into an expected postwar slump. Prices fell and raw fiber output dropped from a wartime high of 121,663 tons in 1943 to a low of 74,561 tons in 1955 (table 1). Chaotic market conditions again brought the industry close to collapse. This time an added element, the Yucatecan cordage industry that had grown rapidly during World War II, further complicated the smooth transition from wartime to peacetime. At times, cordage mills sold finished products at or below the raw fiber prices charged by Henequeneros. Ironically, it was selling the raw material to the local mills at a below-market price. In 1955 President Ruiz Cortines, reportedly reacting to charges of widespread corruption in the administration of the ejidos and seeking a solution to the chaotic and depressed state of the industry, dissolved Henequeneros and replaced it with a new federal credit agency.

Summary and Conclusions

Yucatán's economic, political, and social landscape underwent a radical transformation during the century that followed the end of the active phase of the Caste War. Like many other nonindustrial regions in the world during the latter part of the nineteenth century, the state became a peripheral element in the expansion of a handful of industrializing capitalist nations. Its success in becoming a supplier of raw materials to U.S. agriculture was attributable to a number of factors, not the least being the ingenuity of the Yucatecans themselves. Precapitalist labor laws and practices that permitted the almost slavelike exploitation of the large indigenous labor force were also a key element in the expansion of the commercial henequen monoculture. During the prerevolutionary period, Yucatán's entrepreneurs were limited in their ability to shape their own destiny and that of their region. Their fortunes became closely tied to the vicissitudes of U.S. agriculture and to the decisions of a few large foreign purchasers of fiber.

The very characteristics that allowed Yucatán to emerge as a Mexican success story during the early twentieth century made it vulnerable to the vagaries of the world economy and to revolutionary change. The resistance of Yucatecan hacendados to agrarian reform and their persistence in defending labor practices that were the antithesis of constitutional guarantees to Mexican campesinos made the industry a highly visible political target for Lázaro Cárdenas after 1934. Once established as a participant in henequen production, the federal government would prove reluctant to relinquish control for both economic and political motives. Thus, Yucatán, during the stormy years that preceded the radical reforms of 1937, continued to be subject to external influence—that of Mexico City.

4

Federal Intervention
and Industry Performance:
The Agricultural Sector

▲▲▲▲▲▲▲▲▲▲▲▲▲▲▲▲▲▲▲▲▲▲▲▲▲▲▲▲▲▲▲▲▲▲▲▲▲▲▲

AGRARIAN reform profoundly altered the pat-
tern of land tenure and the structure of property rights in
Yucatán. These changes caused a radical restructuring of production organization in the henequen zone. The ejido replaced the
hacienda as the dominant production unit in the industry; and
the federal government, by virtue of its close economic and political ties to the ejidos, supplanted the hacendado.

Henequen production and cost data after 1955 suggest that the
changes in production organization adversely affected raw fiber
production costs. First, the haphazard distribution of land in 1937
impaired the economic and geographic integrity of the production
unit. The large henequen hacienda ceased to exist after 1937.
Former hacienda lands are cultivated today by three different
types of producers, two of which bear little resemblance to the
hacienda in their organization. Second, the federal presence in the
industry altered the incentive structure of the production unit.
Government institutions came to dominate the demand side of
the raw fiber market and substituted their own set of incentives
and disincentives for those of the market.

It became increasingly evident after the reassertion of the
federal government's presence in the industry in 1955 that agrarian reform did not result in any fundamental change in the relative economic status of the henequen worker. The authority that
Mexico City came to exercise over the ejidos' productive activity
made a mockery of the collectives' control over the former
hacienda lands that had been granted them by Lázaro Cárdenas.
Their restricted rights to the use of their own land and their
dependency on the federal government for financing made the

ejidatarios vulnerable to a new form of economic and political exploitation—that of the state and its agents. The henequen ejidos became controlled collectives.

Further, ex-hacienda owners, far from being destroyed by the reforms, were able to maintain some degree of their former unequal status with respect to the henequen workers. The federal government permitted them to maintain control over most of the industry's capital equipment that was needed to process henequen leaves.

The Economic Organization of the Prereform Henequen Hacienda

The economic and spatial organization of the privately owned, preagrarian reform henequen hacienda was the result of decades of trial-and-error evolution from the subsistence-oriented, cattle-and-corn haciendas that dominated Yucatecan agriculture until the late nineteenth century. Unlike the archetypal hacienda in Mexico and much of the rest of Latin America,[1] the henequen hacienda was a profit-oriented, agroindustrial operation whose production was geared to large external markets. Although the technology used in both the agricultural and industrial operations was relatively simple, management was a complex task that demanded considerable technical and financial skills.

Just before the initiation of land reform in 1934, more than three hundred haciendas were actively producing raw henequen fiber in Yucatán. Although they varied in size from a few hundred hectares up to several thousand hectares, their economic organization was practically uniform throughout the state.

The distinguishing characteristic of raw fiber production was that the agricultural and manufacturing operations were fully integrated in an economic and geographical sense. Rasping and packing equipment were located near the center of the hacienda's fields. A network of portable Decauville railroads connected the leaf-processing facilities with the fields where leaves were being harvested. After the leaves were cut and bundled, they were transported directly to the desfibradora by mule-drawn platforms. There, the raw fiber was extracted from the leaves, dried on nearby racks, and then pressed into 180-kilogram *pacas*, or bales. These were carried to the nearest railhead for shipment to Mérida or Progreso, again by mule-drawn platforms.

Henequen fiber on drying racks. (Photo by Joel Whitman)

The henequen leaves were processed on the hacienda for several reasons. First, leaf-processing is a weight-reducing operation; the raw fiber represents only 10 percent of the weight of the leaf. Second, the quality of the fiber deteriorates if the leaves are not processed within twenty-four hours after being cut. Third, the manufacturing operation probably increased the producers' return. The cultivation and harvesting of the plant were relatively land-extensive and labor-intensive. The leaf-processing operation, on the other hand, was relatively capital-intensive and required only a few unskilled laborers. Before land reform, debt peonage and the limited employment alternatives in the henequen zone kept hacienda workers' wages near the subsistence level.[2] Assuming that the average product of the desfibradora workers was higher in value than that of the field workers and yet their wages were roughly the same, a significant profit differential may have existed between the two operations.

The hacendado's production and investment decisions were complicated by the peculiar life cycle of the henequen plant. During *fomento*, or the first one to two years, the young plants are tended in a separate field. As many as three thousand plants are needed per hectare planted. After this initial phase, the plant is in *cultivo* until its seventh year. Leaves may not be harvested during this phase, but the fields need to be weeded at least twice a year. From the seventh to the twelfth year, the plant is said to be in *mateo*; the fields still require frequent weeding and a few leaves may be selectively cut. The full production phase, or *explotación*, normally lasts from the twelfth to the twentieth year. As many as twenty to twenty-two leaves can be cut from each plant annually during three harvests without impairing productivity. After the twentieth year, leaf production begins to decline and the fields are no longer maintained. When production from a field in the final phase, called *decadencia*, is no longer sufficient to justify its existence, the field is burned over and, ideally, allowed to lie fallow for seven years before being replanted.

To insure that fiber production did not fluctuate widely from year to year, the hacendado was forced to maintain fields in all phases of the plant life cycle. The established practice was to keep at least 50 percent of the land in the nonproductive and least-productive phases.[3]

Agricultural and industrial tasks were structured so that the relatively unskilled hacienda labor force could be used interchangeably in the fields or at the desfibradora and packing facility. Field work had to be closely supervised since improper harvesting or weeding could lower the productivity of the henequen plant by as much as 50 percent. Particular care was given to fields in the mateo phase. Supervisors marked the individual leaves to be cut inasmuch as overcutting retarded plant growth. In view of the perishable nature of the harvested leaves, the desfibradora and packing equipment also had to be maintained meticulously. To minimize breakdowns, each hacienda usually retained a skilled mechanic to service the equipment.

The planning horizon of the hacendado was lengthy because fields continued to be a source of revenue up to the twenty-fifth year of the life cycle. Hacendados did not base their investment decisions upon expected profit streams over the life cycle of a field since they could not predict future prices with any degree of accuracy. Production data suggests that current profits were the major determinant of the hacendados' investment decisions.[4] Their access to long-term investment funds was limited primarily to retained earnings. Profitable years provided the stimulus as well as the funds needed to make new plantings.

Potential raw fiber production in a given year was the result of past investment decisions. The short-run supply of the individual producer was highly inelastic. If prices fell below expected levels, low-productivity fields could be abandoned and harvest levels adjusted to the current price and cost structure. In the event that profits exceeded expectations, the hacendado could produce somewhat beyond normal capacity by overcutting his fields. Both of these short-run supply responses, however, impacted negatively on the expected profit of the hacienda because they lowered the productivity of the affected fields.

The henequen plantation utilized relatively large amounts of capital and produced a single commodity for sale in external markets. The increased risk that this specialization entailed, combined with the complexity of the production process, forced the hacendado to adopt rational management practices and to participate actively in the administration of his estate. As the haciendas increased in size and number toward the end of the nineteenth century, owners often found it expedient to delegate responsibility for the day-to-day management of the large and sometimes far-flung properties to hired managers. This practice led to the creation of a class of technically competent professional administrators, who often supervised production on several haciendas. Most of the henequen haciendas, however, continued to be family enterprises in which the owners played an active role in management.[5]

POST-LAND-REFORM PRODUCTION UNITS

Of the three disparate units that replaced the henequen hacienda, only one, the pequeña propiedad, retained the production organization of the prereform hacienda. The other two major classes of producers, the ejido and the *parcela*, or small parcel, are basically agricultural units that depend on other entities to rasp the harvested leaves and, in the case of the ejidos, to administer production.

The Ejido

The present henequen ejidos differ in four important ways from the prereform haciendas: (1) the legal protection that the law grants the ejido severely limits the ejidatario's freedom to transfer participatory rights and to acquire resources; (2) as production units, they do not possess the same economic and geographical unity as the hacienda; (3) they do not control the production decisions that relate to their own land; and (4) they are political as well as economic organizations.

Production is carried out in the ejido sector by about 500 "economic groups" that receive credit from the Banrural.[6] Since the late 1930s, the proportion of henequen land in full production held by ejidos has fluctuated between two-thirds to three-fourths of the total. At the end of 1977, almost 160,000 hectares of land were classified as being in full production (table 1). In 1980 some 57,259 active and retired henequen workers possessed rights to ejido land.

In theory, each ejido is an independent, self-governing production unit. Members elect a three-man governing body in periodic general assemblies. This committee is charged with the internal organization of the collective production unit and with the representation of ejido interests before outside administrative and judicial authorities. The ejido president, in his role as *socio delegado*, is also the representative of the local credit society that obtains production financing from the agricultural bank, Banrural.

TABLE 1. Yucatán: Raw Fiber Production, Land in Full Production, and Average Yield per Hectare, All Producers, by Selected Years, 1901–1982

Year	Raw Fiber Production (in metric tons)	Land in Full Production (in hectares)	Average Yield (in kilograms per hectare)
1901	83,191	87,600	949
1910	94,789	123,700	766
1916	201,990	198,300	820
1920	160,759	188,600	852
1930	102,899	97,435	1,056
1937	93,821	84,447	1,111
1938	73,236	90,748	806
1943	121,663	124,607	976
1950	90,128	129,547	695
1955	74,651	132,982	560
1956	98,062	140,500	697
1960	137,643	165,472	832
1964	131,267	190,187	690
1970	117,751	150,460	782
1971	113,493	154,591	734
1972	113,848	173,786	655
1973	109,188	174,785	624
1974	111,983	168,928	662
1975	101,421	160,000	633
1976	98,530	157,000	625
1977	85,697	159,556	537
1978	80,007	150,375	532
1979	70,442	135,000	522
1980	71,816	135,000	532
1981	75,772	135,740	558
1982	61,045	. . .	. . .

SOURCES: Gobierno del Estado de Yucatán, *El tercer informe del gobernador* (Mérida, 1979); Secretaría de Agricultura y Ganadería, Agencia General en Mérida, Yucatán, *Henequen 1901 a 1973* (Mérida, 1974); Secretaría de Agricultura y Recursos Hidráulicos, Representación en Yucatán, *Yucatán en cifras, 20 años de estadísticas agropecuarias* (Mérida, 1978); Gobierno del Estado de Yucatán, *El sexto informe del gobernador* (Mérida, 1982); "El declive de la producción de henequen," *Diario de Yucatán,* 30 May 1983.

The Banrural was created in 1974 through a merger of the Banco Nacional de Crédito Ejidal and two other rural credit institutions.[7] In 1980 the peninsula office of the Banrural employed 1,700 people, who served more than 3,700 credit societies in the states of Yucatán, Campeche, and Quintana Roo. The bank is officially charged with stimulating Mexican agriculture and agroindustry by providing financial, technical, and advisory support to producers who are unable to obtain those services from the private sector. In reality, the bank's involvement in rural Mexico goes far beyond the passive provision of auxiliary services. Banrural is the major and, most often, the only source of credit for the more than two million ejidatarios and their families. It is a key marketing channel for ejido production as well as a primary agency through which the federal government introduces innovation and change in agricultural organization and production techniques. Apart from its economic and technical functions, it is also an important political and social arm of the federal government in the area it serves.

The bank's official functions in the henequen industry are financial and advisory. The work plan for each ejido credit society is supposed to be made up on a weekly basis by the socio delegado of the ejido in consultation with an inspector from Banrural. The socio delegado then assigns specific tasks to each economic group. Typically, the division of labor in an ejido consists of cleaning existing fields (chapeo), cutting leaves, and clearing land for the sowing of new henequen plants. After daily tasks are completed, another ejido official, the checkeador, or group foreman, inspects each man's work in his group and reports the day's activities to the socio delegado. The ejido's fields and records are checked weekly by the Banrural inspector to insure that the week's work schedule has been completed in a satisfactory manner. His report is the basis for the credit advance that the ejido receives for the week. The credit advance is delivered to the socio delegado, who is then responsible for distributing the funds to individual ejido members according to work performed.

Credit advances are supposed to be self-liquidating. Ejidal fiber is sold to Cordemex, the government-owned cordage manufacturing monopoly. Sales proceeds are applied against the ejido's loan account. If the proceeds of an ejido's fiber sales exceed the principal and interest of its credit advances, the profit or excess is returned to the ejido for distribution among its members.

The production technology used by the henequen ejidos is virtually the same as that of the prereform haciendas. Similarities end there, however. The hacienda was a highly integrated, profit-oriented agroindustrial operation; the ejido is essentially an agricultural unit that is financed and administered by the federal government to satisfy social and political as well as economic objectives.

The separation of the agricultural and processing functions was a result of the way in which land reform was carried out and, subsequently, the administrative policies of the federal government. In forming the ejidos, federal officials did not maintain the economic and geographical unity that had characterized the hacienda. Because hacienda owners were allowed to retain their leaf-processing facilities, the collectives were deprived of the equipment they needed to process their leaves. Cárdenas's decision in 1938 to place the ejidos under the control of Henequeneros de Yucatán did little to improve their economic status. Dominated by former plantation owners, this organization was hostile to the reform from the beginning and had little incentive to constitute the ejidos as independent production units. Efforts to supply the collectives with processing equipment were simply abandoned.

Efforts after 1955 to integrate the agricultural and manufacturing operations in the ejido sector have been only partially successful. The ejidos themselves, of course, do not enjoy the freedom as owners of the property to engage in transactions that might create a more economically efficient spatial and economic organization of the communally owned resources. The federal government did not begin acquiring desfibradoras and packing equipment for ejido use until 1962. By 1970 forty-one government-owned processing plants were located throughout the henequen zone, or about 20 percent of the total number of plants in the state. Finally, in 1976, Banrural sold these facilities to ejido credit societies, but bank personnel were retained to supervise their operation.

Although the ejidos now possess sufficient capacity to process most all collectively produced leaves, their agricultural and industrial operations continue to be only partially integrated. Banrural, which considers the leaves as security for the credits advanced to the ejidos, has customarily directed most of the ejidos' production to private desfibradoras that operate under a

65

contract with the bank.[8] In 1975 and 1976 ejidos processed less than half of all the fiber they produced.[9] The structure of Yucatán's leaf-processing industry has been the object of a bitter controversy that will be discussed in chapters 5 and 6.

Beyond the differences noted between the ejido and the pre-reform hacienda in the degrees of economic and spatial integration, the ejido, unlike the hacienda, exercises little or no control over its own production decisions. In fact, in recent years the government has abandoned even the pretense that the collectives are economically independent units. Banrural makes all production and investment decisions for the ejidos. The bank's decisions are made effective through its control over production credit advances. Quite literally, not a single "economic group" in the ejido sector could survive for more than a short period as a viable production unit if deprived of agricultural bank credit.

The legal restrictions on ejido ownership have played a major role in the growth of the dependency relationship that exists between the ejidos and the agricultural bank. The rights to ejido grants are vested in the community and are inalienable. Although, according to the Mexican Agrarian Code of 1934, each eligible henequen worker possesses the legal right to four hectares of cultivatable land, he can neither sell, rent, nor encumber his grant. Individual ejido rights can only be transferred at the time of death. The result of these provisions of the law is that the henequen ejidos cannot obtain financing from nongovernmental sources.

Despite the apparent inefficiency of the ejido production unit as it was constituted in 1937, the federal government's interest in the henequen collectives since 1955 clearly has been more political and social than economic. Any serious program to rationalize ejido production would have entailed substantial reductions in the work force and the elimination of marginal production units, as well as efforts to correct the organizational deficiencies discussed above. Successive Mexican presidents chose to subsidize the collectives rather than risk the political turmoil that a radical reorganization might entail. Yucatán's history of rebellion and political discontent has caused the ruling party to be highly sensitive to the potential for political instability in the state.

In 1955 a sizable labor surplus existed in the henequen zone. Although production was below pre-World War II levels, the number of henequen ejidatarios had increased to 44,911 (table 2).

TABLE 2. Ejido Sector: Number of Ejidatarios on the Official Bank Payroll, by Selected Years, 1938–1978

Year	Number of Ejidatarios	Year	Number of Ejidatarios
1938	35,000	1966	58,726
1955	44,911	1967	63,296
1956	48,343	1968	68,748
1957	47,577	1969	71,475
1958	48,992	1970	74,036
1959	52,779	1971	74,096
1960	50,980	1972	66,661
1961	47,777	1973	69,059
1962	52,043	1974	66,988
1963	57,063	1977	90,763
1964	57,038	1978	57,259
1965	58,869		

SOURCES: Banco de Crédito Rural Peninsular, *Resultados del cultivo del henequen para el período 1955–1974*, unpublished report (Mérida, 1976); "Más de un tercio de los ejidatarios inscritos hasta 1977 en el Banrural eran impostores y ya estan incluidos," *Diario de Yucatán*, 15 April 1978; Manuel Pasos Peniche, *La intervención estatal en la industria henequenera* (Mérida: n.p., 1951), p. 84.

To assure each ejidatario a weekly advance, work had to be parceled out so that each man worked no more than two to three days per week. Any significant reduction in the number of ejidatarios on the bank's payroll would have caused serious economic hardship and social disruption.

In 1950 some 167,764 people, or 32.4 percent of the state's population, lived in the fifty-four municipios that comprise the henequen zone (excluding Mérida and Progreso).[10] Of this total, more than 90 percent lived on henequen haciendas or in henequen pueblos.[11]

Most of the land in the henequen zone was, and still is, unsuitable for the subsistence production of traditional staples, such as corn and beans. The state's only urban area, Mérida, offered few employment opportunities for the unskilled and largely illiterate henequen workers. Because of the limited employment alternatives, a reduction in the number of people working in henequen would have required the relocation of substantial numbers of people to parts of the peninsula more suitable for traditional agriculture or the introduction of nontraditional economic activities in the henequen zone. Either of these measures, if undertaken rapidly, would have caused unacceptable levels of social trauma among the conservative indigenous population.

The political realities in Yucatán seemed to argue against any fundamental reorganization of the ejido sector. The henequen ejidatarios, by virtue of their organization, their numbers, and the proximity of the henequen zone to Mérida, have become a volatile and crucial element in the state's sometimes unstable political system. Today, along with the less numerous working and middle classes, they provide the political consensus that is necessary to govern the state. On any given day, as was demonstrated in a January 1978 protest against the reform policies of President López Portillo, large numbers of ejidatarios can be organized quickly to march on Mérida to protest against or lend support to particular policies or political candidates. Fearful of turning the ejidos into a political liability, presidents after Ruiz Cortines doggedly protected the status quo of the collectives in the face of subsidies that were staggering by the mid-1960s.

One of the most influential instruments for political control of the ejido sector is the official agricultural bank that extends production credit.[12] The bank's operating and investment policies have been coordinated with the federal government's overriding political and social objectives in Yucatán rather than with world hard fiber market conditions. This led to a virtual abandonment of economic criteria for credit advances. Through the years, the bank committed itself to the policy of advancing sufficient credits to the ejidos to assure each ejidatario a weekly "salary" irrespective of the value of an ejido's production. The henequen ejidatarios have become, in fact, employees of the federal government.

The Pequeña Propiedad

In 1977 the two classes of private producers owned about 60,000 hectares, or 37 percent, of all henequen land in full production in Yucatán (tables 1 and 3). Of the two private production units, the pequeña propiedad is the more significant in terms of the amount of land under cultivation and the volume of fiber produced. The

68

Food and Agriculture Organization (FAO) of the United Nations estimated that pequeños propietarios owned 76 percent of all privately owned henequen-producing land in Yucatán in 1968.[13]

Most of the estimated 300 pequeñas propiedades in the state today are the remnants of the henequen plantations that were expropriated after 1934. Henequen hacendados were allowed to retain a maximum of three hundred hectares of henequen land and the hacienda's casco. Pequeñas propiedades are economically and spatially organized in much the same way as the prereform henequen haciendas.

In 1976 pequeños propietarios owned and operated 163 of the 223 desfibradora facilities in the state, but some individuals owned as many as ten plants. The contractual agreement with the official bank to process ejidal fiber, together with low labor and capital costs (most of the machines are at least fifty years old), evidently made the activity a highly profitable one.[14] Dozens of privately owned desfibradoras, however, have been abandoned in recent years because of low fiber prices and production. During the late 1970s, a small number of pequeños propietarios began producing cordage products for sale in the domestic market. This activity has placed the private producers in direct competition with Cordemex, both for customers and raw-material supply. Cordemex's recent operating losses have sharpened the conflict and made the continued existence of the private mills the subject of public debate in Yucatán.

The pequeño propietario obtains the labor he needs from the residential population of the hacienda or from nearby ejido villages. Except for a few salaried administrative personnel, workers are hired on an as-needed basis. Because work in the ejido fields is usually restricted to two or three days a week, labor is readily available to private producers even though the rates they pay for the various tasks are somewhat lower than ejido rates. The degree of involvement of the owner of the pequeña propiedad in its day-to-day management varies widely. Among owners interviewed for this study, one stated that he inspected his property only twice a year, leaving the management of daily operation in the hands of a salaried *encargado*, or foreman. At the other extreme, one ex-hacendado indicated that he visited his operations two or three times a week and that his son actively involved himself in its administration almost daily.

Little effort has been made on the vast majority of the small properties to maintain structures that do not perform an immediate economic function. The great houses, their gardens and walls, which were showplaces in the early part of the century, have not been maintained. On many haciendas, the deterioration is so extensive that only the bustle of activity around the desfibradoras contradicts the general impression of abandonment.

Pequeños propietarios have their own association, the Unión de Crédito Agrícola Ganadero del Estado de Yucatán. This is a self-financing institution that is an agent for its members in the henequen market as well as a supplier of warehouse and credit facilities and an unofficial spokesman. The Unión buys raw fiber from its members at a price just below the market price and resells it to either Cordemex or private cordage mills in Yucatán and other parts of Mexico. Some of the smaller private producers who are not members of the Unión sell their leaves directly to Cordemex or to the private *cordelarías*, or cordage mills. The Unión also makes short-term financing available to its members in limited quantities. Banrural is not prohibited from extending credit to private producers; however, since its inception, the bank has limited its advances to ejidos. Long-term loans for investment in equipment and new plants must be obtained from the private financial sector.[15]

The Parcelario

The *parcelario*, or small parcel owner, belongs to a class of private producer that came into being after land reform. The plot of land may be located on ejido land or it may be privately owned. Anyone who cultivates a parcel of less than 150 *mecates*[16] is usually referred to as a parcelario. Ejidal parcelarios utilize small plots of ejido land that are not being cultivated. The privately owned parcels represent land that individual campesinos and their families have accumulated since the revolution. The parcelarios' association claims a membership of more than ten thousand; however, the number of campesinos actively working their plots is estimated by informed sources to be less than half that number. In 1970 the parcelarios accounted for about 9 percent of henequen land in full production and about 9 percent of Yucatán's total output of raw fiber.[17] Parcelario fiber is ordinarily of a higher quality than either that of the ejidos or the pequeñas propiedades.

Henequen parcelas are normally a secondary source of income

for their owners because they produce relatively small amounts of raw fiber. Most of the field work is done by parcelarios and their families. The care and harvesting of the small parcels does not require a large or full-time labor force. Parcelarios do not process their own fiber because the volume of leaves harvested annually is not sufficient to justify investment in rasping and packing equipment. Instead, most of these leaves are transported directly to the nearest Cordemex desfibradora for processing and sale. This arrangement has advantages for both the parcelario and Cordemex.

Unlike the ejidos, parcelarios usually receive no financial support from Banrural. On account of their small size, sources of private bank credit are also closed to them. From 1965 until the mid-1970s, Cordemex subsidized parcelario production by paying them a higher price per kilo for raw fiber than did either Banrural or the Unión. This premium served to guarantee a regular supply of high-quality fiber to Cordemex and to encourage the use of the cordage monopoly's fiber-processing capacity. Early in 1977 parcelarios seeking a resumption of some form of subsidy refused to deliver their fiber to Cordemex's desfibradoras. The strike ended in late May of the same year, when Cordemex's management agreed to pay the same price, seven pesos per kilo, for grade B fiber as for grade A, the highest quality fiber.[18]

The Impact of Federal Intervention on the Competitive Structure of the Market for Henequen Fiber

The federal government's extensive involvement in raw fiber production, and subsequently the nationalization of Yucatán's cordage mill industry in 1964, brought about thoroughgoing changes in the market for raw henequen fiber. Before agrarian reform, the price received by growers was market-determined. By the mid-1970s governmental entities dominated the demand and supply side of the market, and the price of raw fiber was being set by fiat rather than by market forces. Not surprisingly, noneconomic considerations became significant inputs into the pricing decision.

From its inception in the nineteenth century, henequen production was a highly competitive activity. A survey of the henequen zone in 1923 showed that 844 individual hacendados owned 1,164 haciendas.[19] This figure may be misleading, however, because a report published in the following year listed only 433 independent producers.[20] This discrepancy indicates that individual families owned numerous plantations. The practice of vesting legal titles to plantations in the name of nonparticipating family members increased as land reform became imminent during the 1930s. It is unclear, therefore, exactly how many individuals actually controlled the some 350 haciendas that were affected by the reform of 1937. Effectively, a hundred or fewer individuals probably controlled most of the henequen-producing land; in 1924 ninety-one independent producers were said to account for 60 percent of Yucatán's total fiber production.[21] Despite this concentration, it is unlikely that any single producer or group of producers exercised significant control over the price of fiber. Evidence of this is the repeatedly unsuccessful attempts of producers to organize and agree upon common price and production policies from the late 1800s until the 1930s.

After 1880 the demand side of the henequen market was dominated by a few large American companies, primarily International Harvester Company. The interruption of the Allies' sisal and abaca supplies during World War II and the creation of a single agency, Henequeneros de Yucatán, to market Yucatecan fiber strengthened the local growers' position vis-à-vis the American buyers and thus favorably affected both prices and profits. The demand side of the market also became more competitive during the war because of the growth of a significant local cordage industry. In 1934 these mills consumed less than 8 percent of the raw fiber produced in Yucatán. By 1953 more than fifty mills were producing ropes, cables, harvest twine, and sacks and were consuming 55 percent of the raw fiber production.[22] The rapid growth of the Mexican economy during World War II also expanded the heretofore unimportant domestic market. By the early 1950s, some 20 to 30 percent of the cordage produced in Yucatán was being consumed in the nation.[23]

The formation of Cordemex in 1961 and its nationalization three years later brought about a radical change in the demand side of the market. As the principal purchaser of Yucatecan fiber, Cordemex exerted considerable influence over the price of raw fiber from the date it began operations. Its control over growers was strengthened further in 1968 and 1973 by government regulations that limited the raw fiber exports of both private producers and the ejidos. Before 1968 the agricultural bank and private producers had the option of selling to either Cordemex or foreign cordage mills. From 1964 through 1967, some 36.2 percent of all henequen exported consisted of raw fiber sent to foreign mills.[24]

In 1968 Cordemex was given the power to grant export licenses for both raw fiber and fiber manufactures. Its policy between 1968 and 1973 was to permit fiber exports abroad only after it had satisfied its own raw material requirements. The state-owned firm strengthened its position vis-à-vis raw fiber producers even further in 1973 by prohibiting all foreign and domestic exports of the commodity. When Cordemex's sales began to decline in the mid-1970s, this regulation was altered to allow pequeños propietarios to sell up to 30 percent of their output to private domestic cordage mills.

Despite Cordemex's near-monopsony of the raw fiber market, its ability to exploit its position fully is limited by economic and political factors. It does not enjoy the advantage that buyers possessed before agrarian reform of being able to purchase fiber directly from several hundred unorganized or loosely organized producers. Banrural, acting as the sole agent of the dominant ejido sector, supplies more than half of the cordage mills' raw material. The bank, therefore, exercises sufficient market power on the supply side of the market to make raw fiber prices the subject of negotiations between the two governmental organizations.

Private producers are also organized. Although the parcelarios sell much less fiber to Cordemex than does Banrural, they are the primary users of Cordemex's desfibradora facilities. The small parcel owners also produce a higher-grade fiber than do either the ejidos or the pequeñas propiedades. Because of these two factors, the parcelarios' association was successful in forcing Cordemex to alter its pricing policies in 1977 by having its members stop delivering their leaves to Cordemex's desfibradoras.

Pequeños propietarios, though they are Cordemex's second largest supplier, avoid disputing its pricing policies for political reasons. They fear that a conflict with the government-owned firm could be used as an excuse for further expropriations in the henequen zone. The manager of the smallholders association stated that the Unión tried to stay on good terms with Cordemex, limiting public criticism of its pricing policies to the publishing of information on world hard fiber prices.[25]

Cordemex's discretionary pricing power is further limited by the influence of the ejidos. As a major agency of the federal government, Cordemex has an explicit social function to perform in Yucatán. Company policies must reflect a concern for improving the economic welfare of the ejidatarios and the cordage-mill workers. The raw fiber transfer price decision, therefore, must take the political and social realities of Yucatán into account as well as world market conditions. Commenting on this in early 1982, the director-general of Cordemex noted that Mexico is the only country in the world in which the price paid for fiber rises when fiber prices are falling in other producing nations.[26]

STRUCTURAL CHANGE AND PERFORMANCE, 1955–1964

World consumption of natural fibers, such as henequen, sisal, and abaca, increased from an average of 771.1 tons annually during the period 1956–58 to 919.1 tons in 1964, an average annual rate of 2.8 percent.[27] During this period of steadily increasing demand and generally favorable prices, Yucatán's annual raw fiber production rose from 98,062 tons in 1956 to 131,267 tons in 1964, which was the state's third highest output since 1920 (table 1). On the surface, these postwar production figures seem to indicate that the federal government's efforts to reorganize the industry after the dissolution of Henequeneros achieved some measure of success. As previously noted, however, the government did not take steps to correct the organizational and spatial deficiencies of the henequen collectives. In fact, by committing itself to the preservation of the status quo of the henequen ejidos, it effectively insulated the most important and least efficient class of producers from the market. Yields for the period suggest that the decision to subsidize the ejidos adversely affected the productivity of the collectives.

The Ejido Sector

Ejido production fell slightly during the first nine years of active federal involvement in the administration of raw fiber production, declining from 66,533 tons in 1956 to 66,483 tons in 1964 (table 3). The collectives' share in total raw fiber output decreased correspondingly from 67.8 percent to 50.6 percent.

During the same period, Banrural records indicate substantial

TABLE 3. Ejido Sector: Raw Fiber Production, Land in Full
Production, and Average Yield per Hectare, 1955–1982

Year	Raw Fiber Production[a] (in metric tons)	Land in Full Production (in hectares)	Average Yield (in kilograms per hectare)
1955	32,879	102,993	219
1956	66,533	88,180	755
1957	68,733	103,351	665
1958	68,924	107,742	640
1959	81,346	111,753	720
1960	76,522	110,226	694
1961	71,682	103,774	691
1962	69,801	114,940	607
1963	63,793	118,399	539
1964	66,483	116,637	570
1965	68,068	118,289	575
1966	67,927	119,430	569
1967	65,309	120,038	542
1968	64,060	136,681	467
1969	67,126	136,845	483
1970	72,938	141,684	515
1971	73,487	142,574	515
1972	73,116	137,502	532
1973	68,701	134,112	512
1974	64,821	129,288	424
1975	58,773	. . .	. . .
1976	58,532	. . .	. . .
1977	50,870	100,000	509
1978	46,203	. . .	. . .
1979	44,251	. . .	. . .
1980	37,446	. . .	. . .
1981	30,558	. . .	. . .
1982	25,681	. . .	. . .

SOURCES: Banco de Crédito Rural Peninsular, *Resultados del cultivo del henequen para el período, 1955–1974*, unpublished report (Mérida, 1976); Gobierno del Estado de Yucatán, *El tercer informe del gobernador* (Mérida, 1979); Cordemex, *Henequen y sisal producción mundial* (Mérida, 1977); "Medidas para resolver el problema henequenero yucateco," *Diario de Yucatán*, 24 November 1977; Secretaría de Agricultura y Recursos Hidráulicos, *Boletín informativo* (No. 6) (Mérida, March 1980); idem., *Boletín informativo* (Mérida, January 1981); Gobierno del Estado de Yucatán, *El sexto informe del gobernador* (Mérida, 1982); "El declive de la producción de henequen," *Diario de Yucatán*, 30 May 1983.

[a]Ejido raw fiber production data in recent years is suspect because increasing numbers of ejidos have been using the processing facilities of Cordemex.

increases in the ejido labor force and in the amount of ejido land committed to the production of henequen. The number of active ejidatarios rose from 48,343 to 57,038, and the number of hectares in full production increased from 88,180 to 116,637 (tables 2 and 3). These figures indicate that ejido yields declined sharply. This is confirmed by official records, which show that the average yield per hectare of land in full production dropped by 24.5 percent, falling from 755 kilograms of raw fiber per hectare in 1956 to 570 kilograms in 1964 (table 3).

The decline in ejido productivity caused substantial increases in raw fiber production costs. Between 1956 and 1964 the Banco Agrario's annual production advances rose from 84 million pesos to 166.4 million pesos, more than doubling the bank's cost of acquiring a kilo of ejido fiber (table 4). Because the price that the bank received from the sale of ejido fiber rose much less rapidly than acquisition costs, the government's subsidy payments to the collectives increased both absolutely and relatively. In 1956 the bank recovered 72 percent of its credit advances, leaving 23.5 million pesos unpaid. By 1964 the recovery rate on production advances had fallen to 57.6 percent, and unrecovered credits totaled 70.6 million pesos[28] (table 4). Although the bank accumulated the unrecovered portions of annual ejido debt on its books, neither the government nor the ejidatarios considered the debt collectable; the Banco Agrario did not even bother to render annual accounts to individual ejido credit societies. At the end of 1964, the accumulated debt of the ejidos to the bank or, more accurately, the total subsidy paid the henequen collectives since 1955, amounted to 389.7 million pesos (table 4).

The above statistics raise a number of interesting questions. First, why did ejido productivity fall so precipitously after the federal government reassumed control of collective production? Second, why did the government permit the agricultural bank to increase the ejido labor force and substantially expand its financial commitment to the henequen collectives?

One henequen *técnico*, or technician, argues that the major cause of declining productivity is soil exhaustion. A hundred years of constant land use has gradually worn out the soil in the henequen zone.[29] The soil-exhaustion thesis does not hold up well, however, when the productivity of postreform privately held henequen land is compared with productivity of ejido land. The estimations made by Roland Chardon in the late 1950s indicated

TABLE 4. Ejido Sector: Credit Advances Extended, Recuperated, and Carried Forward by the Official Bank, by Selected Years, 1955–1977[a] (in Millions of Pesos)

Year	Credit Advances	Advances Recuperated	Balance Carried Forward
1955	41.0	29.3	11.7
1956	84.0	60.5	23.5
1957	88.7	51.9	36.8
1958	85.4	48.3	37.1
1959	86.5	47.9	38.6
1960	102.2	74.7	27.5
1961	102.1	66.4	35.7
1962	110.4	64.1	46.3
1963	139.0	82.0	47.0
1964	166.4	95.8	70.6
1965	156.5	114.7	41.8
1966	148.4	81.3	67.1
1967	148.7	76.9	71.8
1968	160.9	60.3	100.6
1969	165.0	52.8	112.2
1970	160.5	42.0	118.5
1971	195.4	89.4	106.0
1972	199.0	102.7	96.3
1973	224.2	94.4	129.8
1974	390.1	192.7	197.4
1977	868.0	328.0	540.0

SOURCES: Banco de Crédito Rural Peninsular, *Resultados del cultivo del henequen para el período, 1955–1974,* unpublished report (Mérida, 1976); Gobierno del Estado de Yucatán, *El segundo informe del gobernador* (Mérida, 1978).

[a]Precise data on credit advances and recuperations have not been made available since 1977.

that the yields on private lands were considerably above those obtained on ejido lands.[30] The Food and Agriculture Organization came to the same conclusion in a 1968 study. It estimated that, though the average yield per hectare on ejido land was 750 kilograms, pequeña propiedad and parcela yields averaged 1,150 kilograms and 1,300 kilograms, respectively.[31] Private yields are not only well above those of the ejido sector, but also compare very favorably with the yields of the prereform haciendas.

Although the quality of henequen-producing land is not uniform throughout the henequen zone, it would be difficult to argue that the yield differential is due to ejidos possessing land that is inferior to that cultivated by private producers. Ejido land is located throughout the henequen-producing area. Failing to encounter any substantial evidence that the fertility of privately owned henequen-producing land has declined significantly since land reform or that ejidos possess land inferior to that of private producers, the investigator is forced, like Chardon, to consider whether organizational deficiencies in the ejido production unit itself are sufficient to account for the productivity differentials.

The unlinking of the agricultural and leaf-processing functions undoubtedly had a negative effect on ejido production costs. One ex-hacendado has pointed out that transportation is the "Achilles heel" of the ejido. He estimated that the cost of transporting leaves to the desfibradora is twenty pesos per one thousand leaves for the ejido compared to five pesos per thousand for the pequeño propietario because the collectives normally use trucks rather than mule-drawn platforms for this task.[32] If the ex-hacendado's cost estimates are correct, his assertion that transportation is the Achilles heel of the collectives is an overstatement. Assuming a yield of twenty kilograms of fiber per hundred leaves, the fifteen-peso differential in transportation cost would account for less than a one-peso differential in ejido and private producers' production costs per kilogram. In addition, though the use of trucks rather than mule-drawn platforms may increase production costs, it cannot be inferred that this practice will lower the productivity of ejido land.

A potentially more significant impact of ejido organization on performance is its effect on the management function and on the incentive structure of the production unit. Under the best of conditions, management of the ejido would probably be less efficient and more costly than that of the henequen hacienda. In the first instance, the ejido is physically more difficult to manage than the hacienda because, typically, its fields are sometimes not contiguous. Ejido fields are in many instances several kilometers apart, and the nearest desfibradora may be far from either the collective's fields or the pueblo. The lack of geographical unity obviously increases supervision costs and makes the coordination of production tasks more difficult. On the henequen hacienda, the encargado, operating from the central location of the hacienda's casco, could oversee operations with a minimum of assistance. The processing equipment and workers' homes were located within the casco and all fields could be reached easily by the Decauville railroad system or on horseback.

The problems of ejido management, of course, extend far beyond those related to increased direct supervision costs. The inequality of the relationship between lender and landowners has created disruptive tensions and conflicts between the henequen ejidos and the agricultural bank. A prevalent opinion among industry officials, as well as middle- and upper-class Yucatecans, is that the ejidatarios are incapable of managing their own land, though little effort has been made to provide any kind of training.[33] Ejidatarios have long been aware of this attitude among Banrural officials as well as of the technical deficiencies of many of the bank's own staff; non-Yucatecans who know nothing about henequen have often been assigned to supervise the production and financial activities of the ejidos. The henequen workers also recognize that bank officials, though performing none of the back-breaking, unpleasant tasks that are associated with the production of henequen fiber, are materially much better off than themselves, the owners of the land. The perception that the bank, possessing absolute control over the ejido's productive activities, is exploiting their land and labor has engendered a collective attitude that Nathaniel Raymond describes as "hate, anger, and frustration"[34] toward the bank and its personnel.

Within this environment of mutual hostility and distrust, the efforts of conscientious agricultural bank officials to elicit efficient performance from the ejidos have been made more difficult by the sensitive political relationship that exists between the collectives and the federal government. The agricultural bank that replaced Henequeneros de Yucatán continued the practice of paying a uniform "wage," or credit advance, to all henequen workers. As pointed out earlier, the payments became a guaranteed weekly income because of the federal government's long-standing policy of subsidizing the losses of the ejidos. Ejidatarios have come to view the credit advances as wages to which they are entitled.

The paternalistic attitude that the federal government displays toward the ejidos gives the ejidatarios some measure of power in their dealings with the agricultural bank. Although they feel only in a remote sense that they are owners of the land, they are quick to assert their ownership if a bank official attempts to force them to do something or if they do not like the official who is supervising their work. Because it is technically the ejidatarios' land and orders for weekly payment come from Mexico City, the bank is able to exercise only limited control over the manner in which work tasks are carried out. Bank inspectors who attempt to do their job properly are often intimidated and physically threatened.

Improper care of ejido fields has contributed to the decrease in productivity in the ejidos as well as to a decline in the quality of the fiber. Although the henequen plant needs little soil or water to thrive, excessive weed growth affects its productivity. Properly cared for, the mature plant should produce twenty to twenty-two leaves per year. If the fields are not cleaned properly and on a regular basis, the annual yield can fall to twelve to fourteen leaves per plant. Excessive undergrowth also prevents the plant from sending *vástagos*, or suckers, to the surface. A shortage of these can be a serious obstacle to the expansion of new plantings.

One agricultural bank official likened the ejidos to a union, one whose political power precluded attempts by the bank to rationalize production. The power of the ejido "union" and the consequences of failing to coordinate economic decisions with political objectives was clearly demonstrated in 1966. The Banco Agrario established a policy of paying a bonus or additional subsidy to a small group of ejidos that were producing high-quality fiber. The purpose of this bonus was to give a positive incentive to those ejidos whose fiber was not of export quality. This action produced the opposite of the desired effect because it violated the long-standing practice of paying uniform wages throughout the henequen zone. Hundreds of enraged ejidatarios stormed the center of Mérida. Federal troops finally had to be brought in to stop the rioting and looting. The national head of the official bank restored calm to the henequen zone the following day by suspending the new policy and by promising to grant emergency loans to those ejidos that had not received a bonus.[35]

The agricultural bank has also been obliged to follow policies since 1955 that have led to economically unwarranted increases in the ejido labor force. According to law, the number of ejidatarios is supposed to be fixed; only one child can legally inherit the status of his father. Under pressure from the ejidos, the bank ignored this provision and granted ejidatario status to all children who chose to apply. As a consequence, the labor surplus in the henequen zone became progressively more acute, restricting the earning potential of the individual ejidatario. The necessity to provide some work for all has resulted in the individual being allowed to work for only one or two days a week.

The incentive structure that the federal government established after it reassumed control of the ejidos not only encouraged inefficiency in production, but also produced corruption on an alarming scale. It has been commonplace in both the official bank and the ejidos since land reform, and instances of corrupt practices are well documented.[36]

With the approval and participation of high bank officials, ejido officials and bank employees routinely have inflated ejido rolls and falsified work records in order to obtain additional income. A related problem has been the illegal sale of ejido fiber to pequeños propietarios. Banrural officials have estimated that as much as 20 percent of all ejido fiber is marketed in this way. According to Jorge Tomás Vera Pren, owners of private desfibradoras also extract illegally a quantity of the best-quality ejido fiber as an additional payment for processing the leaves. Ejidatarios do not protest because they understand that it is part of the rules of the game.[37] These practices distort ejido production figures and increase the bank's losses inasmuch as the collectives already have been paid for the fiber through the weekly credit advances. Corruption has persisted on a large scale despite a widespread awareness of its existence because so many people have a vested interest in the system and also because the federal government has simply looked the other way.

The ejidatario who labors in the henequen fields is aware, of course, that ejido and bank officials are profiting illegally and that even flagrant acts of corruption seldom are prosecuted. Lacking a sense of common purpose and perceiving little connection between his individual economic welfare and the efficient functioning of the ejido, the ejidatario may behave in a manner that is antisocial and antithetical to the common welfare. In addition to minimizing the time he spends in performing his tasks and knowing that whatever benefits he does not extract from the ejidos will be taken by others, he often resorts to actions that despoil the common property and impair the profitability as well as the economic functioning of the ejido.[38]

Private Producers

The raw fiber prices of the late 1950s and early 1960s apparently allowed private producers to earn adequate profits because the larger part of the total increase in raw fiber output between 1956 and 1964 was accounted for by the private sector.[39]

The most obvious way in which land reform affected the private producer was to force a reduction in the scale of the production unit. Before agrarian reform, haciendas commonly exceeded a thousand hectares. Inasmuch as no studies have been done on scale economies in the production of henequen fiber, it is difficult to say whether the limitation on private holdings of henequen lands adversely affected productivity. The most commonly used measure of productivity, the average productivity of henequen land in full production, indicates that the forced reduction in scale had little noticeable effect on the yields of privately held land.

The best available current data show that the average yield per hectare on pequeñas propiedades has remained around a thousand kilograms, which compares very favorably with the yields of the prereform hacienda.[40] These estimates, however, are not a reliable measure of the effect of changes in scale for three reasons. First, many pequeños propietarios have begun utilizing their land more intensively by planting as many as twice the number of plants per hectare as was customary in the past. Second, as previously mentioned, ejidos sold or transferred illegally an unknown quantity of their output to pequeños propietarios, which would have inflated the statistics on smallholders' production. Third, production statistics have been collected, or more accurately, estimated, by several different institutions whose estimates have often been at variance with one another.

Although the negative effects of land reform on the organization and technical conditions of smallholder production are inconclusive, smallholders are almost unanimous in their opinion that land reform has altered their behavior by increasing the uncertainty of land tenure. Some of the families that own the pequeñas propiedades are the remnants of the officially despised casta divina, the small group that dominated the state economically and politically before the 1930s. This group, in particular, fears that the federal government might find it politically expedient to make further expropriations if the expanding rural population in the henequen zone puts pressure on the government to provide it with more land. Hence, the ambiguous status of the pequeñas propiedades has negatively affected the rate of private investment in new plantings and equipment. Private lenders are hesitant to extend loans to the smallholders because of the risk of expropriation. The federal government, of course, traditionally has declined to supply any form of financial aid to this group because of its former status. Nevertheless, the pequeños propietarios' limited access to credit was mitigated somewhat by the relatively high prices during the late 1950s and early 1960s as well as some grants or loans under the United States' "Alliance for Progress" program.[41]

SUMMARY AND CONCLUSIONS

During the first decade of renewed federal involvement in Yucatán's henequen industry, governmental policies nurtured and even encouraged the expansion of the marginal and inefficient ejido sector while they restricted the growth of efficient private producers. Inefficiency in the henequen industry was institutionalized. Corrupt behavior became accepted practice. The corrupt and inefficient system was supported by officials in the Banco Agrario and the ejidos who had a vested interest in its continued existence as well as by high governmental officials who were concerned with the maintenance of the political status quo in the state. Productivity in the ejido sector was negatively affected by the passive resistance of ejidatarios themselves to a system that they viewed as being an exploitive one. Favorable market prices between 1955 and 1963, however, reduced the effects of the economically unsound structure on the competitiveness of the industry.

5

Federal Intervention
and Industry Performance:
The Manufacturing Sector

▲▲

THE FEDERAL government nationalized Yu-
catán's cordage industry in 1964. This was the last in a series of
actions, beginning with the first large land expropriations in the
henequen zone in 1934, that ultimately transformed the henequen industry into what is today a predominantly state-owned
and -operated enterprise. No evidence exists that the creation of
Cordemex was the final phase of a master plan to nationalize and
integrate the agricultural and manufacturing sectors of the henequen industry. Like Cárdenas's massive expropriations in 1937
and the dissolution of Henequeneros de Yucatán in 1955, the
decision to nationalize and consolidate Yucatán's cordage mills
was made when the industry was in a state of economic crisis and
it was carried out rapidly. One official justification for governmental intervention in the cordage industry was similar to that
given for involvement in the agricultural sector: to achieve more
social and economic justice for the henequen ejidatarios.

THE ENTREPRENEURIAL ROLE OF THE STATE IN MEXICO

The nationalization of Yucatán's cordage industry was not an
isolated act of intervention by the Mexican government but
another step in a trend toward an expanded role for the state in
economic activity. State ownership of productive enterprises
gained momentum during the 1930s, when President Cárdenas
expropriated the nation's railroads and foreign interests in the
petroleum industry. President Luis Echeverría Álvarez (1970–76)
accelerated the encroachment into private-sector activity. By 1982
the government had a minority or majority ownership in more

than a thousand firms that ranged from banking to the manufacture of bicycles.

The multiple, and often conflicting, policy goals that parastatal firms such as Cordemex and Banrural have been subject to provide a framework for analyzing their economic performance. In Mexico, the motives that have led to direct public participation (through ownership and control) in the economy can be placed in four major categories: (1) economic nationalism; (2) growth and industrialization policies of the state; (3) social justice; and (4) political patronage. As in the 1982 takeover of private banks, Marxian ideology has been a contributing, but not the decisive, factor in the creation of parastatal, or public, enterprise.

When economic sovereignty becomes a paramount goal, the state enterprise is seen as a counterweight to the intrusion of the multinational corporation in the domestic economy. Whether through negotiated nationalization or expropriation, industries initially organized and managed by foreign companies in key sectors of the domestic economy, such as oil, electricity, mining, and railroads, have inexorably moved into the public domain. Major nationalizations in Mexico have been invested with revolutionary mystique and the aura of presidential infallibility.

A major justification for governmental ownership centers on control of natural monopolies, like electricity, ports and harbors, and telecommunications. These industries are characterized by internal economies of scale (in which expanded output yields declining unit costs), capital intensity, and significant forward linkages. A companion argument for state enterprise emphasizes positive externalities associated with investment in public goods such as multiple purpose river projects and pure research, in which benefits cannot sufficiently be captured by private owners to justify private production.[1]

The social-justice motive is operative whenever the national government charges the public enterprise with ameliorating perceived social problems related to income distribution, regional imbalance, and employment creation. In this scenario, the state enterprise subsidizes the relevant target groups by offering its product at below user-cost or competitive market price. Depending on the product or service offered, the price subsidy may, in practice, benefit the lower-income groups or the politically vocal urbanized middle sector. In the interest of maintaining the level of employment, state enterprises may be required to carry redundant labor forces. Bankrupt or ailing private firms may be absorbed by the state, again in the interest of maintaining jobs. Clearly, social-justice considerations figured importantly in the creation of a number of public entities, such as Ayotla Textil, the sugar industry, CONASUPO, and Cordemex.

State enterprises are a convenient and safe mechanism for the discharge of political debts. Referring to Latin American experience, Raúl Prebisch, former executive director of the Economic Commission for Latin America, writes that, "with a few exceptions," directors of state enterprises "are not generally chosen on the basis of efficiency but in the light of political interests."[2] In Mexico, patronage also extends to favored labor union "aristocracies" and their leaders in exchange for their support of the PRI.

The dramatic growth in the number of Mexican public enterprises has enhanced the opportunity for patronage. Because of the constitutional limit on reelection, each sexennial change in the presidency brings with it a massive turnover in personnel within the government. The Mexican political process entails an unceasing conflict between political cliques, or *camarillas*, groups bound by loyalty to an individual leader who is expected to award patronage in return for their support. The high rate of turnover, including the top and middle positions in state enterprises, contributes to the practice of self-enrichment through public office. Consequently, the proliferation of these public entities within the economy has greatly widened the opportunity for corrupt practices. As political scientist Peter H. Smith has observed, the Mexican political system "has purchased stability (through widespread patronage) at the expense of skilled experience."[3]

The ambivalent policy environment within which public enterprises must operate is reflected in official pronouncements. According to Mexico's 1980–82 Global Development Plan, state enterprise policy proposed to "base operation of these entities on greater productivity levels of their human elements and on increasingly efficient management of their physical and financial resources."[4] On the other hand, speaking at a seminar on productivity, Minister of Government Enrique Olivares Santana observed that, with respect to the parastatal enterprises, productivity is measured, "neither by prices, input or wages, nor by the usual criteria of traditional economics."[5] He went on to say that in Mexico the productivity standard applied to public enterprises is more concerned "with social tranquility and stability than with the figures of an accounting firm." He also stated that, with regard to public enterprises, productivity is "measured directly by the social peace of Mexicans and peace, like war, has no price."[6]

THE DEVELOPMENT OF A CORDAGE INDUSTRY IN YUCATÁN

A modern cordage industry did not begin to emerge in Yucatán until the 1930s, more than two decades after the prominent failure of La Industrial, S.A. The large amounts of capital generated by the World War I boom in conjunction with low postwar prices for raw fiber encouraged the hacendados to invest in cordage manufacturing. Mill owners increasingly found themselves able to compete with American mills because production was relatively labor-intensive. The required technology was also uncomplicated and, for the most part, available locally. Yucatán's penetration of the American market for ropes, harvest twine, and other henequen products was reinforced by the peninsula's proximity to the United States and the absence of U.S. tariff barriers on such products. Local manufacture of raw fiber, which had absorbed less than 1 percent of Yucatán's total fiber output in 1925, rose to 24.61 percent, or more than 22,000 tons, in 1940 (table 5).

World War II created highly favorable conditions for Yucatecan mills. Allied military and naval operations swelled the demand for ropes and cables. U.S. mills running at full capacity were unable to satisfy the wartime demand for these articles. Many European mills did not operate during the war.[7] The conflict also disrupted the Allies' supplies of the two other major natural fibers. World production of sisal fell from 260,495 tons in 1939 to 201,301 tons in 1947.[8] More importantly, because the Philippines was in enemy hands, cordage mills in the Allied nations were deprived of their source of abaca, the preferred fiber for rope and cable production. Given these favorable circumstances, exports of henequen manufactures increased from 10,472 tons, valued at 4.4 million pesos, in 1940 to 39,580 tons in 1945 worth 34.7 million pesos (table 6).

Other factors also favored the growth of the industry after 1940. Beginning in the 1930s, the reaper was gradually replaced by the combine harvester, which does not use binder twine. Fortunately for Yucatán, the rise in U.S. farm wages stimulated the introduc-

TABLE 5. Yucatán: Consumption of Raw Henequen
Fiber by Local Cordage Mills, 1925–1946

Year	Local Consumption[a] (in metric tons)	Local Consumption as a Percentage of Total Raw Fiber Production
1925	899	0.70
1926	900	0.90
1927	4,094	3.51
1928	4,035	3.39
1929	3,751	3.41
1930	3,520	3.42
1931	3,400	4.56
1932	5,022	5.52
1933	9,840	10.10
1934	7,192	8.32
1935	12,249	13.80
1936	16,245	14.77
1937	17,168	18.30
1938	11,116	15.18
1939	17,957	22.62
1940	22,142	24.61
1941	24,480	25.00
1942	35,605	33.76
1943	31,508	25.90
1944	38,006	31.67
1945	47,462	49.17
1946	48,656	49.83

SOURCES: Humberto Carranca Tomassi, *La industrialización del henequen en Yucatán* (México, D.F.: Banco de México, 1953), p. 98; table 3.
[a]The original data were in pacas, or bales, rather than tons. Each paca contains 180 kilograms of raw fiber on the average.

tion of automatic baler machines. On account of the fuller utilization of American grasslands to support a growing cattle population, the number of automatic baling machines expanded rapidly, and, at the same time, the demand for baler twine. Henequeros de Yucatán subsidized the expansion of production by selling raw fiber to local mills at less than the world market price.

TABLE 6. Yucatán: Volume and Value of Manufactured
Henequen Exports, 1940–1953

Year	Volume of Exports (in metric tons)	Value of Exports (in thousands of pesos)
1940	10,472	4,434.0
1941	13,708	5,839.7
1942	15,722	8,006.2
1943	25,208	19,953.0
1944	31,025	26,434.9
1945	39,580	34,681.5
1946	33,987	36,586.7
1947	43,644	76,477.1
1948	38,381	78,928.2
1949	23,861	54,002.8
1950	24,681	54,196.1
1951	33,608	90,516.2
1952	29,474	93,074.3
1953	33,094	91,018.5

SOURCES: Armour Research Foundation of Illinois Institute
of Technology, *Technological Audit of Selected Mexican Industries with Industrial Research Recommendations* (Ann Arbor,
Mich.: Edward Brothers, 1946), p. 85; Humberto Carranca
Tomassi, *La industrialización del henequen en Yucatán* (México,
D.F.: Banco de México, 1953), p. 124.

Federal and local export taxes on manufactured articles were also
reduced.[9] Because Henequeneros did not control the manufacture
and sale of finished products as it did with raw fiber, local mills
were free to sell their output at market prices, which were highly
profitable during the war. Within their feverish environment,
factories proliferated. From 1946 to 1948, when the Soviet Union
was making exceptionally large cable purchases, as many as 110
to 120 cordage mills were active in Yucatán.[10]

Most of the mills were located in Mérida, which offered adequate manpower, repair shops, and urban services such as transportation and communication, water, and electricity. Further, the
city's proximity to the United States facilitated the marketing of

cordage products in North American markets and the provision of working capital financing through American banks.[11]

A few large mills that utilized modern equipment and technology dominated production, particularly after World War II. In 1952, for example, eleven firms, or 21.6 percent of the total, absorbed 68.3 percent of the raw fiber consumed by the industry; and twenty-six firms, or 51 percent of the group, absorbed only 8.4 percent. These few large firms also accounted for most of the estimated 50-million-peso industry investment.[12]

During periods of peak demand and prices, dozens of makeshift mills began production. When activity slackened, the small, marginal mills simply ceased operation and waited for market conditions to improve. The ease of entry, in conjunction with the moderate degree of concentration, suggests that any significant economies of scale were exhausted at low levels of output, but that, subsequently, average costs were relatively constant over a large range of output. Entry into the industry was facilitated by the relative simplicity of cordage-making technology and by the highly elastic local labor supply. Most of the equipment used by the smaller shops could be constructed rapidly by machine shops in Mérida, or in the factories themselves. The permanent cordage mill labor force numbered about 2,500 workers. During periods of strong demand, this group was quickly augmented by using underemployed campesinos from around Mérida.[13]

The local entrepreneurial capabilities and technical skills that created the Mexican cordage industry and the backwardly-linked machinery complex were rooted in the earlier experience of Yucatán's Golden Age.

Table 7 lists the thirty-eight active cordage mills operating in April 1951. Their joint production capacity, measured in terms of weekly fiber consumption, was 6,645 bales. Significantly, of the thirteen largest mills, eight were owned by recent immigrants and at least three were in the hands of former plantation owners (Escalante, Manzanilla, and Cáceres). Of the eight immigrant-owned mills, five were controlled by Lebanese (Macari, two plants; Suari, Sauma, and Jacobo, one plant each) and one each by Spanish (Castro), Scotch (Fitzmaurice), and Turkish (Gaber) immigrants.

Although the most advanced machinery used for the elaboration of knotless baler twine was imported from James Mackie & Sons, of England, a large part of the machinery used in the cordage

TABLE 7. Industrial Capacity of Yucatán's Cordage Industry, by Ownership Source, as of April 1951

Name of Enterprise	Weekly Henequen Consumption (bales of 185 ks.)	Owner
Cordelería San Juan, S.A.	800	Juan Macari C.
Industrializadora del Sisal, S.A.	500	Alberto Suari
Sub-Arrendatarios de la Industrial, S.A.	400	José M. Castro
Fabricantes de Hilos Sisal, S.A.	400	J. L. Fitzmaurice
Henequen Industrial, S. de R.L. de C.V.	400	P. Manzanilla
Compañía Industrial Peninsular, S.A.	300	A. Cetina A.
Productores y Exportadores de Artefactos de Henequen, S.A.	300	M. Escalante
Sisal, S.A.	300	Juan Macari C.
Cordelería el Progreso, S.A. de C.V.	300	Halim R. Gaber
Cordelería Modelo, S.A.	250	Augusto Iturralde
Cordelería Tipo, S.A.	200	Humberto Sauma
Cordelería Providencia, S.A.	200	M. Cáceres B.
Cordelería Uxmal, S.A.	200	Chafi Jacobo
Other 25 cordage mills	1,095	. . .
Total	6,645	

SOURCE: Tomás Marentes Miranda, *Notas sobre agricultura, ganadería e industrias de transformación en Yucatán* (México, D.F.: Costa Amic, 1951), Anexo No. 6, pp. 97–101.

industry was of local origin, built in mechanical shops in Mérida or in the repair shops of the mills themselves. "The experience gained in machine shops and foundries in the construction of rasping equipment," writes Humberto Carranca Tomassi, "was later applied to the fabrication of replacement parts and less complicated machines used by cordage mills."[14]

The rapid and somewhat artificially stimulated growth of Yucatán's cordage-mill industry during World War II adversely affected its postwar development. The strong wartime demand, coupled with the decline in foreign competition and the subsidy from Henequeneros, favored the creation of an industry structure in which unit costs of production and quality varied widely among firms. An inventory of the industry after the war revealed that a wide variety of machinery was being used, ranging from the antique to the modern.[15] The sellers' market enabled many firms to engage in shoddy and deceptive business practices that damaged the industry's reputation and weakened its competitive position after World War II. The United States and other foreign buyers complained regularly during the 1940s about the low quality of manufactured goods from Yucatán. One author notes that "some of the factories which exported (manufactured) henequen fiber resorted to fraud in order to add weight to the products which they sold overseas. Some doubled the amount of insect repellent oil with which the fiber was treated, others left in dust and pulp, and yet others simply included rocks in the bales."[16]

The end of the war brought a sharp decline in the demand for rope and cable as well as the resumption of normal levels of production by sisal-producing nations. Total manufactured henequen exports fell from 43,644 tons in 1947 to 23,861 tons in 1949 (table 6). World sisal production, on the other hand, rose from 201,381 tons in 1947 to 351,717 tons in 1951.[17]

Yucatecan mills experienced difficulty in adjusting to the new competitive environment because of the reputation for low quality that the industry had earned during World War II.[18] By 1948 the manufacturing sector, like the raw-fiber-producing sector, was near collapse, plagued by intensified competition, low prices, and oversupply. Price competition among mills became cutthroat. So intense was the struggle for buyers that at times the price of manufactured items fell to the same level as that of raw fiber. This placed the mills in direct competition with Henequeneros, which caused conflict between the mill owners and their benefactor. Finally, in 1949, cordage-mill owners formed the Asociación de Productores de Artefactos de Henequen. The purpose of the organization was to avoid excessive competition among the members, establish minimum prices, and maintain standards of quality for manufactured goods.

The attempt to form a henequen cordage cartel in Yucatán during the 1950s was unsuccessful. Neither the Asociación de Productores nor a similar government-sponsored organization formed in 1953, Cordeleros de Mexico, was able to enforce common pricing policies.[19] These failures are not surprising because

92

market conditions were not conducive to producer cooperation. Divisive forces were present in both the demand and supply side of the cordage market. The large number of producers made coordination difficult. This problem was mitigated somewhat by the concentration of industry output that existed after World War II. Fewer than sixty firms survived the postwar recession, and, as was noted above, eleven of those accounted for almost 70 percent of the raw fiber consumed by the industry. The formation of the Asociación de Productores suggests that one vital precondition for cooperation existed, at least among the dominant firms: the recognition that the price and output decisions of individual producers affected other firms' actions and the level of prices.

Even if the degree of concentration was sufficient to permit the coordination of price policies, which in itself is a questionable proposition, other characteristics of the market provided strong incentives for cheating. First, local plant capacities were designed to meet the strong wartime demand. The abrupt downturn in demand after the war left the industry operating at below full capacity. Under these conditions, owners of the larger, more capital-intensive mills had a strong incentive to cut prices in order to increase capacity utilization and cover overhead costs.

Second, the normal peacetime patterns of demand for manufactured goods did not favor producer cooperation. The demand for cordage products is cyclical and prices are subject to frequent and sharp fluctuations. Because of this, firms faced the same problems with capacity utilization during normal cyclical downturns in demand as they did in the depressed postwar period. In addition, the demand for harvest twine, which is Yucatán's major export, is highly seasonal. Most of the year's production and sales take place in the late winter and early spring. As F. M. Scherer notes, "Profitable . . . collusion is most likely when price quotations on large orders are received infrequently and at irregular intervals."[20] The rationale for this is quite clear. The potential gains from shading price increase as the order size increases relative to total sales.

Finally, after the war, cordage-mill owners had only limited control over either the price or supply of raw fiber, which introduced an additional element of uncertainty. The unreliability of raw-material supply combined with the cyclical and seasonal pattern of demand made the successful operation of a cordage cartel highly unlikely.

Unable to enforce any price discipline among its members, Cordeleros tried but failed to sell its member mills to the Mexican government in 1961 for 250 million pesos. However, federal officials were forced to come to the aid of the industry later that same year when the owners attempted to mortgage fifty-two mills to a Canadian bank as collateral for a 90-million-peso loan. Confronted with the possibility that Yucatán's cordage-mill industry might fall into foreign hands, the federal government agreed to lend mill owners $5 million. The terms of the loan gave Nacional Financiera, a government development bank, the right to subscribe to 125 million pesos, or one-half, of the authorized stock of a new cordage manufacturing firm called Cordemex, with an option to purchase the remaining shares within three years.

Cordemex was formed by consolidating all existing mills under the management of a single firm. The federal government further extended its generosity to the mill owners by declaring cordage production to be saturated in Mexico and prohibiting the opening of any new mills. Between December 1961 and March 1964, Cordemex operated as a private entity because the government did not exercise its right to subscribe to the stock. Favorable market conditions permitted the firm to accumulate a profit of almost 100 million pesos during this period. In mid-1964 the government, through Nacional Financiera, finally exercised its option and mill owners were paid 200 million pesos. The federal government also assumed Cordemex's existing debt of 100 million pesos and forgave 20 million pesos of taxes owed by the firm.[21]

The official explanations given by the government for nationalizing Yucatán's cordage industry were both economic and social. In the first place, governmental control of the local cordage industry allegedly would permit more integration of the agricultural and manufacturing phases of production, which would result in operating and marketing economies. Second, the federal government was in a much better position financially to undertake cost-reducing modernization and amalgamation programs that were necessary if the local industry was to remain competitive in the world market. Third, the creation of a state monopoly to process and sell henequen fiber would improve Mexico's competitive position vis-à-vis foreign buyers. Fourth, the profits realized by Cordemex could be used to raise the standard of living of cordage workers and henequen ejidatarios.[22] The government's decision was also undoubtedly influenced by the increasing pressure from ejidatario and labor groups who wanted a share of Cordemex's profits. Hence, the nationalization measure was viewed by government officials as an expression of nationalism and support for the masses.

Despite the government's stated intentions to operate Cordemex for the benefit of the agroindustry's labor force, the initial beneficiaries were the ex-mill owners, some of whom had been large plantation owners before agrarian reform. The secretary of the treasury's official appraisal of the mills in 1961 was only 139 million pesos. Because of the generous nature of the final sales agreement and fortuitous world market prices during the three years that Cordemex operated as a private entity, mill owners were able to walk away from the enterprise with 300 million pesos. Interestingly, eight stockholders in Cordemex held almost two-thirds of its stock, which was another indication of the failure of agrarian reform to bring about the desired redistribution of wealth and income in Yucatán.[23]

THE ECONOMIC BENEFITS OF NATIONALIZATION: AN EVALUATION

In view of the problems that Yucatán's cordage industry experienced after World War II, the idea of consolidating the numerous private mills had considerable merit. The deterioration in agricultural productivity and fiber quality that accompanied agrarian reform and the chaotic growth of the cordage industry during World War II weakened Yucatán's ability to compete in the world natural fiber market. In the highly competitive environment of the postwar period, the rapid expansion of sisal production in Africa and South America threatened the very existence of the state's major economic activity and employer. The growth of Brazil's sisal industry was particularly spectacular. It began production during World War II; by 1950 the South American nation was producing 10 percent of the world's supply of natural fibers. During the following two decades, it quadrupled the output. By 1970 it was the world's largest producer of natural fibers.[24]

The lack of integration between fiber producers and cordage mills was costly for both sectors. During periods of high demand, the local supply of grade A raw fiber had often been insufficient to meet the requirements of the cordage mills.[25] Grade A, which is the highest quality fiber, is used to produce harvest twine. One potential benefit of vertical integration is to reduce the uncertainty of raw-material supply to the downstream firms.[26]

Government ownership and management of the cordage monopoly could also reduce the potential for costly conflict between Cordemex and raw fiber producers. Before the formation of Cordemex, the agricultural bank, acting as an agent for the ejidos, dominated the local raw fiber market because it supplied between one-half and two-thirds of the fiber consumed by local mills. Individual private producers supplied such a small percentage of total production that they were essentially price takers that based their production decision on the price established by the official bank. The bank's power over price was reduced considerably when the Cordemex monopsony was created. In the absence of vertical integration, the raw fiber market would have resembled a bilateral monopoly that would result in conflict between Banrural and Cordemex over the price of raw fiber.[27] Vertical integration, by internalizing the transfer price decision, may minimize costly negotiation and haggling between two firms because a price can be set by fiat.

Another problem that governmental ownership of the manufacturing sector sought to resolve was the industry's lack of access to long-term external financing. Before the creation of Cordemex, mill owners had almost no access to long-term credit because of the instability of the world market for natural fibers. Funds to modernize equipment and to expand plant capacity were obtained through the retention of earnings or short-term credit arrangements. Cordemex, on the other hand, enjoyed liberal access to external long-term financing because its shares were purchased by the Mexican government's largest development bank. Aided by credits from Nacional Financiera, Cordemex's management could completely modernize and reorganize the industry. Furthermore, the reorganization, by eliminating many smaller mills and consolidating the new and larger ones under a single unified management, would enable Cordemex to realize management and marketing economies as well as production economies. Enjoying broader access to resources, the governmental monopoly was also free to engage actively in research, new product development, and product promotion. Few of these types of demand-increasing and cost-reducing activities had been economically feasible before the federal takeover of the industry.

The new industry structure appeared to possess clear advantages over the previously more competitive one from the viewpoint of industry revenue as well as costs. Establishing the Cordemex monopoly eliminated the price-depressing competition that had existed among the cordage mills after World War II. Although International Harvester Company declined in importance as a manufacturer of cordage after 1940,[28] the large farm-implement manufacturer continued to dominate the U.S. market for harvest twine. In the late fall of each year, International Harvester announced a price schedule for harvest twine. This schedule was the basis for price negotiations between Yucatecan mills and United States buyers, who purchased 60 to 70 percent of the industry's annual cordage output. Inasmuch as Cordemex was the only supplier of Mexican cordage products, the industry could bargain with American buyers on a more equal footing and presumably, by virtue of the monopoly's increased market power, obtain higher prices and income than had been possible under the more competitive industry structure.

The restrictions on the export of raw fiber out of Yucatán in combination with measures taken by the Mexican government to protect the domestic cordage industry effectively eliminated Cordemex's foreign and domestic competition in the home market. These measures enabled the monopoly firm to undertake profitable discriminatory pricing policies, charging higher prices in the internal market, where fewer substitutes were available, than in external markets, where competition from sisal fiber was strong.

As the only manufacturer and seller of henequen products, Cordemex could resolve the quality-control problem that had plagued the industry since the inception of World War II and eroded its competitive position in the world market. Rigorous quality controls were established by Cordemex for both raw fiber purchases and manufactured goods.

INDUSTRY ORGANIZATION UNDER CORDEMEX

After the complete nationalization of local mills in 1964, Cordemex officials undertook the promised reorganization and modernization of Yucatán's cordage industry. The programs had three basic objectives: (1) to lower production costs; (2) to upgrade the quality of cordage products and establish rigorous standards for quality control; and (3) to find new uses and new markets for henequen products.[29]

When the federal government exercised its option in 1964, the industry consisted of forty mills, whose equipment, product quality, and capacity varied widely. Total employment was about 3,000.[30] A dozen years later, in 1976, Cordemex was operating seventeen mills whose total annual capacity was 144,000 tons. Employment had more than doubled to 7,500.

Miguel Olea, the first director-general of Cordemex, was permitted to manage the firm basically as he saw fit. Although it had a board of directors, meetings were infrequent. Olea's actions, therefore, were subject only to the approval of the minister of finance and the president of Mexico.[31] From a technical standpoint, the director's accomplishments were impressive. Most of the mills that the government had inherited were stripped of usable machinery and simply closed. In 1966 the twenty-four mills that remained active produced 69,100 tons, or an average of 2,800 tons per mill. By 1969 manufacturing operations were being carried out in only seven mills whose total production capacity was 100,058 tons per year. Three of the seven mills were new and the remaining four were old ones that had been modernized.[32] In addition to increasing the scale of the firm's manufacturing plants, operations were centralized and modern equipment was installed. According to information released by Cordemex, the changes significantly reduced manufacturing costs and boosted labor productivity. The average number of kilograms produced per man-hour rose from 12 in 1966 to 21.05 in 1970, and direct production costs (excluding overhead) fell from 90 centavos per kilogram in 1966 to 46 in 1969.[33]

Cordemex's new headquarters and major factories are located in an industrial complex just north of Mérida called "The Salvador Alvarado Industrial Henequen Center." The complex has become a showplace for visitors from foreign countries and from other parts of Mexico. The grounds contain guest houses and other facilities for visitors. The factories are new and utilize the most modern equipment. Administrative offices are air-conditioned, carpeted, and soundproofed. Across the highway from the factories, a housing complex has been built for the workers and their families. Workweeks have been reduced to forty hours, and workers' salaries and benefits are said to be the highest in the

Mexican textile industry.[34] Cordemex, to all appearances, represents a triumph for the Mexican system of economic development and the federal government.

Although private cordage mills compete with Cordemex in the highly protected internal market, only Cordemex is permitted to sell to foreign markets. Raw fiber is purchased from ejido and private producers in Yucatán as well as from producers in other parts of Mexico.[35] Because exports of raw fiber were terminated in 1973, all export sales consist of manufactured goods and bear the brand of Cordemex. U.S. agriculture is still by far the largest foreign consumer of the firm's output, but products are now sold in more than thirty nations. Product lines have also been expanded.

Cordemex extended its activities into leaf-processing, an operation that has traditionally been performed in the agricultural sector. Beginning in 1967, fourteen desfibradoras were placed in operation in the henequen zone. Unlike the majority of the equipment owned by pequeños propietarios and the ejidos, Cordemex's equipment consists of new, high-capacity machines that are equipped to extract the potentially marketable by-products of the henequen leaves as well as the fiber.[36] The official rationale for expanding operations into leaf-processing when an excess capacity already existed in the state was multiple. First, the Cordemex machines would loosen the parcelarios' dependence upon pequeños propietarios, who previously had processed all parcelario fiber. By providing an alternative to the parcelarios and offering premium prices for their leaves, Cordemex could also control the quality of the incoming fiber more rigorously as well as insure the firm a steady supply of high-quality fiber. Second, because the desfibradoras were equipped to extract by-products, the new facilities were integral to Cordemex's plans to diversify its product line.[37]

More than 65 percent of the firm's new investment expenditures after 1964 were made during the presidency of Luis Echeverría Álvarez, who was interested in improving Mexico's image among other Third World nations as well as in increasing the efficiency of the industry.[38] In the pursuit of the former goal, Cordemex entered into joint ventures with Tanzania (Tanzamex) and El Salvador (Salvamex) to assist those nations in developing their own cordage industries. In May 1982 Cordemex's investment in Tanzamex totaled about $2 million.[39]

Structural Change and Performance

Despite Cordemex's impressive technical achievements after 1964, little real progress was made toward the firm's major objectives. The problems that the management encountered in trying to carry out cost-reduction programs were largely political and centered around the firm's status as a key representative of the federal government in Yucatán. The introduction of relatively low-cost plastic fiber in the 1960s, on the other hand, tended to neutralize Cordemex's market power, which frustrated its efforts to increase prices and income. As a result of these problems, as well as the heavy fixed costs that were incurred to modernize and to expand production capacity, the federally dominated industry structure that emerged during the late 1960s was relatively inflexible and highly vulnerable to adverse changes in market conditions.

The Politics of Reorganization

During the period of private ownership (1961 to 1964), the role of Cordemex was economic. Cordage production and henequen leaf-processing were overwhelmingly the major industrial activities in the state, accounting for 45 percent of its value-added in production in 1960 (table 8). The importance of the cordage industry to the state economy was heightened by the fact that local mills were the major consumers of Yucatán's raw henequen fiber production. After nationalization in 1964, Cordemex ceased being just a major economic entity in the state. As a publicly owned, semiautonomous corporation, it became the outstanding symbol of the federal presence in Yucatán, closely identified with the administration of President Díaz Ordaz and the dominant political party, PRI. As such, its image, actions, and performance had significant political as well as economic implications.

Cordemex's importance was enhanced further by its potential as an instrument of social and political policy. Under federal management, its function was explicitly socioeconomic. The end of federal ownership was not only to improve the operating efficiency of the henequen industry, but also to elevate the living standards of henequen ejidatarios and mill workers without reductions in employment.[40] Cordemex's social function had extremely important implications for the reorganization and

100

TABLE 8. Yucatán: Manufacturing Output, Employment, Wages and Salaries, and Value-Added, Selected Industries, 1960 (money amounts in thousands of pesos)

Industry	No. of Establish-ments	No. of Employees	Wages and Salaries	Net Investments	Value of Output	Value-Added
Textiles[a]	355	15,485	98,889	425,419	669,216	234,965
Food Products	1,275	3,651	19,660	73,388	230,792	74,884
Beverages	18	2,007	40,293	297,455	232,416	125,001
All other manufac-turing	624	3,932	30,533	119,268	178,768	81,048
Total manufac-turing	2,252	25,075	189,375	897,530	1,311,193	515,898

SOURCE: Secretaría de la Presidencia Naciones Unidas, *Información básica para la planificación regional industrial: Industria de transformación, datos básicos de 1960* (México, D.F.: 1975).
[a]Includes both cordage manufacturing and defibration activities.

modernization program after 1964. Any economic action, however justifiable, was precluded if it upset the status quo of the swollen ejido labor force or reduced the scale of cordage manufacturing activity. The federal government's objectives through Cordemex were to create jobs and income, thereby enhancing rather than diminishing the economic and political stability of the state. The firm, therefore, was constrained much in the same manner as Banco Agrario; economic criteria needed to be subordinated to the social and political objectives of Mexico City.

Cordemex's new status after 1964 strained its relationship with Banco Agrario and, subsequently, hampered efforts to integrate the manufacturing and agricultural sectors of the henequen industry. Before the nationalization of Cordemex, political power in the state was shared by the governor and the head of the agricultural bank by virtue of their command of state and federal resources and their standing in the PRI. Whether the governor or the head of the bank possessed more power depended primarily upon their respective relationships with the president of Mexico and other leading members of the national power structure. The creation of Cordemex upset the balance of power in the state; the director of the cordage monopoly possessed a larger operating budget and the same prestige within the inner circles of the PRI as either the head of Banco Agrario or the governor.[41] Because the individuals holding all three posts were attempting to maintain and enhance their own prestige and power within the party, a rivalry arose between the three institutions as soon as the first director of Cordemex was appointed.[42]

The problem of coordinating the investment, pricing, and output decisions of Cordemex and Banco Agrario was complicated further by the absence of a unified commission or agency possessing the authority to resolve conflicts in the best interests of the industry as a whole. Cordemex and the official bank came under the jurisdiction of different government ministries, the Treasury Department and the Department of Agriculture, respectively. The only gesture that either governmental entity made to enhance cooperation was to give the rival agency a seat on its board of directors. Although nominally this gave each firm an input into the other's operations, these kinds of suggestions were rarely considered by the boards of the respective agencies.[43]

Developments in the World Hard Fiber Market
during the 1960s

During the latter half of the 1960s, when rivalries between Cordemex and the official bank were negating many of the potential benefits of industry integration, the favorable demand and price conditions that had characterized the world natural fiber market during the late 1950s and early 1960s began to deteriorate.[44]

Natural fiber demand in the developed nations began to slacken in the early 1960s. World consumption of sisal and henequen, which had increased at an average annual rate of 2.8 percent between the Korean War and 1963, declined at an average annual rate of more than 1 percent after 1963. Net exports of the two fibers fell from a high of 603,800 tons in 1962 to 502,900 in 1969. The effect of the fall in demand on producers' incomes was devastating. Export earnings from sales of hard fiber fell from $201 million in 1963 to $94 million in 1970 as prices plummeted to a post-Korean War low.

The problem that natural fibers faced during the late 1960s and early 1970s was primarily a result of two factors: oversupply and decreasing demand. Prices rose substantially in the early 1960s as political uncertainties in East Africa (where two major sisal producers are located) sparked abnormally large purchases of fiber. The higher prices caused world supply to expand from 1960 to 1966. Demand, on the other hand, began to fall during the same period. This resulted primarily from increased substitution of synthetics for natural fibers in the developed nations.

Before the introduction of low-cost polyolefin fibers in the early 1960s, synthetics, because of their higher production costs, competed with natural fibers only on a limited basis. High natural-fiber prices in 1963 and 1964 stimulated increased investment in facilities to produce polyolefin plastics. By 1970 the synthetics, which possess advantages over natural fibers in many end uses, had captured almost half of the rope and cable markets in developed nations and had made serious inroads into the packing and industrial twine markets. An estimated 115,000 tons of natural fiber were displaced by synthetics between 1966 and 1970. The market that was least affected by the increased substitution of synthetics for natural fibers was harvest twine because of its low cost. The synthetic's share of this market in developed countries rose from 2 to 7 percent, absorbing the market growth. Sisal and henequen's absolute share, however, remained virtually unchanged until 1970.

Major producing nations tried after 1968 to establish export quotas for each nation through informal agreements. The major goal of the cooperative effort was to maintain natural fiber prices at levels that were remunerative for the industry, but still below the level that would encourage the substitution of synthetics. These efforts at cooperation were hampered by persistent oversupply in the late 1960s and early 1970s that encouraged member nations to exceed their quotas.

During the 1960s Yucatán's problems were aggravated by intensified competition from sisal producers in the United States harvest-twine market. The major market for Yucatán's raw fiber and manufactures has always been the United States. Efforts to penetrate European markets have usually proven to be unsuccessful because of the high tariff barriers that protect the domestic cordage industries in Western Europe and because of high transportation costs. From 1940 until the early 1960s, Yucatán was able to hold a 50-percent share of the United States harvest twine market. The state's success in maintaining a competitive edge over sisal during this period was attributable primarily to the price differential that existed between sisal and the lower-quality henequen as well as the rapid expansion of Yucatán's cordage industry after 1940.

Both of these advantages began to disappear after 1960. During the 1950s and early 1960s, the gap between henequen and sisal began to narrow. Buyers from the United States reacted to the narrowing price differential by substituting the higher-quality sisal twine for henequen twine.[45] To add further to Yucatán's problems, sisal-producing nations, such as Haiti, Brazil, and Tanzania, began manufacturing harvest twine for the United States market in the late 1960s. The overall result of the increased competition from sisal fiber and sisal manufactures was that Yucatán's share of the United States harvest-twine market fell from 44 percent to 26 percent between 1964 and 1970.[46]

Monopoly Management: A Study in
Sociopolitical Decision Making

The deterioration of world demand for hard fibers generally and for henequen specifically during the 1960s clearly signaled the need for producing nations to begin shifting public and private resources out of natural fiber production. Major African producers adjusted quite rapidly. Total employment in the sisal industries of Tanzania, Kenya, and the Malagasy Republic dropped by two-thirds from 1964 to 1970.[47] The Mexican government, on the other hand, unable for political and social reasons to reduce the number of workers in the henequen ejidos and committed to a sweeping reorganization of the manufacturing sector, expanded its resource commitment to Yucatán's henequen industry. Banco Agrario subsidies to the henequen ejidos totaled 470.2 million pesos from 1966 through 1970, an amount that exceeded the accumulated subsidies for the previous eleven years (table 4). Bolstered by the generous access to government sources of financing, Cordemex's total gross investment in land, buildings, and equipment rose to an estimated 485 million pesos in 1970.[48]

104

Cordemex's expansion program during the late 1960s was predicated on the assumption that it would be able to maintain its share of the world natural fiber market and that raw fiber production levels would be consistent with its production capacity. By the mid-1970s its annual production capacity was 144,000 tons. This was sufficient to elaborate all raw henequen fiber then being produced in Mexico.[49] World hard fiber market conditions, however, did not justify the optimism of Cordemex's investment strategy. But, because management was not constrained to go to private capital markets to acquire funds, neither the depressed market conditions of the 1960s nor the pessimistic global outlook for natural fibers altered the firm's investment plans.

In view of the increased competition from synthetic fiber, the success of Cordemex's investment strategy depended crucially upon the firm's ability to compete with sisal producers in the U.S. harvest-twine market. Inasmuch as henequen was inferior to sisal in quality, the price of henequen twine would need to be significantly lower than that of sisal for Cordemex to be able to maintain or increase its level of sales. The reorganization of the cordage industry left the inefficient and corrupt ejido sector intact. This meant that the whole burden of cost reduction and control was placed on Cordemex. Management, on the other hand, had only limited control over certain manufacturing costs because of the sociopolitical functions that the firm was required to undertake by the federal government.

Nationalization strengthened the position of the two unions that represented the cordage-mill workers.[50] One of the explicit goals of the government-owned monopoly was to enhance job security and income for the workers. The union's leverage was enhanced further by the strength of organized labor in the political hierarchy; Mexico's labor unions have traditionally been one of the strongest bases of support for the PRI. Under agreements reached between Cordemex and the unions, the work force became permanent, virtually immune to layoffs even during periods of low production. The company's labor force exceeded 3,700 by 1970. Tappan de Arrigunaga observed that "the wages paid to Cordemex workers set entirely new standards for Mérida and for Yucatán as a whole."[51] Workers were also provided with unprecedented fringe benefits, including social-security rights and subsidized housing.

Cordemex's social commitment to its labor force seriously

hampered the firm's flexibility. Before the company's formation, factory owners protected themselves against the frequent fluctuations in demand by maintaining a relatively small permanent work force and hiring temporary workers during periods of peak demand. Cordemex's labor costs became part of its already heavy overhead costs. During the 1970s one of the factors that most critically undermined the cordage monopoly's financial position and its ability to compete with sisal and synthetics was its lack of control over labor costs.

The other major weakness of the new industry organization that would seriously affect Cordemex's future performance was the absence of a mechanism to coordinate the production and investment decisions of the cordage monopoly with those of the raw fiber producers. The heavy costs involved in expanding manufacturing capacity presumably were incurred under the assumption that raw fiber production would be sufficient to allow Cordemex to operate at or near capacity. The only direct input, however, that its management had into the decisions of private producers or the ejido sector was the price it paid for raw fiber.

Cordemex encountered problems early with raw-material supply because inadequate quantities of high-grade fiber were being produced. To improve Yucatán's image with cordage buyers, Cordemex adopted high standards for the grading of its raw fiber purchases. The highest prices were paid for long, unstained grade A fiber that Cordemex used to manufacture its major export item, harvest twine. Lower prices were paid for shorter, stained fiber, which could not be utilized to produce top-of-the-line export items without undermining Cordemex's efforts to improve its reputation for quality in external markets.

Significantly, the grading procedure and structure of price incentives only slightly affected the quality of fiber produced by the largest supplier, the henequen ejidos, for all ejidatarios were paid a flat, uniform wage by Banco Agrario regardless of the quantity or quality of the fiber they produced. Because of the general atmosphere of noncooperation that existed between the bank and the manufacturing monopoly, as well as the sensitive political status of the ejidos, Cordemex could not alter the existing ejido incentive system to its advantage.

To circumvent the bank and to reduce the uncertainty of its grade A fiber supply, the firm, as mentioned previously, constructed its own desfibradora facilities throughout the henequen zone. To encourage delivery to them, it charged less for leaf-processing than either the ejidos or the pequeños propietarios. In 1972 it started the practice of directly purchasing leaves, graded according to their length, as a further inducement to producers. By 1976 Cordemex's desfibradoras were processing almost a fourth of Yucatán's total leaf production.[52] Although the new programs alleviated somewhat the organization's raw-material supply problems, they also served to worsen its relations with the pequeños propietarios and Banco Agrario.[53]

The smallholders saw the new desfibradoras as a threat to their income because they had been processing the parcelarios' leaves. The bank perceived the action as a first step toward Cordemex's objective of dominating the agricultural sector of the industry.

The Economic Performance of Cordemex, 1964–1970

In spite of the low fiber prices and the declining external demand for henequen fiber and manufactures, Cordemex managed to earn a cumulated 11-million-peso profit on total sales of 1,842 million pesos during the period 1964 through 1970.[54] This modest accomplishment was primarily the result of two factors: (1) the price discrimination policies the firm pursued in the growing and highly protected domestic market; and (2) the firm's success in limiting the demands of Banco Agrario for a higher raw fiber transfer price.

Total external sales of henequen manufactures from Yucatán fell from 70,549 tons in 1964 to 45,993 tons in 1970. The decline in foreign sales was caused by a sharp decline in sales of harvest twine and packing and wrapping twine to United States buyers. Cordage exports to the United States fell from 67,500 tons to 41,808 tons during that period (table 9). The losses in sales and income that Cordemex suffered in that country were partially offset, however, by the growth in internal cordage consumption.

When Cordemex was established in 1961, it possessed a virtual monopoly in the Mexican internal market. Competition from independent domestic cordage mills was all but eliminated because the majority of Mexico's cordage mill capacity was located in Yucatán and, subsequently, became part of Cordemex. Fewer than ten independent mills operated in Mexico by 1962.[55] These mills posed little threat to Cordemex's dominant position in the market because the cordage monopoly could control

TABLE 9. Yucatán: Volume of Manufactured Henequen Exports, by Destination, 1959–1970 (in metric tons)

Year	United States	Other Countries	Total
1959	82,813	622	83,435
1960	72,338	822	76,160
1961	79,272	1,592	80,864
1962	82,146	979	83,125
1963	68,929	4,325	73,254
1964	67,500	3,049	70,549
1965	54,766	2,580	57,346
1966	51,753	3,677	55,430
1967	43,136	5,234	48,370
1968	34,362	4,901	39,263
1969	44,160	5,300	49,460
1970	41,808	4,185	45,993

SOURCE: Carlos Tappan de Arrigunaga, "Trade, Development, and Structural Change: The Future of Mexico's Henequen Industry" (Ph.D. dissertation, Texas A&M University, 1971), pp. 71–72.

exports of raw fiber from the state. The firm's predominant position in the home market was strengthened further by the established barriers to the import of sisal and synthetic substitutes for henequen fiber. Domestic consumption of henequen manufacturers, which had accounted for only 9,000 to 10,000 tons of Yucatán's output during the early 1950s,[56] climbed rapidly during the 1960s. During the period 1964–69, the domestic market absorbed 140,053 tons, or 31.5 percent, of Cordemex's total output (table 10). The impact of the domestic market was even more significant during those seven years because of the firm's successful price-discrimination strategy. The average price per kilogram of cordage sold in Mexico was 5.28 pesos, and the average for foreign sales was 3.61 pesos per kilogram. Due to this price differential, income from home sales was 40.2 percent of total income during the period (table 10).

Cordemex's control over the destination and quantity of raw fiber shipments out of the state also permitted it to set favorable raw fiber transfer prices. According to Margaret Goodman, its director, Miguel Olea, tried to purchase fiber from Banco Agrario

TABLE 10. Cordemex: Volume and Value of Sales, by Destination, 1964–1969

Destination	Volume of Sales (in metric tons)	Percent of Total Sales Volume	Value of Sales (in millions of pesos)	Percent of Total Sales Value	Average Price Received per Kilogram (in pesos)
External markets	305,000	68.5	1,102.4	59.8	3.61
Domestic markets	140,053	31.5	740.1	40.2	5.28
Total	445,053	100.0	1,842.5	100.0	4.14

SOURCE: Cordemex, Seis años de labores (Mérida: 1976).

at the lowest possible price in order to generate maximum profits.[57]

From 1965 through 1970 Cordemex successfully stabilized the transfer price of grade A fiber at 1.65 pesos per kilogram. This was competitive with the world market price for grade A Mexican henequen fiber during that period.[58] However, the price structure was still favorable for Cordemex because of the control it possessed over the destination of raw fiber sales. First, its virtual monopoly over the manufacture and sale of henequen articles in Mexico enabled it to pay world market prices for raw material and yet market manufactured items internally at prices substantially above what it received on the world market. Second, much of the fiber that the firm obtained from the agricultural bank was purchased at prices well below 1.65 pesos per kilogram inasmuch as it was not of grade A quality.[59] Official bank records for the period 1965 through 1970 show that the average price received by the bank per kilogram of raw fiber produced by the ejidos was only 1.06 pesos.[60] Even in the absence of any restrictions on the export of raw fiber, Cordemex would have been the sole purchaser of low-grade ejido fiber because U.S. cordage mills used only grade A fiber to produce harvest twine. Cordemex used the lower-grade material to produce bags, filters, and padding, much of which was sold in the protected home market.

109

Although these pricing policies during the 1960s for the short term favorably affected the firm's profits, they caused both the pequeños propietarios and Banco Agrario to reduce their investment in new plantings.[61] Cordemex management was apparently unaware or unconcerned about the impact of their "profit maximizing" policies on the firm's raw-material suppliers. Incredibly, as late as 1974, the annual report confidently predicted that sufficient new sowings had been made to increase Yucatán's henequen production to 250,000 tons.[62] Barely five years later, the state's raw fiber production had fallen to 80,000 tons, and Cordemex had begun to close factories because of a shortage of raw material.

Summary and Conclusions

The federal government's purchase of Yucatán's cordage mills in 1964 was followed by a massive program of reorganization and modernization during the late 1960s. By 1970 Mexico's cordage industry was the most modern in the world. Cordemex, however, was frustrated in its efforts to improve the overall cost-competitiveness of the agroindustry because of the lack of coordination and political tensions with the agricultural bank. The government monopoly was also constrained by its commitment to social and political goals that conflicted with its economic objectives. These commitments caused the firm to be highly vulnerable to the adverse market conditions that began to confront natural fiber producers in the late 1960s.

6

Henequen Politics:
The Political Economy of
Crisis Management

▲▲▲▲▲▲▲▲▲▲▲▲▲▲▲▲▲▲▲▲▲▲▲▲▲▲▲▲▲▲▲▲▲▲▲▲▲▲▲

THE FEDERAL government's administration of
Yucatán's henequen industry turned into a national scandal and a
nightmare for Mexico City during the 1970s.

Between 1955 and 1964, Banco Agrario's annual subsidy to the
henequen ejidos fluctuated between 11.7 million and 70.6 million
pesos. By 1977 credit advances to the collectives were exceeding
recuperations by more than 500 million pesos (table 4), and the
accumulated debt of the henequen ejidos was in excess of 2
billion pesos.[1] Despite the rapid growth of federal aid to the
ejidos, raw fiber production in the state declined sharply during
the 1970s.

Cordemex's financial problems were even more severe than
those of the ejidos. After 1970 the publicly owned monopoly
sustained losses every year except for the period 1973–74, when
the price of hard fiber reached artificially high levels because of
the world petroleum crisis. Accumulated losses from 1970
through 1978 totaled 2,173.8 million pesos (table 11). During the
same period, the outstanding debt increased by more than 460
percent, rising from 482.2 million pesos to 2,700.9 million pesos
(table 12). As of December 31, 1978, total liabilities and capital
accounts were 3,241.3 million pesos.[2] This total was a rough
measure of the federal investment in the cordage industry, for
Cordemex is wholly owned by the government and the largest
share of its debt is held by government banks. This figure does not
include the funds it received from the government's export-incen-
tive program. Assuming that this subsidy has averaged from 8 to
10 percent of the value of total foreign sales, federal investment
could have been as high as 3,600 million pesos.

TABLE 11. Cordemex: Operating Results, 1970–1981[a] (in millions of pesos)

	1970	1971	1972	1973	1974	1975	1976	1977[b]	1978	1979	1981
Total revenue	299.2	408.9	514.6	888.4	1,330.2	826.1	1,375.2	853.0	1,365.8	...	2,266.3
Total expense	360.4	436.1	551.7	756.6	1,212.2	1,139.6	2,364.0	1,150.0	2,064.6	...	2,900.0
Profit (Loss)	(61.2)	(27.2)	(37.1)	131.8	118.0	(313.5)	(988.8)	(297.0)	(698.8)	(667.4)	(633.7)

SOURCES: Cordemex, *Informe anual de Cordemex* (Mérida, 1977); idem, *Seis años de labores* (Mérida, 1976); idem, *Sesión del consejo de administración de Cordemex* (Mérida, January 1978); "Cuantiosas pérdidas de Cordemex en 1978," *Diario de Yucatán*, 31 July 1979; "Pérdidas de Cordemex: 633 millones en 1981," *Diario de Yucatán*, 31 March 1982.

[a]Operating results for 1980 were not reported by Cordemex.
[b]Operating results for 1977 include only the last nine months of the year.

TABLE 12. Cordemex: Outstanding Debt and Social Capital, 1971–1978 (money amounts in millions of pesos)

Year	Outstanding Debt	Social Capital	Outstanding Debt as a Percentage of Social Capital
1971	482.2	250.0	192.9
1972	574.0	250.0	229.6
1973	666.8	250.0	266.7
1974	350.9	500.0	70.2
1975	553.2	500.0	110.6
1976	1,266.1	500.0	253.2
1977	2,376.6	500.0	475.3
1978	2,700.9	500.0	540.2

SOURCES: Cordemex, *Informe anual de Cordemex* (Mérida, 1977); idem, *Seis años de labores* (Mérida, 1976); idem, *Sesión del consejo de administración de Cordemex* (Mérida, May 1978); "Cordemex en 1978," *Diario de Yucatán,* 2 August 1979.

The huge losses prompted a storm of criticism. The firm's management reacted by releasing less and less information on its operations. In December 1979 an annual report still had not been issued for 1978, and the *consejo de administración*, or board of directors, had not met for sixteen months. The "stonewalling" by management fueled suspicions that the firm had been grossly mismanaged and plundered by its administrators. In the view of one critic, the supreme irony of the situation to Yucatecans was that Cordemex, which was purchased in the name of the ejidatarios, had become "a small island of wealth surrounded by an immense sea of misery."[3]

In the absence of federal intervention, the henequen industry and the state economy would have undergone a painful readjustment during the 1970s. The decline in the world demand for hard fibers that began in the early 1960s continued unabated into the 1970s. The magnitude of industry losses, however, was attributable to the organizational deficiencies, corruption, and the limited economic flexibility of the governmental entities that administered production. Political crises and bureaucratic inertia prevented the federal government from making timely and adequate responses to deteriorating conditions in the world hard fiber market. As representatives of the authorities in Mexico City, both Banrural and Cordemex pursued policies designed to minimize political and social unrest in the state rather than to minimize industry losses. The economic consequences of this strategy were devastating. By 1977 the losses were so overwhelming and production so disorganized that the bank and Cordemex had almost ceased performing a legitimate economic function in the state. Instead, the two government organizations had become the major disbursing agents for a massive, corrupt, and largely ad hoc social welfare program.

TRENDS IN THE WORLD MARKET FOR HARD FIBERS AFTER 1970

After 1970 several factors combined to worsen both the relative and absolute position of henequen and sisal producers vis-à-vis synthetic fibers.

Until the early 1970s, Mexico was the only producing nation that had a modern cordage industry. As late as 1969, some 83 percent of world sisal and henequen exports were shipped in raw form to cordage mills in North America and Western Europe for further elaboration. The remaining 17 percent consisted primarily of Mexican exports of harvest twine manufactured in Yucatán.[4]

The composition of natural fiber exports changed significantly after 1970. Low fiber prices during the late 1960s and early 1970s stimulated the rapid growth of cordage industries in other major producing nations. In 1978 some 181,000 tons, or 39.1 percent, of the total hard-fiber exports of henequen- and sisal-producing nations were elaborated or semielaborated.[5] European cordage mills, which operated behind high protective tariffs, found they were unable to obtain adequate supplies of natural fiber. They, therefore, turned to synthetic fibers as a source of raw material. This accelerated the substitution of synthetic harvest twine in European agriculture during the 1970s.[6]

Technological changes also improved the competitive position of plastic twine and adversely affected the demand for harvest twine. The price of the polypropylene resins, which are used to manufacture artificial fibers, fell by more than a half after their introduction in the early 1960s. By 1976 the cost advantage that

114

henequen and sisal possessed in the 1960s had almost disappeared. In Western Europe, the price of polypropylene twine actually fell below that of natural fiber twine.[7] The demand for both natural and synthetic twine weakened, particularly in the United States, because of the changes in collection and storage techniques. Farmers began to collect and store hay in large rolls that required little or no twine rather than baling it. The increasing use of silos to store grain in bulk produced a similar effect on the demand for binder twine.[8]

The stability of the world hard fiber market was threatened further by the sharp decline in fiber prices that took place at the end of the world petroleum crisis in 1974. Shortages of oil-based resins, and subsequently, synthetic fiber, precipitated the speculative purchase of abnormally large quantities of natural fiber twine in late 1973 and 1974. As an immediate result, the price of sisal and henequen fibers rose to more than twice the level of 1970. The price of the superior-grade East African sisal, for example, increased to a record level of $1,070 per ton. The unusual stockpiling that took place during the crisis caused a sharp decline in both prices and imports following the end of the oil embargo. Hard fiber imports of consuming nations fell from

TABLE 13. World Production of Sisal and Henequen Fiber, 1974–1981 (in thousands of metric tons)

Year	World Production
1974	778.4
1975	606.0
1976	552.5
1977	490.0
1978	442.0
1979	478.1
1980 (preliminary)	504.5
1981 (estimate)	475.3

SOURCE: Table 1; Commodity Research Bureau, Inc., 1982 Commodity Yearbook (New York, 1982), p. 165.

427,000 tons in 1974 to 294,000 tons in 1975 and prices plummeted to near the record lows of 1970.[9]

After 1974 the world recession and increased competition from synthetic fibers prevented hard fiber prices from rising appreciably above the 1975 level. World production of sisal and henequen decreased steadily, falling from 778,400 tons in 1974 to 490,000 tons in 1977 (table 13). In spite of this decline, the Intergovernmental Group on Hard Fibers was unable to fix a minimum price for harvest twine because of the large carry-over stock from the petroleum crisis.[10]

THE REEMERGENCE OF POLITICAL REGIONALISM IN YUCATÁN

Increased competition from sisal and synthetic fiber after 1960 virtually neutralized Cordemex's market power vis-à-vis North American buyers. Efforts to boost prices would have triggered a massive substitution of the rival fibers for henequen. In this highly competitive environment, governmental efforts to maintain existing industry production and employment levels while minimizing income transfers to the industry depended heavily on Cordemex's success in controlling and reducing production costs. The firm's control over costs, already limited because of its status as a publicly owned enterprise, was loosened further by a series of political and social crises in Yucatán during the late 1960s and early 1970s.

In 1967 the Partido de Acción Nacional (PAN), the PRI's nominal conservative rival, pulled a stunning upset in the Yucatán state elections. A PAN candidate, Victor Correa Racho, was elected as *alcalde*, or mayor, of Mérida by an almost three-to-one majority. Two PAN candidates were also elected to the nine-member state legislature, which made Yucatán the first Mexican state to have a two-party legislature in the twentieth century.[11] This strong challenge to the PRI's political dominance of the state sent shock waves throughout Mexico, for it represented an open rebellion by a large urban population against Mexico City's policies and highly centralized decision-making apparatus.[12]

The elections of 1967 were preceded by an intense outburst of regional sentiment in Yucatán. On July 12, 1967, Mexican President Gustavo Díaz Ordaz, who was by many accounts never fond of either the state or its people, suspended all federally funded public works projects there, accusing the inhabitants of mis-managing the newly constructed potable water system in Mérida. Later that same month, he increased anti-Mexico City sentiment in Yucatán by publicly humiliating a group of its prominent citizens who had traveled to the neighboring state of Campeche to try to iron out the misunderstandings between themselves and the president.[13] His actions and remarks were interpreted as a direct attack on the Yucatecan upper class and an affront to regional pride. Social tensions in Yucatán were already high because of the ejidatario riots at Mérida in 1966. From the end of July until the elections in November 1967, conservative, anti-PRI, anti-Mexico City elements in the state, including the private business sector and the influential regional daily *Diario de Yucatán*, waged a successful campaign to unseat PRI candidates in the municipal election. Economic conditions also favored PAN candidates. Low raw-fiber prices caused unrest among both ejido and private producers and produced a general worsening of economic conditions.

The PRI and government officials set out immediately to undo the results of the elections of 1967. Reversing his previous stand, Díaz Ordaz committed the Mexican government to large increases in public expenditures in the state in order to stimulate agricultural diversification and the growth of the fishing industry. To counter continuing discontent in the henequen zone over raw fiber prices, Banco Agrario's subsidies to the ejidos were also increased substantially.[14] Total public expenditures per capita in Yucatán during Díaz Ordaz's term in office (1965–70) were 3,390 pesos, or almost triple those of the previous administration of Adolfo López Mateos.[15]

Efforts to undermine the panistas also included a frontal assault on the PAN mayor of Mérida. Correa Racho's efforts to govern the capital were constantly frustrated by the political machinations of the PRI-dominated state legislature.[16] In 1969 the state legislature actually took control of Mérida's police force away from the mayor and vested it in the governor of Yucatán, where it remains to this day.

Correa Racho's tumultuous term as mayor of Mérida set the stage for another confrontation between the PRI and the PAN in the governor's election in the fall of 1969. Correa resigned his post as mayor to run against the PRI's handpicked candidate Carlos Loret de Mola, who was a former senator from Yucatán. The PRI conducted a concerted campaign to prevent the panista from being elected to a six-year term as governor. The campaign itself was one of the most violent that Mexico had witnessed for several decades.[17] Numerous confrontations occurred between the followers of the PRI and the PAN throughout the summer and fall of 1969. At one point, mobs of PRI supporters stormed the *Diario de Yucatán*, burning newspapers and threatening to sack the offices. The local police and military, under the control of the PRI, seldom intervened to control the excesses of the PRI forces. Not unexpectedly, the election was a resounding victory for Loret de Mola. To the present day, supporters of the now-deceased Correa contend that the election was stolen through fraudulent voting and counting procedures. Because the Federal Election Commission was controlled by the PRI, the PAN's allegations were never proven or even seriously investigated. In 1970 the PRI regained complete control of the state's political apparatus by sweeping the municipal and state legislative elections.[18]

Yucatán's brief anti-PRI rebellion was significant on several levels. First, it demonstrated that, despite the many years of federal dominance of the local economy and political system, a strong undercurrent of anticentralist, anti-Mexico City sentiment that could be politically exploited still existed in the state. Second, the core of the PAN's support was composed basically of the same elements that opposed the reformist policies of the Mexican Revolution: the conservative, pro-Catholic upper class, a remnant of the prereform landowning aristocracy. This group gathered additional support from an emerging business elite and the *Diario de Yucatán*. Mass support came from the growing urban middle class of Mérida, which was disaffected with the policies of the PRI and the federal government in Yucatán. Finally, the elections showed that one of the PRI's best organized and strongest base of support was in the populous rural areas. Outside Mérida, except for a few scattered enclaves of PAN support, the campesino population remained solidly in the PRI camp.

The lesson of the elections was not lost on either the PRI or Mexico City. Economic initiatives after 1970 clearly reflected the crucial role that Yucatán's rural population played in the PRI's efforts to dominate the state political system.

Serious disruptions in the henequen zone continued to threaten the political stability of the state during the early 1970s. Angry and sometimes violent demonstrations by mobs of ejidatarios against the agricultural bank and Cordemex provoked numerous interventions by the Mexican Army and the state police in the henequen zone. These disturbances culminated in the stoning to death of a high bank official by a group of ejidatarios at Izamal in 1972.[19]

Both as a candidate in 1970 and as president of Mexico in 1972, Luis Echeverría Álvarez was met by restive groups of ejidatarios demanding higher fiber prices, an end to the corruption in the agricultural bank, and a reorganization of the henequen industry that would give the ejidos more control over both agricultural and manufacturing operations. Although the president paid lip service to the ejidatarios' demands for change, the organization of the henequen industry remained basically unchanged during his term in office. Like his predecessors, he eschewed any action that would have upset the status quo.[20] His basic strategy for dealing with the unrest was to increase the salaries and benefits of the ejidatarios. In 1972 henequen ejidatarios were granted social-security benefits, the premiums for which were paid by the Banco Agrario. This was a significant action because the health-care needs of only a small percentage of the nation's rural population were then provided for by the National Social Security System. More importantly, Echeverría permitted the transfer price of raw fiber to rise from 1.55 pesos per kilogram in 1972 to 7.00 pesos per kilogram in November 1974. The price increases were immediately passed on to the ejidos in the form of higher salaries.

The federal government's economic offensive in Yucatán did not end with the granting of wage increases to the henequen ejidatarios. In a dramatic reversal of the niggardly policies of past administrations toward the state, hundreds of millions of dollars were poured into the economy after 1970 through a bewildering array of credits, subsidies, and investments. In 1978, for example, total federal expenditures in Yucatán were estimated to be 6 billion pesos, or almost 43 percent of that year's gross state product of 13.99 billion pesos[21] (the reader should bear in mind that Mexico City was not even connected by highway with Mérida until 1961). The state budget, which is heavily subsidized by the federal government, was 1.1 billion pesos in 1979, or ten times greater than it was in 1969.[22]

Although the expenditures of the some two dozen government agencies active in the state were directed at all sectors of the local economy, a major target was the rural population, specifically the impoverished population of the henequen zone. In 1979, for example, Banrural, Banco Agrario's successor and the major federal agency involved in Yucatán's agriculture, projected that it would extend credits totaling 2.7 billion pesos in the state, an amount equivalent to 81 percent of the value-added of all agriculture production in 1978. Of this sum, 1.5 billion pesos were programmed for henequen production and diversification projects in the henequen zone.[23] Strong efforts have also been made to improve the social infrastructure in rural areas.

President Echeverría's economic policies were highly successful from a political standpoint. The deluge of well-placed federal expenditures during his term reduced the friction between the state and Mexico City, brought peace to the countryside, and produced a general improvement in economic conditions in the state during the first half of the 1970s. Opposition parties, including the PAN, were simply left without an issue that could excite popular support. In 1976 the PRI hierarchy further solidified their party's strength in rural Yucatán by selecting Dr. Francisco Luna Kan, a man of self-proclaimed campesino origins, to be the next state governor.

It would be an oversimplification to imply that political objectives alone dictated the federal government's economic policy in Yucatán during the past decade. On the other hand, heavy governmental subsidies to the henequen industry during the 1970s undoubtedly played a major role in reducing social unrest among henequen ejidatarios.

HENEQUEN POLITICS AND INDUSTRY PERFORMANCE DURING THE 1970s

The agricultural bank-Cordemex nexus enhanced the federal government's control over the state of Yucatán. During the late 1960s and 1970s, the destabilizing effects of adverse conditions in the world hard fiber market on employment and income were countered by increasing the amount of federal subsidy to the henequen industry. Federal management of the industry became a social, and ultimately a political, exercise. Profits and losses were discarded as a guide to economic decisions and as a measure of management performance in both the agricultural bank and Cordemex. Social and political criteria and the self-interests of industry officials were placed in their stead. The noneconomic orientation of the federal entities during the near decade-long turbulence in Yucatán is not surprising. The legitimacy of the PRI's continued dominance of the state rested precariously on the government's real or perceived ability to meet the economic and noneconomic demands of a selected constituency. The successful political strategy, however, turned out to be an economic disaster.

The Agricultural Sector

Between 1966 and 1977 the number of ejidatarios on the agricultural bank's payroll, which had been relatively stable before the mid-1960s, rose sharply from 58,726 to 90,763 (table 2). This 54.5 percent increase in the ejido labor force bore little relation to the labor needs of the industry. Ejido land in full production declined from 119,430 hectares to 100,000 hectares, and the raw fiber output of the ejido sector fell from 67,927 tons to 50,870 tons during the same period (table 3). Notwithstanding the precipitous decline in productivity and the swollen labor force, individual ejidatario wages almost doubled during the twelve-year period. The end result of these seemingly irrational policies was that the governmental subsidy to the henequen ejidos rose from 67.1 million pesos annually in 1966 to 540 million pesos in 1977 (table 4).

The above figures seem to indicate that the federal government, in pursuit of noneconomic objectives in Yucatán, either lost or relinquished economic control of the ejidos. Efforts by bank officials to link credits with ejido raw fiber production were abandoned after the mid-1960s. The federal government's neglect fostered corruption on a scale almost without precedent in Mexico. The extent of the corruption was revealed in early 1978, when President José López Portillo ordered a *depuración*, or "cleansing," of both the henequen ejidos and Banrural. By comparing social-security rolls with bank payrolls, investigators discovered that more than 33,000 of the ejidatarios on the bank's weekly payroll were imposters. Of this number, approximately 21,000 were "phantoms" who were either dead or had never existed. The remaining illegal recipients were individuals who did not possess ejido rights. Mexican officials estimated that the "phantom" ejidatarios had been costing the bank 200 million pesos per year.[24]

An internal investigation of Banrural also revealed numerous irregularities. During the course of 1977 and 1978, some 133 bank employees were discharged for fraud.[25]

López Portillo's decision was largely unavoidable in view of the serious deterioration in production conditions that had occurred in the ejido sector during the 1970s. Between 1970 and 1977, ejido raw fiber production fell by 30.2 percent, despite the almost fivefold increase in raw fiber prices that occurred during the period (table 3). The bank's annual credit dvance to the ejidos, on the other hand, rose by 707.5 million pesos while the bank's receipts from the sale of the collectives' fiber increased by only 286 million pesos (table 4). In 1977 it cost Banrural an average of 17.05 pesos to produce a kilogram of ejido fiber, compared with 2.20 pesos in 1970 (tables 3 and 4). The average price received by the bank from the sale of a kilogram of ejido fiber increased by less than five pesos during the same period. Clearly, the government's patronage system was not only out of control in a financial sense, but it was destroying the ejidatarios' incentive to produce efficiently, or for that matter to produce at all. López Portillo was also aware that corruption had reached levels that were unacceptable even for Mexico. The government's continued tolerance of the situation could have produced a major embarrassment for his administration, which was then conducting a high-profile campaign against corruption in government.

The disclosure of massive corruption in the ejidos and Banrural came as no surprise to Yucatecans. As discussed earlier, corrupt practices have been commonplace in the ejido sector and the agricultural bank since the agrarian reform of the 1930s. That federal officials were aware of the corruption and yet allowed employment and bank subsidies to reach unprecedented levels from 1966 to 1977 is a measure of the anxiety with which Mexico City viewed the political and social disturbances in Yucatán during that period.

Some of the illegal payments, including those made to widows, disabled ejidatarios, and persons who worked in the fields without possessing ejido rights, represented a genuine attempt of the government to ease the plight of the unemployed and underemployed in the henequen zone. Despite the generally depressed state of the henequen industry throughout much of the post–World War II period, the population of the henequen zone (excluding the municipio of Mérida) increased from 183,512 in 1950 to

241,056 in 1970.[26] Total employment in the manufacturing and services sector of the state economy, the bulk of which was located in nearby Mérida, increased by less than 13,000 during the same period. Another portion of the illegal payments was utilized routinely to pay off ejido leaders who were the key elements in the political organization of the countryside. Many of the illegal payments, however, were received by individuals who were using their positions in the ejido or bank for their personal advantage.

The output of private producers also declined during the 1970s, falling from 44,813 tons in 1970 to 34,827 tons in 1977 (tables 1 and 3). Low prices, the uncertainty of land tenure, and the lack of access to credit discouraged pequeños propietarios from investing in either new fields or equipment. Cordemex's aggressive entry into leaf-processing and the expansion in the number of ejido desfibradoras also negatively affected pequeños propietarios' profits by reducing the volume of leaves that the smallholders processed. By 1978 fewer than a hundred private desfibradoras were operating in the state.[27] As a result of the production declines of both ejido and private producers, the state's total raw fiber output fell to 85,697 tons in 1977 (table 1), which was almost 60,000 tons short of Cordemex's production capacity.

The Manufacturing Sector

During the presidential term of Luis Echeverría Álvarez (1970–76), Cordemex became an instrument of international as well as domestic political policy. He was vitally interested in pressing Mexico's claim, as well as his own, to a position of leadership among Third World nations. In 1970 Mexico was the only major natural-fiber-producing nation that had a significant cordage manufacturing capacity. Under Echeverría, Cordemex's modernization and expansion program was accelerated in order to make the Yucatán cordage manufacturing complex a show place of Third World economic accomplishment. During the Echeverría administration, 413 million pesos of federal funds were invested in mills, equipment, and leaf-processing facilities. Manufacturing capacity was increased from 100,000 tons annually to 144,000 tons, and the Cordemex labor force rose from 3,700 to 7,500.[28] In the company's 1976 annual report, management could boast that: "Cordemex is known the world over as the largest, most modern, and most integrated hard fiber producer. Mexico, through Cordemex, is the principal exporter of hard fiber manufactures in the world . . . the only producing nation which exports only manufactured products."[29]

President Echeverría capitalized on Cordemex's prestige and progressive image to strengthen Mexico's ties with the various hard-fiber-producing nations in Africa and Latin America. In 1973 the FAO Intergovernmental Group on Hard Fibers, meeting for the first time in Mexico, was attended by Echeverría and heads of other fiber-producing nations. The next year, Julius Nyerere, the Tanzanian head of state, traveled to Mexico City to sign an agreement with the Mexican president to create Tanzamex, a joint venture between Cordemex and the African nation for the purpose of initiating cordage manufacturing in Tanzania. By 1976 Cordemex was also engaged in a joint venture with El Salvador and planned to sell cordage-making technology to Brazil, Haiti, and Venezuela.[30] Echeverría's noneconomic aspirations for both Mexico and himself clearly were a key factor in Cordemex's ambitious expansion program during the early 1970s, for world hard fiber market conditions continued to be depressed. During the first three years of the 1970s, the cordage monopoly accumulated losses of 125.5 million pesos (table 11).

In Yucatán, Cordemex became deeply involved in the government's efforts to placate the restive ejidatarios in the henequen zone. Under pressure from ejido groups, the firm agreed to turn over its leaf-processing facilities to the henequen collectives. In November 1974, by presidential resolution, the first of the facilities was turned over to four ejidos near the town of Motul. Ejido agrobusiness units were formed to administer and operate the desfibradoras and to exploit the by-products of leaf-processing. The ejido-run facility faltered from the beginning because of poor planning and covert opposition to the plan by Cordemex and Banco Agrario. By 1976 the program had been abandoned and Cordemex regained control of its leaf-processing facilities.[31]

The debacle of the ejido agrobusiness program was symptomatic of the chaotic manner in which the federal government attempted to deal with the unrest in the henequen zone. The demands on Cordemex were made by the Confederación Nacional del Campesino (CNC) and the Secretaría de la Reforma Agraria (SRA) in the name of the ejidos. The former is a union of rural workers that is closely tied to the PRI; the latter, a government agency charged with conducting agrarian reform programs.

TABLE 14. Cordemex: Volume of Sales, by Destination, 1970–1981 (in metric tons)

Destination	1970	% of Total Volume	1971	% of Total Volume	1972	% of Total Volume	1973	% of Total Volume
External markets	51.7	66.7	63.9	66.1	78.6	63.8	82.5	64.7
Domestic markets	25.8	33.3	32.8	33.9	44.6	36.2	45.1	35.3
Total	77.5	100.0	96.7	100.0	123.2	100.0	127.6	100.0

Destination	1974	% of Total Volume	1975	% of Total Volume	1976	% of Total Volume	1977	% of Total Volume
External markets	63.5	66.4	40.8	53.8	73.6	63.6	64.5	73.4
Domestic markets	32.2	33.6	35.0	46.2	42.2	36.4	23.4	26.6
Total	95.7	100.0	75.8	100.0	115.8	100.0	87.9	100.0

Destination	1978	% of Total Volume	1979	% of Total Volume	1980	% of Total Volume	1981	% of Total Volume
External markets	60.2	67.2	54.2	63.2	31.5	58.4	37.4	58.5
Domestic markets	29.4	32.8	31.6	36.8	22.4	41.6	26.5	41.5
Total	89.6	100.0	85.8	100.0	53.9	100.0	63.9	100.0

SOURCES: Cordemex, *Informe anual de Cordemex* (Mérida, 1977); idem, *Seis años de labores* (Mérida, 1976); idem, *Sesión del consejo de administración de Cordemex* (Mérida, January 1978); Secretaría de Programación y Presupuesto, Delegación en Yucatán, *La economía del estado de Yucatán en 1978* (Mérida, 1979), pp. 20–21; Gobierno del Estado de Yucatán, *El sexto informe del gobernador* (Mérida, 1982); Cordemex, *Sesión del consejo de administración de Cordemex* (Mérida, March 1982).

TABLE 15. Cordemex: Value of Sales, by Destination, 1970–1981
(in millions of pesos)

Destination	1970	% of Total Value	1971	% of Total Value	1972	% of Total Value	1973	% of Total Value
External markets	152.5	50.9	234.7	57.4	326.3	63.4	634.8	71.5
Domestic markets	147.0	49.1	174.2	42.6	188.3	36.6	253.6	28.5
Total	299.2	100.0	408.9	100.0	514.6	100.0	888.4	100.0

Destination	1974	% of Total Value	1975	% of Total Value	1976	% of Total Value	1977	% of Total Value
External markets	995.0	74.8	359.5	43.5	752.5	54.3	. . .	. . .
Domestic markets	335.2	25.2	466.6	56.5	632.5	45.7	. . .	. . .
Total	1,330.2	100.0	826.1	100.0	1,385.0	100.0	853.0[a]	100.0

Destination	1978	% of Total Value	1979	% of Total Value	1980	% of Total Value	1981	% of Total Value
External markets	804.5	59.0	886.1	55.1	782.2	50.9	871.9	40.4
Domestic markets	559.1	41.0	722.0	44.9	754.6	49.1	1,287.5	59.6
Total	1,363.6	100.0	1,608.1	100.0	1,536.8	100.0	2,159.4	100.0

SOURCES: Same as listed for Table 14 plus Cordemex, *Valor de ventas, 1975–1980,* as published in *Diario de Yucatán,* 26 January 1981.
[a]Sales figures for 1977 include only the last nine months of the year.

TABLE 16. Cordemex: Average Price Received per Kilogram of Sales, by Destination, by Selected Years, 1970–1981 (in pesos)

Destination	1970	1971	1972	1973	1974	1975	1976	1978	1979	1980	1981
External markets	2.94	3.67	4.15	7.69	15.67	8.81	10.22	13.36	16.35	24.83	23.31
Internal markets	5.70	5.31	4.22	5.62	10.41	13.33	15.00	19.02	22.85	33.69	48.58

SOURCES: Tables 14 and 15.

The desfibradora transfer program was wholly unrealistic unless the ejido agrobusiness could obtain financing, technical, and administrative assistance from Cordemex and the agricultural bank. Because all the groups involved were allowed to continue to pursue their own particularistic interests, the program became yet another example of the poorly planned, and sometimes demagogic, programs that the federal government has tried to establish in the henequen zone since land reform.

Although Cordemex was able to maintain the integrity of its production facilities in the face of demands for a broader participation of ejidatarios, it was unable to limit their petitions for higher fiber prices. In 1972 President Echeverría encouraged the CNC to petition for higher raw fiber prices for producers.[32] Fortuitously, the increase in hard fiber prices and demand that accompanied the world petroleum crisis allowed Cordemex to grant generous increases to the ejidos. Its total sales, which had been only 77.5 thousand tons in 1970, rose to 127.6 thousand tons in 1973 (table 14). More significantly, the average price the firm received per kilo of henequen manufactures sold abroad increased from 4.15 pesos in 1972 to 15.67 pesos in 1974, and the value of total sales rose from 514.6 million pesos to 1,330.2 million pesos (tables 15 and 16).

Reacting to the unexpected bonanza and increasing pressure for a higher transfer price, Cordemex rapidly increased the price it paid for raw fiber. Between July 1972 and November 1974, it raised the transfer price of grade A raw fiber from 1.55 pesos per kilogram to 7.00 pesos per kilogram. The maximum weekly wage paid to henequen ejidatarios rose from about 85 pesos to 118 pesos, which helped to quiet the unrest in the henequen zone.

During the same period, Cordemex also granted generous wage and benefit increases to its expanding labor force. Salaries, wages, and benefits more than doubled between 1970 and 1974, rising from 75.8 million pesos to 180.3 million pesos (table 17). Despite these large increases in raw-material and labor costs, record world market prices allowed the organization to generate profits of 131.8 million pesos in 1973 and 118.0 million pesos in 1974 (table 11).

Ironically, the brief period of high prices and profits that the new director, Dr. Federico Rioseco, hailed as a "new henequen bonanza"[33] proved to be extremely damaging for the firm's future performance. Rather than recognizing that the high prices that coincided with the oil embargo were an aberration, the management reacted as if the increases in prices and demand were permanent. Between 1973 and 1976 almost 180 million pesos were invested in new plant and equipment.[34] Correspondingly, the labor force was increased from 6,400 to 7,500 to staff the new plant capacity and leaf-processing facilities. This action represented a large increase in the firm's fixed costs because a reduction in its labor force was difficult to accomplish. Management's failure to assess more cautiously the implications of the surge in world market prices reflected both the low priority that the firm assigned to economic criteria and its desire to increase the monopoly's power and prestige in the state.

The management soon realized that the seven pesos per kilogram transfer price they had so generously established was a price floor. Both Presidents Echeverría and López Portillo decided to maintain the price at seven pesos per kilogram or above. A large portion of Cordemex's raw-material costs, therefore, became fixed costs because the firm was committed to purchase the ejidos' production at prices that had been set during the petroleum crisis. As a result, the firm, by the middle of the 1970s, had virtually no control over its major categories of cost.

The consequences of this lack of flexibility became painfully

TABLE 17. Cordemex: Wage, Salary, and Benefit Expense, by Selected Years, 1970–1978 (money amounts in millions of pesos)

Year	Wage, Salary, and Benefit Expense	Total Revenue	Wage, Salary, and Benefit Expense as a Percentage of Total Revenue
1970	75.8	299.2	25.3
1971	99.0	408.9	24.3
1972	128.8	514.6	25.0
1973	180.3	888.4	20.3
1974	264.1	1,330.2	19.8
1975	271.9	826.1	32.9
1978	677.3	1,365.8	49.6

SOURCES: "Cuantiosas pérdidas de Cordemex en 1978," *Diario de Yucatán*, 31 July 1979; Cordemex, *Seis años de labores* (Mérida, 1976).

evident in 1975 as the petroleum crisis subsided. Demand for hard fiber twine declined dramatically. Cordemex's foreign sales plummeted to 40,800 tons, less than half the level of 1973 (table 14). The average price that the monopoly received per kilogram of product sold abroad fell to 8.81 pesos, which was just barely above the price the firm was paying for grade A raw fiber (table 16). Cordemex's labor and transfer pricing policies had a predictable effect on its operating results for that year. The average cost per kilogram of total sales, 5.93 pesos in 1973, rose to 15.03 pesos in 1975, causing the firm to sustain a loss of 313.5 million pesos (tables 11 and 18).

After 1975 the situation continued to deteriorate badly. Total sales in 1976, 1977, and 1978 were 115,800, 87,900, and 89,600 tons, respectively (table 14). Accumulated losses during the three-year period were a staggering 1,984.6 million pesos (table 11). By 1978 the average cost incurred per kilogram of sales had risen to 23.04 pesos, almost 8 pesos higher than the average price Cordemex was receiving per kilogram (table 18).

The firm's leaf-processing operations contributed heavily to its losses during the late 1970s, despite the greater speed, versatility, and technical efficiency of its seventeen modern desfibradoras.

In 1979 the owners of the 80-odd private desfibradoras were being paid by Banrural 1.50 pesos per kilo of ejido raw fiber processed. In the same year, the desfibradoras of Cordemex processed 19,000 tons of fiber at an average cost of more than 16.6 pesos per kilo. In 1978 and 1979 the reported losses on leaf-processing operations were 161 million pesos and 167 million pesos, respectively.[35] Interestingly, Cordemex only received an average of 16.35 pesos per kilo on foreign sales of finished goods in 1979 (table 16).

A major reason for the firm's high leaf-processing costs is the large, permanent labor force it employs at its seventeen facilities. In 1978 and 1979 the desfibradoras processed 28,200 and 19,000 tons of fiber, respectively. The labor force, on the other hand, rose from 1,550 to 1,585.[36] Processing cost per kilo of fiber, therefore, rises sharply when fiber volume decreases on account of the fixed payroll outlays. Privately owned desfibradoras are able to produce at lower costs because they employ far fewer full-time workers, pay lower wages, and offer no benefits such as social security and paid vacations.

Cordemex's difficulty in controlling its costs was exacerbated

TABLE 18. Cordemex: Average Cost, Price Received, and Profit (Loss) per Kilogram of Sales, 1970–1981 (in pesos)

Year	1970	1971	1972	1973	1974	1975	1976	1977	1978	1979	1981
Average price	3.86	4.23	4.18	6.96	13.90	10.90	11.88	16.40	15.24	. . . .	33.79
Average cost	4.65	4.51	4.48	5.93	12.67	15.03	20.42	22.12	23.04	. . . .	45.38
Profit (Loss) per kilogram	(0.79)	(0.28)	(0.30)	1.03	1.23	(4.13)	(8.54)	(5.72)	(7.80)	(7.78)	(11.59)

SOURCES: Tables 12, 14, and 15.

by the Mexican rate of inflation, which fluctuated between 15 and 30 percent. Principally because of inflation, the firm was forced to grant large wage increases to its workers. In the midst of the worst year in its history in 1976, it increased mill workers' wages first by 13 percent and then by 23 percent.[37] Between 1975 and 1978 total wages, salaries, and benefits rose from 271.9 million pesos to 677.3 million pesos (table 17).

Cordemex's marketing problems were not limited to the external market. A substantial increase in the peso price of fiber on foreign markets took place after the Mexican government allowed the value of the peso to float in 1976. Because the cordage monopoly was still actively pursuing a price-discrimination policy, domestic prices increased sharply. In 1978 the price received per kilogram of product averaged 19.02 pesos and 13.36 pesos, respectively, in domestic and foreign markets (table 16). The firm's effort to maintain internal prices at a profitable level in the face of substantial increases in operating costs stimulated a resurgence of private domestic cordage production. In early 1978 at least forty-nine independent mills (including fourteen in Yucatán), whose total annual production capacity was estimated at 47,060 tons, were operating in Mexico.[38] The increased private competition had a noticeable impact on Cordemex's sales in the highly protected domestic market. In 1978 internal sales were 29,400 tons, which was 16 percent less than in 1975 and only 14 percent more than in 1970 (table 14).

Three factors help explain the erosion of Cordemex's monopoly in the domestic market. First, internal prices rose to a level where independent producers who employed low-cost, unorganized labor could compete with the monopoly in some product lines, even when forced to pay higher prices for raw fiber. Second, economies of scale in the production of some cordage products are exhausted at relatively low levels of output, thereby making the financial barriers to entry quite low. This is suggested by the fact that the average production capacity of the forty-nine independent mills was less than a thousand tons per year. Finally, independent mills were able to obtain regular supplies of raw material from private producers. After 1975 private producers were permitted to ship up to 30 percent of their raw fiber production out of state because Cordemex was unable to absorb their total output. It admitted publicly in 1978 that the increase in independent mills was an obstacle to its continued sales growth in the Mexican market and urged that any further expansion of independent production capacity be curbed. Interestingly, most of the private *cordelarías* used equipment that Cordemex discarded.[39] It has been alleged that officials of the cordage monopoly are silent partners in some of the competing mills.

Summary

Political instability in Yucatán during the late 1960s and early 1970s prompted the federal government to make a major boost in expenditures in that state and subsidies to the henequen industry. Cordemex and the agricultural bank, which were the major conduits for the subsidies and expenditures, pursued goals that were primarily political and social during this period. The behavior of these institutions in the face of deteriorating world market conditions for natural fiber produced losses on an unprecedented scale. The economic situation of Cordemex and Banrural was exacerbated by political bickering and massive corruption. President José López Portillo ordered a "cleansing" of both the ejidos and the agricultural bank in 1978 as the first step toward what the government hailed as fundamental reorganization of the industry.

7

Industry Reorganization
and Its Aftermath

▲▲

PRESIDENT José López Portillo, a former secretary of the treasury, was well acquainted with the problems of both the henequen ejidos and Cordemex. His dramatic actions that disclosed the existence of 33,000 "phantom" workers and workers without ejido rights seemed to indicate that he was resolved to break the vicious cycle of corruption and inefficiency in Yucatán's henequen zone. Referring to the ejido sector in 1977, he stated:

> The subsidy, confused with credit or salary is the permanent poison of the henequen zone; it has created inefficiency, insufficiency, and corruption. A very rigorous analysis has to be made of the Banrural. It must be disclosed how the hundreds of millions of pesos are being spent. Once and for all that amount which is credit should be separated from that which is salary and that which is subsidy.[1]

The "cleansing" was followed in 1978 and 1979 by a reorganization of the credit-granting system in the henequen zone. Cordemex was also streamlined through the closing of factories and the termination of workers. In an apparent attempt to absorb excess labor, federal expenditures on agricultural diversification were stepped up. The president also approved plans in 1979 to construct mills in Yucatán that would produce cellulose from henequen pulp and employ several thousand people.

Despite these actions, the henequen zone remains a blighted area. Production of this commodity is at its lowest ebb in this century and diversification based on it is a largely unfulfilled promise. Cordemex is operating at 50 to 60 percent of capacity and suffering near-record losses. Evidence of the physical deterioration of the once-prosperous industry is widespread throughout the henequen zone. Many ejido fields are weedy and poorly maintained. Others simply have been abandoned. Ejido-owned processing facilities have fared no better. Most private producers have reduced the number of hectares planted in henequen, or have abandoned raw fiber production altogether. Cattle raising has become increasingly popular among pequeños propietarios as a profitable, more liquid, and less controversial alternative to henequen production. Although Cordemex's manufacturing complex is still impressive, it has an abandoned air about it. Guest houses have been closed and the once-meticulous grounds are no longer maintained.

The human costs of the failure of the López Portillo administration's program to increase productive employment in the henequen zone are even more striking. Yucatán's ex-governor General Graciliano Alpuche Pinzon estimated in mid-1983 that the rate of open unemployment in the state was 30 percent and that 55 to 60 percent of the economically active population earned less than the minimum wage.[2] Ironically, federal government expenditures there have continued to increase rapidly and provide an estimated 50 percent of the state's income.

The meager subsistence that employment in the henequen fields provides for the more than fifty thousand ejidatarios and their families is readily apparent in the many small villages that dot the henequen zone. Alcoholism and illiteracy are endemic, and widespread apathy exists toward the productive exploitation of the henequen lands.

The fundamental failure of the López Portillo program, as with those of previous administrations, was that it was not thoroughgoing. The long-existing defects in production organization and incentive structures discussed in previous chapters were not corrected. Thus, entrenched political interests, bureaucratic inefficiency, and corruption dissipated any beneficial influence that reorganization might have had on the industry. Further, the efforts to rationalize production in light of the continuing secular demand for natural fibers have been haphazard and rife with political conflict. The welfare of the population of the henequen zone and of the Mexican taxpayers who spend billions of pesos to subsidize the industry remain subordinated to individuals or organizations who have a vested economic or political interest in maintaining some semblance of the status quo.

This chapter analyzes the program that President José López

Portillo initiated in 1978 in Yucatán to rationalize henequen production, eliminate corruption, and foster economic diversification. In the final part of the chapter, we outline the measures that his successor, Miguel de la Madrid Hurtado, proposed to accomplish what neither López Portillo nor his predecessor was able to do: eliminate the state's obsession with henequen.

THE FIDEICOMISO HENEQUENERO

Shortly after the *depuración*, a trust was formed to administer the credit advances for the henequen ejidos. The Fideicomiso Henequenero, or Henequen Trust, took over the task of administering ejido credit and production on January 1, 1978. The directors who supervise its operation include representatives of the governor of Yucatán, Banrural, Cordemex, and other key federal agencies in the state. Initially, Cordemex and the governor were excluded from formal representation, which indicated that the reorganization did not eliminate the long-standing and destructive conflicts among the state, Cordemex, and Banrural.

One of the first actions of the new agency, according to the instruction of President López Portillo, was to delineate what proportion of the advances to the ejidos was credit, and therefore legally recuperable, and what proportion was subsidy. Seventy percent of the advances related to the harvesting of leaves and the maintenance of existing fields was to be considered credit; and only 30 percent of the advances for the establishment of new fields, purchase of equipment, and other long-term investments was to be legally recuperable.

Although the above change did allow the government to distinguish more clearly the subsidy being paid to the henequen ejidos, the organizational changes associated with the creation of the Fideicomiso were largely illusory. It is funded by and operated within Banrural. Credit extension procedures and criteria basically remain unchanged. The 57,000 ejidatarios still on the bank's payroll are paid a weekly salary.

The initial reaction of the ejidatarios to the new system, which not only excluded several thousand campesinos without ejido rights but also set a new system of wage rates for the various tasks, was confusion rather than anger. About a thousand campesinos from around Motul, a large town thirty kilometers from Mérida, tried to march on the capital to protest the new rates, which increased the wages for some tasks and decreased them for others. The mood of the workers, who for the most part had only a vague idea of why they were marching, was good-humored and almost festive. State police, who were out in force both around Mérida and in major towns in the henequen zone, stopped the contingent at the city limits of the capital, though they finally allowed eighteen people to proceed to Banrural to protest various aspects of the new program.[3]

Despite the number of "workers" purged from the bank's payroll, the *depuración* threatened neither the political nor economic stability of the state. The primary reason for this is that the federal government did not reduce its expenditures on the henequen-zone population. In fact, it increased them.

The saving realized by Banrural from the purging of its payroll lists was used to raise the salaries of ejidatarios. The maximum wage that one of them could earn working in the henequen fields was raised from 113 to 185 pesos per day in 1978. This increase, however, apparently entailed a longer workweek for those who remained on the bank payroll.[4] Banrural also began paying ejidos a premium that varied from 1 peso to 1.60 pesos per kilogram of fiber, based upon productivity. On another front, the government stepped up its efforts to provide alternative sources of employment and income, such as fishing, cattle and pork production, and fruit-growing, in the henequen zone.

Information on the activities of the Fideicomiso since its inception is sketchy and sometimes contradictory; actual expenditures seem to have often diverged from the authorized budget. Total expenditures apparently doubled between 1978 and 1982, rising from 1.77 billion pesos to 3.65 billion. Of the sum authorized for 1982, some 1.8 billion pesos were designated for henequen-related activities and 1.5 billion pesos for nonhenequen (diversification) activities. The remaining 0.35 billion pesos consisted of administrative expenses.[5] The 1.8 billion pesos authorized for henequen activities is a little more than twice the credit extended in 1977 (table 4), the last year in which 90,000 ejidatarios were on the Banrural payroll. The average amount of credit extended per individual per year, therefore, approximately tripled between 1977 and 1983, rising from 10,000 pesos to about 30,000 pesos.

The percentage increase in credit extended per ejidatario paralleled the rise in the price paid by Cordemex per kilo of raw fiber. This price, which had been 7.00 pesos per kilo for grade A fiber until May 1979, was progressively increased to 27.7 pesos in October 1982. Ejidatario incomes, as pointed out above, rose by approximately 300 percent over the same period. Therefore, although the Fideicomiso was successful in stabilizing the ejido labor force at around 57,000, it was not able to prevent large increases in total outlays on the ejido sector nor to stem the deterioration of ejido production.

PRODUCTION TRENDS AFTER REORGANIZATION

World production of sisal and henequen continued to fall throughout the late 1970s and early 1980s, reflecting rising production costs, declining demand, competition from synthetics, and stagnant world prices.[6] Global production was estimated to be 475.3 thousand tons in 1981 (table 13) and was projected to fall to 300 thousand tons by the late 1980s. In 1980 producing nations for the first time exported more manufactured articles than raw fiber.[7] World prices recovered briefly from 1978 to 1980 because of the rapid escalation in petroleum prices, but by 1982 that had settled again at near mid-1970 levels.[8]

Yucatán's production of henequen fiber continued to decline, but at a faster rate than world production. From 1977 to 1981 world output of sisal and henequen fell by 3 percent (table 13); output in Yucatán declined by 11.6 percent (table 1). The state's fiber production in 1982 was 61,045 tons, the lowest production level of the twentieth century (table 1). Average yield per hectare in full production continued to decline, falling to 558 kilos in 1981 (table 1). Land in full production (ejido and private producers) dropped to 135,740 hectares in 1981 (table 1). Both private and ejido production declined during the last decade. Ejido output suffered most, falling from 72,938 tons in 1970 to 25,680.8 tons in 1982 (table 3).

The precipitous decline in production in the ejido sector has created problems for Cordemex. Because of insufficient raw-material supply, it has been unable to comply in some instances with already-established sales contracts and has experienced a loss in its share of the external market.[9] The shortage became so severe in 1980 that the firm began importing sisal fiber from Brazil. The production decreases reflect not only world market conditions, but also the lack of coordination between the Banco Agrario and Cordemex durng the late 1960s and early 1970s. New sowings have been insufficient to permit the cordage monopoly to supply its traditional markets.

Despite efforts by the Fideicomiso to raise productivity through incentives, a general lack of interest among the ejidatarios in henequen production continues to impact negatively on productivity. According to Jorge Tomás Vera Pren, a Mexican expert on henequen production, ejidatarios at first resisted the new program because of past exploitation by the rural bourgeoisie and government officials. Resistance took place in the form of productivity-reducing acts, such as the overcutting of henequen leaves and the ignoring of fires in the ejido henequen fields. Recalcitrant campesinos finally were brought into line by official repression and manipulation.[10]

The 57,000 ejidatarios who work in the fields are still twice the number that are needed to generate current levels of production. The income that henequen provides for each worker is not sufficient to give him the incentive to utilize his land productively. A large proportion of the ejidatarios, particularly the younger ones, prefer nonhenequen activities when they can be found.[11] Nonetheless, the guaranteed payments and additional incentives, such as free medical care and retirement,[12] have been sufficient to keep thousands of campesinos in a holding pattern of misery and ignorance.

In December 1978 President López Portillo forgave the 1,969-million-peso debt that the henequen ejidos had accumulated from 1960 through 1977. According to a spokesman for Banrural, the action was taken because the ejidatarios were "for the most part not responsible (for the debts) and the debts only tied them in an unjust and inconvenient manner, without any hope of terminating the bond of dependency to the Banrural."[13]

Erasing seventeen years of debt to the official bank, however, did not serve to break the henequen ejidos' bond of dependency on the federal government. In October 1978 the bank was recuperating less than 70 percent of the credit advances made to 497 credit societies. A year later, ejido debt (including funds advanced for diversification activities) has risen to 2,100 million pesos.[14] The amount of subsidy paid to the henequen ejidos in 1981 is reported to have been 1,350 million pesos; the value of raw fiber production in the same year was estimated at 1,363.9 million pesos.[15]

The economic and financial status of Cordemex continued to worsen after the reorganization of the ejido sector. Although the prices that the firm received for finished products rose substantially after 1978, increasing raw-material, labor, and financial costs, as well as a reported shortage of raw fiber, prevented the government-owned cordage monopoly from taking advantage of world market conditions. Significantly, its relative shares in both the domestic and external market diminished. Pricing policy and a relatively price-inelastic supply appear to be the major factors in these market-share losses.

Total sales volume fell from 115.8 thousand tons in 1976 to 53.9 thousand tons in 1980, and then recovered slightly to 63.9 thousand tons in 1981. From 1976 through 1981 foreign sales volume declined by 49.2 percent and domestic sales by 37.2 percent (table 14). Cordemex's total revenue from sales, on the other hand, climbed from 1,385.0 billion pesos to 2,159.4 billion because of the devaluation of the peso in 1976 and the sharp increase in world prices that took place after 1978 (table 15). In 1981 the firm received an average price of 23.31 pesos per kilo on foreign sales and 48.58 pesos per kilo on domestic sales compared to 10.22 pesos and 15.00 pesos, respectively, in 1976 (table 16).

Costs also rose rapidly. As pointed out earlier, the price that Cordemex paid for raw fiber increased almost 400 percent between May 1977 and October 1982. Cordage workers received pay increases of 20 percent in 1980, 29.7 percent in 1981, and 33 percent in 1982. The firm's labor costs reached 845.3 million pesos, or more than 70 percent of total revenue for the first six months of 1982. This compares to 677.3 million pesos and 49.6 percent, respectively, for the entire year of 1978 (table 17).

The firm's annual losses exceeded 600 million pesos in 1978, 1979, and 1981 (table 11). Losses for the first half of 1982, part of which were accounted for by increased financing costs created by the devaluation of the peso, totaled 777.4 million pesos.[16] Operating results for 1980 have yet to be reported as this is written in late 1984.

A major reason for the decline in Cordemex's share of the external market has been its persistent inability to compete with sisal producers like Brazil, Cuba, and Haiti. As indicated earlier in this volume, to be competitive henequen fiber must be priced below sisal because of the latter's superior qualities. During the late 1970s and early 1980s, sisal producers often undersold Cordemex, which caused buyers to substitute sisal for henequen.[17]

Cordemex has been experimenting with the production of a

synthetic henequen fiber mix material that would permit it to compete more effectively with synthetics in some product lines and also ameliorate the raw-fiber shortage. The firm purchased machinery and began experimenting with the manufacture of synthetics in the early 1980s. At first, it announced publicly that it would not sell to the internal market and compete with existing Mexican private synthetic producers. However, in August 1983, an official of the National Association of the Plastics Industry accused the company of trying to obtain orders for plastic sacks from two of the private sector's largest government customers, Fertimex and Azucar, S.A.[18] Although Cordemex has several million dollars worth of equipment and the technology to produce synthetic products, it has, to date, not begun large-scale manufacture and distribution; and the present financial difficulties make it unlikely that it will do so in the near future.

The firm's share of the 60,000-ton internal market for cordage products was steadily eroded in the late 1970s by competition from private cordage mills. By 1980 it was supplying only 50 percent of what had once been a captive domestic market.[19] As noted before, its domestic pricing strategy must bear most of the blame for the rebirth of the private cordage industry in Mexico. This pricing strategy may also be motivating the substitution of synthetic fiber products for those produced from natural fiber. In 1976 more than half of Cordemex's domestic sales were made to other government-owned agencies, which tended to stabilize its market share. The firm reported in 1980 that the Mexican postal service, a large customer, had stopped ordering henequen mailbags and had begun using those made of canvas and synthetic fiber.[20]

The cordage monopoly, supported by the state government, has attempted to counter private competition by continually questioning its legal status and by stiffening the state law that controls the interstate movement of raw fiber. Yucatán has passed legislation that would again prohibit the export of raw fiber to major private mills in San Luis Potosí, Mexico City, and Puebla. If the law were enforced, Cordemex would obtain more control over the domestic distribution of fiber. The pequeños propietarios who are shipping the fiber out of state want to continue this practice because the private mills pay higher prices than Cordemex. Both the state government and Cordemex contend, however, that the continuation of out-of-state shipments will worsen the current

TABLE 19. Yucatán: Raw Fiber Exports and Prices,
1897–1917

Year	Raw Fiber Exports (in metric tons)	Price (in U.S. cents per pound)
1897	70,545	2.64
1898	68,834	6.23
1899	73,191	6.16
1900	81,093	6.33
1901	83,191	6.21
1902	83,993	9.84
1903	93,058	8.22
1904	67,205	7.47
1905	96,534	6.96
1906	97,198	6.35
1907	100,174	5.70
1908	108,794	4.33
1909	95,756	4.79
1910	94,790	4.25
1911	116,547	3.71
1912	139,902	4.73
1913	145,280	6.35
1914	169,286	7.34
1915	162,744	5.89
1916	201,990	5.59
1917	127,092	13.25

SOURCE: Enrique Aznar Mendoza, "La industria henequenera desde 1919 hasta nuestros días," *Enciclopedia yucatanense*, vol. 3, ed. Carlos A. Echanove Trujillo (México, D.F.: Edición Oficial, 1946), pp. 727–787.

fiber shortage. Ironically, a prohibition of out-of-state sales would probably exacerbate the fiber shortage because private producers would have a diminished incentive to invest in the planting of new fields.

A recent suggestion by Cordemex management for increasing external sales is indicative of the attitude of the firm's decision-makers and of the ineffective marketing strategy that has evolved since 1964. On the occasion of a visit by President Miguel de la Madrid to Yucatán in 1984, Cordemex proposed that the government's grain-purchasing agent, CONASUPO, force U.S. farmers to accept henequen products as partial payment for their grain sales to Mexico.[21]

Although Cordemex has continued to invest large, but undisclosed, amounts of federal funds in diversification schemes, some adjustments have been made in the cordage-producing operations to bring them in line with production and sales possibilities. After 1977 the firm cautiously began to close factories and terminate part of its work force. Between 1977 and 1979 the force was reduced from 7,500 to 5,978 permanent workers.[22] These terminations were made only after lengthy negotiations with the two cordage-mill workers' unions in which Cordemex agreed to pay large bonuses to the released workers. It also closed a number of its smaller factories both in and outside Yucatán. By the end of 1982 it was operating only seven of its fourteen factories, but, even after this adjustment it was still producing far below its reduced capacity of 115,000 tons. Yet, the cutbacks have exerted little influence on its financial status because of the rapidly escalating labor and financial costs.

Cordemex's losses and investment expenditures have been supported by loans and direct payments from the federal government. In 1978 the firm was permitted to capitalize a debt of 1,368 million pesos owed to Banrural for raw fiber.[23] In 1980 the director-general reported that debts totaled 2,541 million pesos and that Banrural would be asked to absorb 1,700 million pesos of that amount.[24] In January 1982 it was reported that Cordemex's debts to Banrural and private suppliers had risen to 1,650 million pesos. The company's budget for 1982 also contained an item of 3,527 million pesos to amortize revolving debt. The total 1982 budget was 7,666 million pesos, or more than 300 percent of the 1981 sales revenue.[25]

DEMAGOGY AND DIVERSIFICATION

Even in the face of the huge losses that Cordemex suffered during the late 1970s and early 1980s, the federal government continued to subsidize or vigorously stimulate the firm's various diversification programs in Yucatán. Cordemex's ambitious plans caused the existing enmity between the governor and the director to erupt into open conflict over their control.

Cordemex's most ambitious diversification scheme was its

plan to create a milk industry in Yucatán. The plan called for the establishment of sixty milk production modules by 1990, each of which would possess a thousand head of dairy cattle. The animals would be fed bagasse, or henequen pulp, from the firm's desfibradoras. Initially, Cordemex planned to invest 600 million pesos to establish twenty production modules, involving 20,000 dairy cattle. The ultimate goal was to produce 300,000 liters of milk daily. At the time of the announcement, Cordemex was experimenting with milk production at two of its desfibradoras.[26]

Cordemex's plan was further elaborated by the state director of the Mexican Food System (SAM). SAM was a federal program begun by President José López Portillo in 1979 whose purpose was to coordinate the various federal agencies involved in agricultural production toward the end of making the nation self-sufficient in basic foodstuffs. According to a study by SAM, sixty agroindustrial units would be formed in the henequen zone. Each unit would support a thousand campesinos and their families. In addition to producing raw henequen fiber for sale to Cordemex, they would carry out the dairy operations proposed by the firm, manage livestock, and produce vegetables. No estimate was given of the total investment that would be required to put the production modules in place.[27]

The federal government's diversification plans for Yucatán became even more ambitious when President José López Portillo announced that he had approved the construction of a giant cellulose mill in the state. In November 1979 the president apparently approved construction of this mill, which would use henequen pulp as the major raw-material input. The approval of this mill was based on feasibility studies made by the National Council of Science and Technology. The original plan was to sow an additional 30,000–32,000 hectares of henequen in the henequen zone. Owners of affected land could become shareholders by pledging the land to the project or they could simply sell henequen leaves to the factory. The cellulose plant itself would have the capacity to produce 90,000 tons of paper per year of the varieties that would hasten the import substitution of paper products in Mexico. Projected operations included the growing of henequen plants for planting the new fields, the harvesting and processing of the leaves, and the production of cellulose. The total required investment was estimated at 3.5 billion pesos, which would result in the creation of 7,000 additional jobs in the state. Similar plants that produce cellulose from sisal fiber were already operating in Brazil and the United States. The creation of a new federal research institute in the state, the Center for Scientific Research of Yucatán, was announced almost simultaneously. One of its major goals would be to seek new uses for henequen.[28]

In January 1980 the undersecretary of programming and budget visited Yucatán to discuss the paper factory with state and other federal officials. He made it quite clear at that time that final approval must await further study. He also commented that, though the objective for the factory was mainly social, it should not be the subject of permanent subsidy.[29] It was estimated that further studies would delay the inception of the project for six months. Dr. Rioseco, the director-general of Cordemex, also announced that the cordage monopoly would probably manage the new industrial activity.

Federal support of such a vast program, which excluded the participation of the state government, threatened to diminish the economic and political status of the governor. Public displays of hostility between Dr. Rioseco and Governor Luna Kan surfaced in 1980, when the former asserted that Cordemex would manage a giant cellulose-producing complex. The conflict was exacerbated by a continuing bitter fight over control of the state's leaf-processing facilities.

Francisco Luna Kan, Yucatán's governor from 1975 to 1981, had repeatedly backed measures that would place all or some of Cordemex's functions under the control of the state government. In 1980 Governor Luna Kan intensified his criticism of the monopoly by challenging Rioseco's veracity and by calling for a separation of the firm's leaf-processing operations from its manufacturing operations. The unions joined the fray by claiming that Governor Luna Kan was conspiring to deliver Cordemex into the hands of Banrural, which would result in the firm's desfibradoras falling into the hands of the private sector.[30]

In early 1980, apparently under pressure because of its huge losses, Cordemex agreed to open talks that would lead to the eventual delivery of its fourteen functioning desfibradoras to the agricultural sector.[31] A short time later, the head of the Banrural in Yucatán stated that the bank would help organize and finance the transfer of the desfibradoras to ejidatarios in the henequen zone. This suggestion met with instant opposition from Cordemex's unions, for it threatened the jobs of the more than 1,500 desfibradora workers. Although Governor Luna Kan continued to call for completion of the transfer, Cordemex made no move in that direction during the remainder of his term. The question of which entities would administer the cellulose mill also remained unresolved.

The struggle for control of the desfibradoras is symptomatic of the larger conflict that was alluded to earlier in this volume between local political and economic interests and those of the federation. Cordemex's strategy to become a major factor in leaf-processing became more aggressive after 1970 because of a growing shortage of fiber and its plans for diversification. Through the policy of paying a higher price for fiber than the private desfibradoras, the firm increased its share of leaf-processing to 45 percent of the state's total fiber production in 1981. In that same year, it was reported that forty-five private desfibradoras were forced to shut down because they were unable to compete with Cordemex.[32]

The perception held by the group that has traditionally controlled henequen activity is that Cordemex wants to replace the older, less-efficient private and ejido desfibradoras with its own. If the firm were successful in this undertaking, the political and economic interests of the pequeños propietarios, the state government, and the Banrural would be jeopardized.[33] The closing of the private processing facilities would directly affect the profitability of private smallholders who contract with the bank to process ejido fiber. Just as important, such an action would displace a substantial number of agricultural bank personnel and state government employees who are involved in the political and economic administration of the ejido desfibradora facilities. In the light of the political and economic implications of Cordemex's efforts to rationalize leaf-processing activities, the threatened groups, whose spokesman was the governor, mounted an offensive to protect their own interests and reduce the influence of the cordage monopoly.

The governor who succeeded Luna Kan in 1982, General Alpuche Pinzon, stepped up the criticism of Cordemex. He stated that only the people of Yucatán possess more power than the governor and that the firm should subordinate itself to the state government. Further, he declared that he would not permit Cordemex to make unilateral decisions that did not take the welfare of the people into account.[34] He also formed in 1982 the Consejo

Consultivo Henequenero (Henequen Advisory Group), which was to serve as a forum for discussion among all interested and involved parties of the problems of the henequen industry.

In May 1982 a presidential decree created the Promotora Agroindustrial del Henequen, which was to be organized as a parastatal firm. It was to manage both Cordemex's desfibradora and dairy operations as well as carry out a research and development function. The administrative council of the Promotora included representatives of Cordemex, Banrural, the governor, and the Fideicomiso Henequenero.[35]

The struggle between Yucatecan interests and Cordemex over control of the henequen industry has been complicated by an internecine conflict between Alpuche Pinzon and other elements of the PRI in the state. He is a Yucatecan by birth, but he has lived most of his life outside the state. When he became governor in 1982, he brought much of his staff from Mexico City. The "foreignness" of his administration caused it to be unpopular from the beginning with Yucatecans. The general also proved to be inept in dealing with groups within his own party, particularly the campesinos and their leaders.

In February 1984 Alpuche abruptly asked for a *licencia,* or license, to leave office for six months to attend to a personal matter. He was replaced in the interim by Victor Cervera Pacheco, who was a federal deputy and former mayor of Mérida. Rumors circulated that Alpuche had been forced to step down because of fears within the PRI that his unpopularity would harm local party candidates in future elections. He did not return after his license expired. Cervera Pacheco, who is a professional politician and well liked in the state, will serve the remainder of the ex-governor's term.

The diversification plans that created so much discord during the early 1980s had ground to a halt by 1983. Through the previous two years, it had become increasingly clear that local officials were overoptimistic about obtaining funding for this ambitious program. Although Banrural advanced some funds for the cultivation of the millions of additional *vástagos,* or suckers, that would be needed to make the new planting, no other work went forward on the project. Clear evidence of the reluctance of the federal government to finance it was evidenced in January 1982, when the local representative of the secretary of agriculture and water resources unveiled a proposal for a much-scaled-down version of the paper factory, which would only produce 7,500 tons of cellulose per year.[36] Cordemex's plan to produce milk in Yucatán is also far behind schedule. By the middle of 1982, the firm had 3,300 cows there, but was only milking 900. Because this quantity of milk production was insufficient to permit the pasteurizing plant (a reported investment of 65 million pesos) to operate at capacity, the operation was unprofitable.[37]

It is unlikely that either the dairy venture or the cellulose factory will proceed on the originally planned scales. Mexico is mired in its worst economic crisis since the Mexican Revolution. President Miguel de la Madrid Hurtado has been forced to slash expenditures on government investment projects and the Mexican Food System has been completely dismantled. Both plans were grandiose in scope and exaggerated the state's capacity to absorb large quantities of capital rapidly. Worse still, neither project adequately confronted the most serious potential problem: the question regarding their honest and efficient administration. The major result of the federal government's efforts to reorganize and diversify activity in the henequen zone has been to display more evidence of ineptitude and demagogy to an already cynical state population.

In May 1984 President de la Madrid made what has become for Mexican presidents an obligatory trip to Yucatán to outline his program for resolving its economic woes. He, like his predecessors, announced plans for rationalizing the industry in order to bring it in line with the possibilities presented by the world market. He stressed the need for productivity increases, a reduction in the number of workers employed in henequen, and a reorganization of the credit-granting system. To complement his plans for reordering the henequen industry, he announced that the federal government would spend 55 billion pesos in the state in 1984 on projects designed to stimulate economic diversification.[38]

The most surprising action of the president during his visit was to give the governor responsibility for the henequen industry. The governor will exercise this responsibility through his appointment by the executive to the presidencies of the Administrative Council of Cordemex and the Fideicomiso Henequenero. On the surface, this move seems to indicate that local interests have, at least temporarily, blunted Cordemex's drive to control the industry. It is highly unlikely, however, that de la Madrid contemplates giving Yucatecans the latitude they enjoyed when Lázaro Cárdenas created Henequeneros de Yucatán. Most likely, the control over the resources of Banrural and Cordemex will remain with officials of those institutions and be subject to policies emanating from Mexico City. It would be an unprecedented move for the federal government to vest that magnitude of financial authority in a state governor.

Under the new arrangement, it is possible that the governors may be formally charged with responsibility for the conduct of the henequen industry without the corresponding authority to make the decisions that bear on its performance. The political advantages for the federal government of dividing responsibility and authority in this manner are fairly obvious: the blame for the poor economic performance of Cordemex and the ejidos can be shifted partially to Yucatecans themselves.

SUMMARY AND CONCLUSIONS

President José López Portillo initiated a sweeping reorganization of the henequen industry in 1978. The credit-granting system that served the ejidos was placed under the control of a *fideicomiso*, or trust, in an effort to eliminate corruption and improve the accounting procedures of Banrural. The number of ejidatarios on Banrural's payroll was reduced to 57,000. The Fideicomiso Henequenero was also charged with carrying out a diversification program that would create permanent nonhenequen-related activities to absorb excess labor in the henequen zone. Cordemex continued to be plagued by large losses, declining sales, and raw-material shortages throughout the late 1970s and early 1980s. Seven of the cordage monopoly's factories were closed and the work force was reduced in an effort to bring the firm's activities in line with the realities of the world market.

It became apparent by 1982 that López Portillo's program in the henequen zone had produced little in the way of positive benefits for its residents, despite the substantial sums that the federal government had spent on henequen and henequen-based diversification activities. The López Portillo administration, like its predecessors, lacked the will to pursue badly needed reforms and simply threw money at Yucatán's problematic industry as a short run palliative.

In 1984 López Portillo's successor, Miguel de la Madrid Hurtado, in the wake of renewed political strife in Yucatán, announced the guidelines for a new program to rationalize henequen production and stimulate economic diversification in the henequen zone. The most unusual feature of the new program was that it formally gave the governor of Yucatán increased control over Cordemex and the production of henequen fiber.

8

Economic Diversification:
Yucatán's Viable Alternative

▲▲

THE MEXICAN government's economic role in Yucatán has been characterized by ambivalence. On the one hand, federal intervention in the henequen sector has reinforced the state's traditional monocrop pattern and delayed the necessary industry adjustment to the decline in the global demand for hard fiber since the early 1960s.

On the positive side, the Mexican government has made a major commitment to Yucatán's diversification drive, as reflected both in policy initiatives and public investment projects:

- Completion of the railroad linkage between the state and central Mexico in 1950 and its conversion to standard gauge in 1957.
- Completion of the highway linking Yucatán to other parts of the nation in 1961.
- Promulgation in the mid-1960s of the federal government's policy of industrial decentralization and regional development as well as the resultant creation of an "industrial city" in Mérida.
- Federal investments in the state's infrastructure, including farm-to-market roads, electric power, irrigation works, communications, and a sheltered commercial fishing port near Progreso.
- Presence of Nacional Financiera, the federal government's comprehensive development bank, in Yucatán through the establishment of a regional office at Mérida in 1972.
- Development of Cancún, a major international tourist resort in the neighboring state of Quintana Roo, under the auspices of the Mexican government's Fund for Tourism Development (FONATUR).

151

• Inauguration in 1984 of the Henequen Rationalization and Integral Development Program for Yucatán.

Significantly, during the recent period of accelerated diversification, Mérida has emerged as the major urban center for the southeast, and as such Yucatán's capital has become the focal point of the region's industrial, commercial, and professional services.

Yucatán—an economically backward area in a semi-industrialized nation—occupies 43,379 square kilometers, or 2.2 percent of the total. The state had an estimated 1.5 percent of the national population in 1980, but contributed only 1.2 percent of Mexico's gross domestic product (GDP) that year.[1] The state's per capita output of 49,243 pesos in 1980 was only 77.6 percent of the national figure of 63,466 pesos and compared unfavorably with such relatively prosperous states as Nuevo León, Tabasco, and the Federal District. Yucatán's comparative economic backwardness is also reflected in the small share that manufacturing contributed to the state's GDP (16 percent) compared with the national share of 23 percent.

This chapter analyzes Yucatán's recent diversification experience and prospects, including the often ambivalent supporting federal role. Diversification opportunities encompass industrialization based on relatively low wage rates, introduction of nontraditional agricultural commodities, growth of the livestock and commercial fishing sectors, and the promotion of tourism.

OCCUPATIONAL STRUCTURE AND ENTREPRENEURSHIP

The tenth general population census (1980) conveys only a rough impression of the composition of Yucatán's labor force, by sector and industry. Considering that 24.4 percent of the labor force was classified as "unspecified," it may be concluded that at least 31 percent of the working population in 1980 was engaged in the primary sector (agriculture, forestry, and fishing); at least 29.3 percent in the tertiary sector (commerce, transportation, and other services); and at least 15.3 percent in the secondary sector (manufacturing, construction, mining, and electric power and gas).[2] About half of the agricultural labor force, as has previously been noted, is engaged part time in the growing of henequen. Within the industrial sector, 35,671 persons were employed in manufacturing; 22,433 in construction; 929 in electric power, gas, and water; and 406 in mining and quarrying. The labor force of 367,825 represented about 36 percent of the state's total population in 1980.

Even though the birthrate has steadily declined from 46/1000 in 1960 to 37.7/1000 in 1980, Yucatán's natural population growth rate has remained virtually stable because of the parallel decline in the deathrate from 12/1000 in 1960 to 7.7/1000 in 1980. The natural population growth rate was estimated at 3.4 percent in 1960 and 3.3 percent in both 1970 and 1980. During the 1950s and 1960s substantial net emigration served to moderate the natural increase in the population. Between 1950 and 1960 the actual population growth rate was only 1.74 percent and from 1960 to 1970 it was 2.13 percent.[3] During the 1970–80 decade, however, the much-reduced rate of emigration resulted in a sharp acceleration of the actual growth rate to 3.15 percent per annum. The population grew by nearly 100,000 between 1950 and 1960, by 144,000 between 1960 and 1970, and by 276,000 from 1970 to 1980, nearly twice the absolute increase registered the previous decade. This accelerated demographic trend dramatizes the importance of economic growth and diversification for Yucatán if the goals of raising living standards and attaining full employment are to be met.

Economic development must be planned, organized, directed, and financed in the context of uncertainty, that is, functions associated with a special human resource: entrepreneurship. In Yucatán, the rise of the modern plantation economy was largely associated with the enterprise of the great Creole families. Their economic initiative extended beyond the agricultural estate to encompass as well the organization of railroads, electric power service, ports and docks, banking, commerce, and the beginnings of industry during the final decades of the nineteenth century. Among the family names that loom importantly in the entrepreneurial landscape of that formative period are Escalante, Ancona, Cámara, Cásares, Espinosa, Cantón, Gutiérrez, Molina, Peón, Bolio, Regil, Palma, and Peniche.[4] Following the uncompensated expropriation of the large estates associated with the agricultural reform of the latter 1930s, many of the old plantation families left Yucatán for Mexico City or the United States. Of those that remained, some continued to work their diminished estate, the pequeña propiedad, and others diversified into such activities as industry, including the manufacture of henequen products (*cordelerías*), commerce, tourism services, and cattle raising.

Some of the largest organizations operating in contemporary Yucatán are agencies and semiautonomous enterprises of the Mexican government. The principal administrators of Cordemex, the dominant industrial firm in the peninsula, and Banrural often come from other parts of the nation and normally change every six years with new presidential administrations. Nacional Financiera, the Mexican government's comprehensive development bank, through its branch office in Yucatán, has stimulated and financed numerous industrial enterprises, including those located in Mérida's industrial park. Several of these recently established plants are owned and controlled by Mexicans from outside the region. Cementos Maya, S.A., the second largest industrial enterprise in Yucatán, is controlled by Monterrey interests; and the brewery, Cervecería Yucateca, recently changed hands from Yucatecans to a group in central Mexico.

As is true of many other parts of Latin America, immigrants have played a vital role in the modern development of Yucatán. Their contribution as entrepreneurs has been vastly disproportionate to their small numbers. Attracted by the henequen-based affluence of the late nineteenth century, the number of foreign-born residents in Yucatán numbered 2,500 in 1900 (less than 1 percent of the population), of which 1,479 were Spaniards and 576 were classified as "Turks," that is, persons who immigrated from Middle Eastern places under Turkish control.[5] The latter, particularly Christian Lebanese, played a decisive role in the growth of the forwardly-linked, export-oriented cordage industry from the mid-1920s until its nationalization in the early 1960s. Today, they dominate the commerce of Mérida and the manufacture of guayabera shirts. They also operate several of the finest restaurants in the city and own ice-making plants as well as food-processing firms, including Yucatán's only flour mill, Harinas del Sureste, S.A. Recently, Lebanese interests have diversified into cattle ranching in the eastern part of the state. Most of the Middle Eastern immigrants arrived in Yucatán between 1890 and 1910. Upon finding the commerce of Mérida and the other cities preempted by local and Spanish merchants, they settled in small interior towns as peddlers. After the Mexican Revolution, their commercial interests became increasingly centered in Mérida and the other cities.[6]

Caracashian machine shop-foundry at Mérida in the early twentieth century. (Courtesy, the Caracashian family)

Among the economically prominent Arab family names are Miguel Angel Xacur (owner of Harinas del Sureste), Alfredo Abhimerí, Asís Abraham, Juan and Aniceto Macarí, Tufic Charruf (owner of Hotel Panamericana), José Mena, Alejandro Abud, the Chapur group, and Abraham Jorge. Many of the sons and daughters of these enterprising Arab families have intermarried with the sons and daughters of the old, socially prestigious hacienda families.

Spanish immigrants initiated ice-making plants in cities and small towns, and Spanish mechanics figured prominently in the creation of the backwardly-linked machine industry that served the requirements of the large agroindustrial henequen estates. On the eve of the First World War, the leading metalworking shops and foundries had acquired the capability to build defibration machines and even to improve upon their design.[7] The most important metalworking shops and foundries were established by two immigrants, the Armenian Carlos Pascal Caracashian and the Catalan mechanic José Torroella. Both men found ways to improve on the old equipment and invented new, more efficient machines. Whereas the earlier standard rasping machine could only handle long fibers, a new model invented by Caracashian could process both short and long ones. Two of the machines developed by him, "La Pascalita" and "La Reforma," were recognized for their advanced technical features and were adopted throughout the henequen zone. At the peak of its operation, Caracashian's mechanical shop and foundry employed eighty individuals, worked in both bronze and steel, and contributed substantial tax revenue to the government. The experience gained in these early machine shops and foundries was later applied more generally throughout the economy, including the fabrication of replacement parts and less complicated machines used by the cordage mills.[8]

AGRICULTURAL STRUCTURE AND DIVERSIFICATION

Until recently, the prevailing assessment of Yucatán's agricultural potential was pessimistic. In this view, the state was deemed to be a semiarid region that offered extremely limited possibilities for the production of such crops as henequen that thrive on capricious seasonal rainfalls, require large quantities of unskilled labor, and grow in soils deficient in organic matter. In

156

view of the rapid expansion of the highway network since the mid-1950s and more recent federal investment in irrigation, pessimism has yielded to a guarded optimism concerning the prospects for a diversified agricultural-pastoral economy. In 1981 the state was served by 5,355 kilometers of roads, of which nearly 2,600 kilometers were paved.[9] Few communities in any part of the state are isolated, and every region has at least one paved and generally well-maintained road that allows the population fast and efficient access to major marketing centers. The substantially improved internal transportation has provided a major stimulus to commercial livestock raising, production of vegetables, and fruit-growing.

Of the 836,000 hectares under cultivation in Yucatán in 1980, only 20,287 were irrigated.[10] This small share (2½ percent of the land cultivated), however, generated a disproportionate share of the value of agricultural production. Because rivers and streams are virtually nonexistent in Yucatán, newly irrigated land derives its water resources from underground wells.

The problem of agricultural development in Yucatán represents a special challenge to farmers and agronomists. More than 95 percent of the soil is rocky; most of it is neither arable nor adaptable to large-scale mechanization. The other conditions that constrain the agricultural economy are the deficient and erratic rainfall and the low productivity of labor in most farm enterprises. The labor-productivity problem is aggravated by the rudimentary technical capacity of most of the farm workers and a high rural population growth rate. This heavy demographic pressure and limited harvesting periods for the traditional crops result in high unemployment and underemployment rates in the rural sector.

For analytical purposes, the landmass of Yucatán is divided into five agricultural zones. The sparsely populated coastal zone comprises an area of 235 square kilometers, and its predominantly sandy soils are ideal for coconut plantations. The state's economic life is concentrated in the henequen zone (11,482 square kilometers), located in the northwestern part of the state, where the soil is characteristically stony. A good transportation network joins cities, villages, and farms in the zone, which also contains abundant ground water at shallow depths from four to fourteen meters. Beyond the coastal and henequen zones, corn is grown by traditional slash-and-burn methods (the eastern and central corn zones, consisting of 8,896 and 3,686 square kilometers, respectively). Of increasing importance as a source of rural income is the cattle zone (7,625 square kilometers), in the northeastern portion of the state. Finally, the fruit-growing zone (5,311 square kilometers), which includes both sides of the Sierrita Baja de Ticul, from Muna to the municipio of Tekax, is characterized by the production of nontraditional crops, including citrus fruit, avocados, and mangoes. Isolated patches of high-quality soil are found in this part of the state, and, where they occur, lend themselves to mechanical farming.

The traditional slash-and-burn, or *milpa*, system in Yucatán, as in many other parts of Latin America, can be characterized as subsistence agriculture. The basic foodstuffs produced by this system—corn, beans, and squash—are consumed directly by the campesino family. When a small surplus of corn is available, it is used to fatten the family's pigs and poultry, whose number is determined by the surplus; little of the milpa's harvest is destined for the market. This seminomadic, indigenous Maya system of agriculture has given a reasonably good but declining return on the campesino's investment.[11]

Ideally, the milpa system requires about fifteen years of fallow to recuperate soil vigor and reach optimum yields. Because of the growing population pressure upon the land, however, the fallow has been reduced to only about five years, which lowers per hectare yields.[12] Even though Yucatán produced 130,000 tons of corn and 9,000 tons of beans in 1980, 150,000 tons of corn and 19,800 tons of beans still needed to be imported to satisfy the state's basic dietary requirements.

Given the limited opportunities for work in the henequen fields, many ejidatarios have diversified into truck gardening and the growing of fruit; others have become stonemasons and gatherers of stone. For many campesinos, these supplementary agricultural endeavors bring substantially more income than the wages earned from the one or two mornings of work in the henequen fields. The typical truck farmer requires a small section of land, say a *mecate* (an ancient surface measure, found principally in Yucatán, used for evaluating the sowing of grains or henequen; it is the equivalent of twenty meters square, also a lineal measure of twenty meters). He also needs a well with an electric pump, hose pipes, and henequen bagasse for fertilizing and mulching the soil. He takes his produce—melons, cucum-

TABLE 20. Yucatán: Crop Production and Area Harvested, 1976–1981

Crops	Area Harvested (in hectares) 1976	1981	Production (in thousands of MT) 1976	1981	Change in Production 1976–1981 (in percent)
Henequen	157,000	135,740	98.5	76.8	−22.0
Corn	104,829	183,400	94.6	156.5	65.4
Beans	15,700	29,000	5.5	12.2	121.8
Squash	n.a.	11,043c	17.8d	28.1c	57.9
Citrus fruit	5,946	7,707	80.6	111.4	38.2
Other tree cropsa	3,117	5,642	25.7	42.9	66.9
Vegetablesb	2,500	2,900	17.1	30.6	79.0
Total		375,432	339.8	458.5	34.9

SOURCE: Secretaría de Agricultura y Recursos Hidráulicos, *VI informe de gobierno* (Mérida, 1982).
aAvocado, guava, and papaya.
bIncluding tomatoes and watermelons.
c1980.
d1977.

bers, tomatoes, cabbages, chilies, radishes, parsley—to the nearest wholesale market and collects his earnings there.

Table 20 shows the changes in the state's crop production and harvested area during the 1976–81 period. For henequen, a declining production trend occurred over the six-year period. The output of corn and beans, as well as the production of squash, also a traditional staple, advanced sharply during this period, mainly as a result of more land being brought under cultivation. Significantly, the harvesting of nontraditional crops—citrus fruit and other tree crops as well as vegetables—also expanded rapidly. The combined tonnage of these three crops rose from 123,000 tons in 1976 to 185,000 tons in 1981, an increase of 50 percent. Of the total area harvested in 1981 (375,432 hectares), only 16,249 hectares (4.3 percent) were devoted to nontraditional crops, but their combined tonnage represented 40 percent of total crop production.

Investment in citrus fruit and other tree crops expanded dramatically during the decade from 1966 to 1976. The number of orange trees increased from 241,000 in 1966 to 780,000 in 1976

(224 percent); lemon trees from 50,000 to 135,000 (170 percent); papaya trees from 36,000 to 99,000 (175 percent); and the number of avocado trees roughly doubled from 28,000 to 59,000. Although the number of trees planted has grown since 1976, as reflected in expanded harvesting of fruit noted above, no data are available that indicate the precise numbers.

Income from cattle and beef production has come to exceed that from growing henequen fiber. In 1980 cattle industry sales, including milk, exceeded 1,220 million pesos (table 21). Yucatán's cattle herd is concentrated in the eastern part of the state, around Tizimin, but smaller concentrations are also found in the henequen zone and in the south. The narrow-gauge railroad between Tizimin and Mérida was replaced by a standard-gauge in the late 1970s to facilitate the shipment of cattle. Large ranches dominate

TABLE 21. Yucatán: Production of the Agricultural-Livestock Sector, 1980

	Millions of pesos	Percent of total
CROPS		
Henequen	1,083.1	21.17
Corn	577.1	11.28
Citrus fruit	157.1	3.07
Vegetables	135.0	2.64
Calabaza	112.6	2.20
Beans	103.3	2.02
Subtotal	2,168.2	42.38
LIVESTOCK		
Beef	1,159.7	22.66
Poultry	558.6	10.92
Pork	538.5	10.52
Eggs	382.6	7.48
Honey	248.2	4.85
Milk	60.9	1.19
Subtotal	2,948.5	57.62
Grand Total	5,116.7	100.00

SOURCE: SPP, Yucatán: Informe económico, 1980 (Mérida, 1981), pp. 96, 102.

in the Tizimin area, and these privately owned estates are the principal source of cattle exports to the Federal District. As of 1981 some 233 cattle ejidos were in operation, mainly in the henequen zone. Assisted by federal credits, they occupied some 52,000 hectares on which 11,430 cattle ranged. Compared with the much larger private ranches in the east, these operations average less than 50 head per ejido. Still, the cattle ejidatario receives a modest income from the sale of animals to the local slaughterhouse. Including both ranches and ejidos, an estimated 15,000 persons are directly engaged in the cattle industry. Its potential for continued growth, based on intensive grazing, is promising. Among the measures that need to be taken are the introduction of new feed cultivation practices, directed herding, and improved sanitary conditions.

The poultry-products industry has been expanding rapidly, mainly in the vicinity of Mérida; total sales, including eggs, exceeded 940 million pesos in 1980. Meat output increased by 232 percent between 1970 and 1980 and egg production nearly tripled, reaching a volume of 17,400 tons in 1980.[13] Growth in the industry's bird population reflects both Yucatán's accelerated urbanization trend and the high income sensitivity of demand for poultry products. In poultry products, the state has reached self-sufficiency.

The state's output of pork has advanced slowly, mainly as a result of the official swine development program formulated specifically for ejidatarios. As table 21 shows, income from pork slaughter approximated 540 million pesos in 1980, a figure roughly equal to the value of poultry-meat production and one-half the production of beef.

Commercial honey growing and processing provides Yucatán with a secondary, if highly variable, source of foreign exchange. There exist in the state an estimated 200,000 beehives that yielded 14,600 tons of the syrup that possessed a value of 248 million pesos in 1980. Apiculture, which is classified as a livestock activity, offers part-time work to an estimated 15,000 persons. As a significant rural activity, it enjoys a long tradition in the peninsula, dating back to the preconquest period. Most of the raw honey is processed in Yucatán for export to such customers as West Germany, the United Kingdom, Japan, and the United States. The peninsula ranks among the world's major honey-exporting areas, including Argentina, Canada, and mainland

China, a recent entrant in the market. Competition among these leading exporters for the global markets is vigorous, and honey prices fluctuate widely from year to year and over the business cycle.

If improved managerial as well as technical methods are applied and further investment made in irrigation facilities, Yucatán has the potential to become not only self-sufficient in the growing of many varieties of fruits and vegetables but also to penetrate the United States market as well. The northern Mexican states already export substantial quantities of fruits and vegetables to that country. Considering that the port of Progreso is only sixty hours by ship from Miami and seventy-two from New Orleans, it would be economically feasible to transport fresh produce on a regular basis from Yucatán to these destinations, particularly during the winter months, when prices of fresh produce reach their peaks in the United States.

Federal authorities, through Banrural and its *técnicos*, have tried to induce campesinos to change their production methods through such sophisticated agricultural ventures as the "Santa Rosa" experiment, "Dzonot Carretero," "Plan Chac," and "Plan Tabi." These government-directed approaches usually involved expensive sprinkler irrigation systems and other capital-using methods in addition to the provision of houses, schools, and related infrastructure. Thus far, however, the officially planned approaches have failed, and the spontaneous diversification efforts of the campesinos have succeeded.

Initiated in 1964, the federally directed "Santa Rosa" project was designed as a large-scale vegetable export operation.[14] Located in the municipio of Peto, near the border of Quintana Roo, "Santa Rosa" was developed on 3,200 hectares of land owned by the Banco Agrícola. A total of thirty-four deep wells were created, and sprinkler equipment as well as irrigation canals were put into use. Modern farm machinery was introduced for land-clearing and cultivation. The bank's main strategy was to ship vegetables to the United States during the winter season, from September to April. In 1964 a contract was signed between the Banco Agrícola and Champion Growers and Packers, a U.S. firm, which agreed to purchase the "Santa Rosa" output for resale in the American market. To facilitate marketing, the project managers imported from the United States specialized equipment to select, clean, and preserve the vegetables destined for export. By

162

1967 nearly a thousand men and women were employed in the cultivation and harvesting of vegetables and another hundred were working in Progreso, where the processing equipment was initially located. To transport the produce, the bank purchased refrigerated trucks and rented three ships to move the processed vegetables from Progreso to Pompano Beach, Florida, where the American firm took possession of the cargoes. Because "Santa Rosa" was not on ejido land, the bank needed to build houses and related facilities to attract workers from nearby towns and villages. Pork- and beef-raising operations were also started in 1967. Because the export-oriented infrastructure was in place, bank officials hoped that the success of the "Santa Rosa" experiment would stimulate private and ejido production in the south of Yucatán.

Although a number of vegetable shipments were made to the United States between 1964 and 1967, exports reaching 4,000 tons in the 1966–67 season, many people soon suspected that the project was experiencing substantial losses. In the absence of project financial information, these suspicions were confirmed when in July 1967 the Banco Agrícola announced it was abandoning the "Santa Rosa" venture and renting the land and equipment to a private firm. In 1970 the private firm, Frutas y Verduras de Yucatán, S.A., returned the land and equipment to the bank. Apparently, both the bank and company encountered excessive production costs and failed to meet the quality-control standards required for selling produce in the U.S. market.

Three years later, in 1973, "Santa Rosa," now encompassing 5,200 hectares, was delivered to 104 ejidatarios and became the ejido "Justicia Social" (social justice). Today it is one of the model ejidos in the state, and well it should be, for the 104 campesinos possess more than 5,000 hectares of the best land in Yucatán and receive strong backing from the official bank. Among the hundreds of collective estates, Justicia Social is one of the four ejidos in the state that is reducing its debt obligations and earning modest profits for its members. On the other hand, total losses of the Banco Agrícola from the "Santa Rosa" enterprise are estimated at 100 million pesos (about $8 million) between 1964 and 1972.[15]

A failure on an even larger scale was the federal government's attempt to develop project "Dzonot Carretero" on the ejido called by that name.[16] Located in the northeast, some 40 kilometers

ECONOMIC DIVERSIFICATION

from Tizimin, the ejido Dzonot Carretero encompassed nearly 300 ejidatarios on 11,000 hectares. Before 1970, when the Banco Agrario launched its modernization project, the ejido's land was well suited for corn-growing. From 1970 to 1975, the federal government, through the bank, invested more than 200 million pesos in land-clearing, irrigation works, and structures and machinery. The project's infrastructure included a landing strip for aircraft, an office building, warehouses, barns, and feeder roads. Crops scheduled for production included, in addition to corn and beans, sorghum, oil seeds, melons, yuca, peanuts, and vegetables. Hog- and beef-raising operations were also funded.

By 1975 "Dzonot Carretero" was acknowledged to be a failure, and between 1977 and 1980 most of the 11,000 hectares were abandoned along with the buildings and equipment. Only the cattle operation continued to show a profit. Of the 200 million peso ($16 million) investment, only a nominal amount is being recovered, and the debt of the ejidatarios to the official bank exceeded 100 million pesos as of June 1980.

Ejidatarios and bank officials cited two major reasons for "Dzonot Carretero's" failure:[17]

1. Major land-clearing operations resulted in irreparable ecological damage.
2. Little coordination occurred among the official bank, the other federal agencies involved in the project, and the ejidatarios themselves. The campesinos did not understand their role in the venture and were unfamiliar with both the modern equipment and the new crops and methods that were introduced by the bank officials.

The failure of the federally sponsored diversification projects reflects both the reluctance of the official bank to make long-term commitments to these ventures and the shortcomings of bank officials: their lack of expertise, their apathy, and their corrupt dealings with the campesinos.

INDUSTRIAL STRUCTURE AND DIVERSIFICATION

Yucatán's industrial growth rate of 5.5 percent annually between 1976 and 1981 compares unfavorably with a more dynamic national growth rate of 8.2 percent.[18] Because of the preeminent position of the henequen industry in 1975, the state's comparatively moderate advance masks the impressive momentum of industrial diversification achieved during the 1976–81 sexennium—a period marked by a sharp decline in Cordemex's production. In contrast with the declining fortunes of henequen, electric-power generation expanded rapidly, as did the production of plastic products, vegetable oils, clothing and nonalcoholic beverages. In addition, the 1976–81 construction boom reflected federal infrastructure investment, the demands of the burgeoning tourism industry, private expenditures in new and expanded plant, and investment in residential housing. Dramatic growth during this sexennium in the production of cement and steel products (mainly corrugated rods) was closely linked to the requirements of the building industry. Yucatán's commercial fishing activities were paralleled by the expansion of the marine-products industry, and, within Mérida's "industrial city," the number of plants and the associated direct employment more than doubled from 1976 to 1981.

As recently as 1975, as the tenth industrial census reveals (table 22), hard fiber textiles—comprising the henequen defibration and manufacturing stages—completely dominated Yucatán's industrial landscape. As a share of total manufacturing in the state, henequen textiles employed 47 percent of the labor force, paid 56 percent of wages and salaries, comprised 57 percent of the assets, and generated 43 percent of the value of gross output and 39 percent of value-added in the manufacturing sector. On the basis of data for 1980, it can be stated unequivocally that both the absolute and relative contributions of the henequen industry to Yucatáns' industrial profile have been much diminished. The gross value of industrial production is estimated at 14.5 billion pesos for 1980 (see table 23). Of this sum, the cordage industry contributed 1,537 million pesos, or about 11 percent of total industrial output and about 11.5 percent of the gross value of total manufactures. A comparison between the last percentage figure and the henequen textile industry's contribution to gross output in 1975 (43 percent) reflects the simultaneous contraction of Cordemex operations and the emergence of newer, dynamic industrial branches during the years 1975–80. Although estimates are given for gross production in a number of industrial branches—construction (1,075 million pesos), cement (891 million pesos), vegetable oils (621 million pesos), clothing (500 million pesos), and steel products (329 million)—information is not available for

TABLE 22. Yucatán: Manufacturing Output, Employment, Wages and Salaries, Assets, and Value-Added, by Industry, 1975 (money amounts in thousands of pesos)

Industry	No. of Establishments	No. of Employees	Wages and Salaries	Assets	Value of Output	Value-Added
Textiles[a]	162	12,500	424,982	1,327,312	1,502,926	527,896
Food products	1,903	6,408	96,881	334,218	828,396	236,127
Apparel	355	1,749	27,247	53,958	106,615	51,354
Beverages	15	1,717	81,433	239,932	470,584	206,510
Nonmetallic mineral products	59	1,016	37,124	201,908	235,341	115,916
Shoes and leather products	84	706	18,413	12,625	44,162	30,090
Printing and publishing	57	558	21,463	37,522	76,328	33,724
Other	366	2,086	46,609	135,914	260,312	92,813
Total	3,001	26,740	754,152	2,343,389	3,524,664	11,294,430

SOURCE: Dirección General de Estadística, X censo industrial, 1976, Volume I, Secretaría de Programación y Presupuestos (México, D.F., 1979), pp. 59–87.
[a]Principally defibration and manufacture of henequen.

TABLE 23. Yucatán: Value of Industrial Production, 1980 (in millions of pesos)

Industry	Value of Production	
Cordage	1,537	
Construction	1,075	
Cement	891	
Vegetable oils	621	
Clothing	500	
Steel products	370	
Food products	329	
Flour milling	291	
Subtotal		5,614
Other industries	8,886	
Total		14,500

SOURCE: Adapted from Gobierno del Estado de Yucatán, *Monografía de Yucatán, 1980* (Mérida, 1981) and Gobierno del Estado de Yucatán, *Plan de desarrollo estatal, 1982–1988* (Mérida, 1982).

other important Yucatecan industries: marine products, salt mining and processing, plastic products, and beverages. The final results of the eleventh industrial census (based on 1980 data) are, unfortunately, not available as of 1986.

The dynamics of Yucatán's recent industrial diversification is highlighted in table 24, which lists the thirty leading industrial firms, by declining order of employment in 1980. The table also reveals the capitalization of the enterprise, its location, major product line, and its market reach. Of these thirty, twenty-seven are located in Mérida, and fifteen began operations in 1970 or thereafter. Eight serve the peninsular market, including the states of Campeche and Quintana Roo, and fourteen claim the Southeast as their market area, including the states of Tabasco and Chiapas. Enterprises manufacturing products characterized by high ratios of value to weight, such as designer shoes, guayabera shirts, and marine products, penetrate markets well beyond the immediate region: central Mexico, the United States, and Puerto Rico. It should be noted, however, that Hong Kong, Korea, and

TABLE 24. Yucatán: Thirty Largest Industrial Firms, 1980

Firm	Employment	Location	Product	Year Initiated	Market
Cordemex	5,589	Mérida	Harvest twine ropes, cables	1961	U.S., Canada, Mexico
Embotelladora Penínsular	500	Mérida	Coca Cola	1946	Peninsula
Cervecería Yucateca	457	Mérida	Beer and ice	1900	Peninsula
Cia. Embotelladora del Sureste	460	Mérida	Pepsi Cola	1945	Peninsula
Ind. Salineras de Yucatán	330	N.E. coast	Salt mining and refining	1946	Mexico, U.S., Cuba
Cementos Maya	326	Mérida	Portland cement	1955	Peninsula
Galletera Palma	326	Mérida	Bakery products	1977	Peninsula
Productos de Harina	300	Mérida	Bakery products	1933	Southeast
Productos Pesqueros de Yucalpeten	207	Progreso	Marine products	1975	Peninsula
Siderúrgica de Yucatán	185	Mérida	Steel products (laminated rods)	1978	Southeast
Embotelladora de Sidra Pino	156	Mérida	Soda drinks	1951	Peninsula
Hidrogenadora Yucateca	130	Mérida	Vegetable oils, soap	1949	Southeast
Fábrica de Calzado Cananéo	120	Mérida	Shoes	1978	Southeast, Mexico City
Ind. Métalicas Yucateca	117	Mérida	Office equipment	1974	Southeast
Alimentos Balan-ceados de México	114	Mérida	Animal feeds	1972	Southeast
Productos Plásticos Alcasmo	105	Mérida	Plastic products	1965	Peninsula
Luis Achurra Suc.	105	Mérida-Uman Hwy.	Liquor and bottles	1957	Southeast

168

(Table 24, continued)

Firm	Employment	Location	Product	Year Initiated	Market
Genuina Yucateca	90	Mérida	Guayaberas	1968	Mexico
Cía. Manuf. de Ropa del Este	86	Mérida	Guayaberas, clothing	1971	Mexico, U.S.
Harinas del Sureste	71	Mérida	Wheat flour	1975	Southeast
AIMMSA	70	Mérida	Metallic construction	1979	Peninsula
Nutrimentos del Sureste	60	Mérida	Poultry feed	1972	Peninsula
Offset Peninsular	58	Mérida	Printing	1972	Southeast
El Faro	53	Mérida	Candles and paraffin products	1950	Peninsula
Oléoproductos del Sureste	50	Mérida	Vegetable oils	1975	Southeast
Manufacturera de Ropa Meridana	50	Mérida	Guayaberas, clothing	1953	Mexico
Bufete de Ing. del Sureste	49	Mérida	Industrial construction	1975	Peninsula
Guayaberas Unidas	48	Mérida	Guayaberas and blouses	1970	Mexico and Puerto Rico
Ind. Químicas de Yucatán	47	Mérida	Limestone products	1975	Southeast
Acumuladores Hércules	45	Mérida	Batteries	1978	Southeast

SOURCE: Gobierno del Estado, *Directorio industrial* (Mérida, 1980).

Taiwan captured foreign guayabera markets formerly held by Yucatecans. A major reason for Yucatán's competitive disadvantage is the Mexican government's unwillingness to permit its own manufacturers to buy cheaper imported cloth.

On the basis of capitalization as the criterion of size, four firms dominate the industrial landscape of Yucatán: Cordemex (500 million pesos); the brewery Cervecería Yucateca (400 million pesos); Cementos Maya (100 million pesos); and Industrias Salineras de Yucatán, which mines and processes salt for both national and foreign markets (100 million pesos). Firms employing seventy people or more, but capitalized at levels below 100 million pesos, include the three major bottling plants, two large-scale bakeries, the steel-products plant (Siderúrgica de Yucatán), a shoe factory, a marine-products plant, a plastics manufacturer, an animal-feeds producer, a vegetable-oils plant, three manufacturers of guayabera shirts, a flour mill, and two metal construction firms.

Industrial development has increasingly focused on metropolitan Mérida, an urbanized regional center of 400,000 inhabitants in 1980, whose market reach extends beyond the peninsula to the new oil-rich states of Tabasco and Chiapas. A classic regional center, Mérida is the major source of nonagricultural employment in Yucatán. According to the tenth population census, 60 percent of the state's industrial labor force and 90 percent of those engaged in manufacturing were concentrated in the municipio of Mérida in 1980. Institutions of higher education and research located there serve the entire peninsula. As the seat of state government and regional offices of the federal government, Mérida is not only the hub of an extensive network of highways and railroads, but is also connected through the nearby port of Progreso to global maritime trade. A well-equipped international airport connects the city with sections of the United States and with other parts of Mexico. Mérida also offers adequate electric power and petroleum distribution as well as a good telecommunications system.

The "industrial city" of Felipe Carrillo Puerto is located about a mile from the international airport on the Mérida-Campeche highway. Including the installations of Pémex and the Federal Electricity Commission (CFE), the industrial city contained sixty plants at the end of 1981, which represented a total investment of 5 billion pesos and provided direct employment for 8,000.[19] During the course of that year, thirty plants were under construction that employed 3,500 workers in the building trades.

The 1980 industrial directory, the source of table 24, listed three hundred enterprises, of which the preponderant majority includes small factories employing between ten to twenty-five workers that manufacture modern products, such as plastics, clothes, furniture, ice, boats, and processed seafood. Most of these smaller firms are also located in Mérida.

Because of its rich artisan tradition, which antedated the Spanish conquest, Yucatán also has a flourishing traditional small-scale industry. Unlike small, modern factories, these home-centered production units use traditional techniques to produce traditional goods. The value-added by these household enterprises is much below factory output, but, in terms of employment and as a way of life, the work of craftsmen and artisans continues to be a vital element of Yucatán's industrial economy. Thousands of individuals are still engaged in weaving, shoemaking, woodworking, stone carving, sewing and embroidering, and pottery making— activities carried on by one or more members of the family in the *solar*, the Mayan residential compound. Handicraft industries require little capital investment because their key resources are labor and local raw materials. They help increase income for people in rural areas, especially women and agricultural workers who are idle part of the year and who lack other employment opportunities. Craft industries mobilize rural entrepreneurship and, when efficiently organized, can open new external markets and generate foreign-exchange earnings.

Unlike factory production, which is concentrated in Mérida, household industries are scattered throughout the state in villages and small towns. The town of Ticul, for example, specializes in pottery, hats made of palm leaves, and women's shoes.[20] The technology of pottery making, learned within the family, has changed little from pre-Hispanic times. Clay and tempering ingredients found in the vicinity of Ticul have long provided the pottery-making community with basic raw materials. Utility potteryware is also produced by Maya families in villages scattered throughout the state, including Maxcanú, Akil, and Uyama.[21] Handmade men's shoes are produced in the village of Hunucmá, and objects of wood, such as kitchen utensils, in the village of Dzityá, near the north coast of Yucatán. This primitive woodworking industry uses locally grown trees, and all members of the family participate in elaborating the product. Stone sculptors in Caucab, Tixhualactun, Muna, and Halacho apply their skilled craft to decorating churches and palaces and to adorning fountains and gardens.

The embroideries of Yucatán are famous not only in the state and nation, but also increasingly abroad. Home-centered embroidering is a ubiquitous activity. Indeed, it is often said that in Yucatán at least one daughter of every family is engaged in embroidering, sewing, or weaving. Beyond the application of the craft to traditional clothing, such as the *huipil*, the dress of indigenous women, embroidering has rapidly expanded and diversified to include guayaberas, blouses, tablecloths, and the like. Hammocks, the "Yucatecan bed," are woven by women and children throughout the state: henequen hammocks for sale are made in Chemax, Tekom, Tixkokob, and other villages; cotton and nylon hammocks are produced in Izamal, Mayapan, Teabo, and Mérida. Embroidering and hammock-weaving employ thousands of individuals and constitute the premier artisan industries in Yucatán.

Handcrafted products are marketed directly in open-air markets throughout the state or are sold to middlemen. The traditional feast days and fairs offer excellent opportunities for moving large quantities of these goods to the final consumer. Yucatecan industry is thus characterized by a pronounced dualistic structure. Large-scale units, employing modern technology, coexist with a traditional sector of small-scale household units that uses labor-intensive techniques and little capital.

TOURISM

Tourism has become the most dynamic component of Yucatán's economy during the past two decades. In 1980 gross state income from tourism (1,774 million pesos) for the first time exceeded Cordemex's total sales (1,537 million pesos). And, as a source of foreign-exchange earnings that year, tourist outlays in Yucatán (736 million pesos) approached the export sales of Cordemex (782 million pesos). As table 25 shows, the number of tourists visiting Yucatán increased from a negligible 32,000 in 1960 to 285,000 in 1970 and 901,465 in 1980. During the 1970–80 decade, the number of tourists increased more than threefold and peso outlays tenfold. Nationals comprised 62 percent of all visitors to the state in 1980 and foreigners 38 percent. Because foreigners spent more per visit, their contribution to Yucatán's tourism income was relatively greater (43 percent), compared with 57 percent for expenditures by nationals.[22] Of the foreigners visiting the state in 1980, 48 percent were U.S. travelers, 37

TABLE 25. Tourism in Yucatán: Number of Visitors and Their
Expenditures, 1960–1981

Year	Nationals	Foreigners	Total	Total Expenditures (in pesos)
1960	8,422	23,361	31,783	19,069,800
1961	29,199	16,421	45,620	27,373,800
1962	76,977	20,465	97,442	58,465,200
1963	90,865	24,106	114,971	68,874,600
1964	92,347	25,548	117,895	70,137,000
1965	109,942	31,048	140,990	84,940,000
1966	130,975	41,282	172,257	103,204,200
1967	144,300	50,701	195,001	117,000,600
1968	146,429	78,847	225,276	135,165,600
1969	133,399	87,594	220,993	131,391,600
1970	159,600	125,400	285,000	171,000,000
1971	128,791	93,362	222,153	180,868,300
1972	226,377	131,693	358,070	286,306,400
1973	330,096	146,657	476,753	379,563,300
1974	382,321	172,518	554,839	442,902,700
1975	402,548	184,131	586,679	731,634,000
1976	436,664	200,724	637,388	794,974,000
1977	443,007	258,806	701,813	986,568,000
1978	465,386	295,457	760,843	1,229,902,000
1979	528,890	321,583	850,473	1,372,184,000
1980	566,965	335,400	901,465	1,773,522,000
1981	587,404	251,404	839,148	3,166,467,000

SOURCE: Dirección General de Turismo del Gobierno del Estado.

percent were Europeans, and the remainder came from other
parts of the globe. Among the Mexicans vacationing in Yucatán,
31 percent came from the Federal District, 25 percent from the
neighboring states of Campeche and Quintana Roo, and the balance (44 percent) originated in other states.

Yucatán's capacity to serve tourists has increased substantially.
As an example, the number of tourist agencies grew from 11 to 44
between 1970 and 1980, and the number of hotel rooms available
in Mérida expanded from 2,534 in 1975 to 3,528 in 1981.[23] Also,

the number of quality restaurants in the capital city has grown appreciably during the past decade.

The state also benefits economically from the expanding tourist activity in the beach resorts of the neighboring state of Quintana Roo. The islands of Cozumél, Isla Mujeres and, most recently, Cancún attract service and construction workers from Yucatán, especially the eastern city of Valladolid. To the extent that tourists bound for these beach resorts stop over in Mérida, the impact will be favorable on the city's hotels, restaurants, travel and auto rental agencies, and other facilities. Also, most of the food and nonalcoholic beverages consumed in Cancún are supplied by Yucatán.

Cancún, the most ambitious tourist attraction in the region, is a fourteen-mile stretch of powdery coral beach located in the Caribbean Sea off the coast of Quintana Roo. The site possesses abundant natural resources, including broad beaches, fine white sand, clear waters, and an excellent year-round climate, as well as proximity to a number of Mayan archaeological sites. Cancún's airport can accommodate all types of aircraft and is located twelve miles southwest of the resort. New York City, Washington, D.C., and Miami are nearer by air to the island resort than they are to Puerto Rico, Jamaica, the Virgin Islands, and other Caribbean destinations, except the Bahamas.

The development of Cancún was begun in 1971 under the auspices of the Mexican government's Fund for Tourism Development (FONATUR), aided by an Inter-American Development Bank (IDB) loan for $21.5 million.[24] FONATUR's creation was part of a broader national policy to encourage regional growth and to generate new sources of employment and foreign exchange. The Mexican government has invested more than $100 million, including the initial IDB loan, to turn the island into a planned beach resort that is designed to remain unspoiled and safe from overdevelopment. Private investment in Cancún (most of it Mexican) substantially exceeds official outlays.

The first to benefit from the transformation of the island into a tourist center were the 130 local inhabitants, who until recently were barely making a living from small-scale fishing and subsistence farming. Better jobs were created for them and the thousands of new settlers, most of them from the state of Yucatán.

What explains the tremendous growth in Yucatán's "invisible" exports? To begin with, there are the monumental archaeological sites of the Mayan civilization; the churches, plazas, and other remains of the Spanish colonial period; and the beach resorts. Second, tourism expenditures are highly sensitive to a rise in per capita income. For this reason, economic growth in the United States, Western Europe, and Mexico—the peninsula's major geographical sources of tourism receipts—has benefited Yucatán disproportionately. The demand prospects for international tourism are superior to those for Yucatán's traditional exports. The dramatic growth of the peninsula's tourism infrastructure, including transportation facilities, both internal and external, has contributed to the region's capacity to attract travelers. Promotional efforts by both the Mexican and state governments, as well as private tourist agencies, have helped market Yucatán's unique attractions to potential tourists.

Beyond its locational advantage and the factors mentioned above, the state's international competitiveness is also affected by the rate of exchange. In a statistical study of the impact of devaluation and revaluation on tourism earnings, an International Monetary Fund (IMF) economist found good, if imperfect, evidence that tourist receipts are very sensitive to the price factor.[25] For example, as the peso became increasingly overvalued relative to the United States dollar between 1980 and 1981, the number of foreigners visiting Yucatán fell by 84,000, thereby abruptly reversing a two-decade growth trend. Following the sharp devaluation of the peso in 1982, a vacation in Mexico suddenly became a bargain for American and other foreign visitors.

Tourism in Yucatán grew at 18.4 percent annually in real, inflation-discounted terms from 1960 to 1980, and in the latter year employment generated directly by the industry reached an estimated 6,137.[26] Because tourism is service-oriented, it provides the advantage of being labor-intensive and capital saving, a desirable situation in a state where capital is scarce and labor abundant. Figures from a recent input-output study in Mexico showed that, for $80,000 invested in tourism, forty-one jobs were created. The same investment would create only sixteen in petroleum, sixteen in metal products, or eight in electricity.

Although the state's tourism industry is quite sensitive to the United States business cycle, seasonal variations of tourist outlays in Yucatán tend to be offsetting: Mexican visitors are concentrated from July to October, and the high season for visits by foreigners extends from November to March.

Arguing from a Marxian perspective, Rosemary Lee concludes that tourism offers little promise toward advancing the state's development.[27] But the analysis of Yucatán's diversified economic base by the authors of this volume suggests that local residents, including workers, keep a large share of what tourists spend in the state. According to the Secretary of Tourism, travel expenditures in Yucatán were allocated in the following ways in 1980: food, 29 percent; lodging, 25 percent; purchase of artisan products, 14 percent; the purchase of other goods, 6 percent; and the remaining 26 percent was spent on local transportation and other services.[28] Most of the food and nonalcoholic beverages consumed by tourists in Yucatán are produced in the state. Building materials such as cement, steel rods, and stone are supplied locally for the construction of new hotels and tourism infrastructure. Although a number of handcrafted items from other parts of Mexico are featured in Yucatecan tourist shops, probably a majority of the goods purchased by visitors consist of such items as embroidered dresses and blouses, guayaberas, and hammocks that are locally made. Furthermore, the nearby beach resorts of Quintana Roo—Cancún, Cozumél, and Isla Mujeres—exert a strong indirect market impact upon these same industries and firms.

COMMERCIAL FISHING

Commercial fishing is becoming an increasingly vital contributor to the Yucatecan economy. It provides a livelihood directly or indirectly for an estimated 16,500 individuals, including some 9,000 fishermen. Commercial fishing in 1950 could hardly be considered an industry, for in that year the volume of catches barely exceeded a thousand tons, whose total value was less than 1 million pesos. The limited catch and absence of refrigeration and processing equipment, combined with primitive organizational and marketing know-how as well as the lack of good harbors, precluded the possibility of exporting fish products to other parts of Mexico or abroad.

In 1981 the volume of the catch reached 38,844 tons, whose value exceeded 1 billion pesos. Fishing is a promising economic activity because of the state's 360-kilometer northern littoral and the extensive continental shelf that is so rich in marine species. Within this shelf, corresponding to the Sound of Campeche, can be found red snapper, grouper, sea bass, octopus, anchovy, shrimp, and lobster. Thirteen communities along Yucatán's Gulf coastline depend on fishing for their principal source of income and employment.

The state's commercial fishing industry is organized into more than eighty private enterprises, twenty-six cooperatives, two fishermen ejidos, and a branch of Productos Pesqueros Mexicanos (PPM), a federal parastatal firm. Of the 8,757 individuals engaged in commercial fishing in 1980, some 1,048 were members of cooperatives, 387 were ejido members, and the remaining 7,322 were independent.[29] The fishing fleet in 1981 numbered 1,928 boats, of which 317 were longer than thirty feet and equipped for deep-water fishing and 1,611 small boats for shallow-water fishing.[30] The largest and best-equipped boats in the fleet were those in the over-fifty-ton net displacement class. Most of these boats were owned by major private fish-processing plants in Progreso and Yucalpetén.

Backward and forward linkages associated with the expansion of the fishing industry have been substantial. The most important forwardly-linked operations in 1981 included twenty-two freezing plants and forty-one ovens for processing fish meal. Backward linkages extend to an incipient boat-building industry, including twelve small plants for making wooden craft and nine factories for the construction of fiberglass boats. Furthermore, commercial fishing activities are serviced by twenty-one ice plants, located at the leading fishing towns and in Mérida. Progreso and Celestún, the two major fishing ports, together accounted for 84 percent of the volume and 80 percent of the value of the state's fish catch in 1980.[31]

Yucatán's fishing industry was one of the earliest targets of the federal government's diversification efforts within the state. Nevertheless, as in other economic sectors, the federal role in the promotion of commercial fishing (both in the nation and the state) has been characterized by ambiguity of objectives.[32] Domestic sales of Yucatecan marine products received a significant boost in 1961 when the federal highway linking Mérida with Mexico City was completed. This highway for the first time gave Yucatecan fishermen reliable and relatively low-cost access to the large population clusters in central Mexico. Another federal project, a technical training school for fishermen, was initiated at Yucalpetén in 1981. Most notably, in response to local business interests backed by strong support from Mexican Navy officials, the federal government completed construction in 1971 of a modern sheltered harbor, named Yucalpetén, which includes an industrial park.[33] A Yucatecan close to the industry indicated that private investors had been eager to invest in both boats and processing equipment but had been hesitant because of the absence of secure harbor facilities. This opinion has been supported by the fact that the private sector has been the dominant participant in the expansion of the fleet and processing facilities since 1967.

President José López Portillo's administration quickly designated fishing as one of three principal priorities for national investment and development. The National Plan of Fishing Development, which proposed to increase production by 361 percent within the next five years, however, disregarded, according to Thomas Sanders, the Mexican fishing industry's key problem: "the relationship between the technical objective of expanding fishing and the sociopolitical culture in which it takes place."[34] As in the henequen industry, the federal government's role in the promotion of commercial fishing (both in the nation and the state) has responded to ambivalent and conflicting goals. On the one hand, the economic infrastructure projects mentioned above have greatly stimulated private investment in fleet modernization and processing facilities; on the other, federal direct intervention through PPM and the organization of fishing cooperatives have mainly served "social" and political ends. Founded in 1971, PPM is one of hundreds of public enterprises created during the Luis Echeverría administration. As with Cordemex and most other government companies in Mexico, it has carried a redundant labor force and has provided lucrative financial benefits to the politician-bureaucrats who administer it. In the Mexican context, administrators of parastatal firms are appointed by the president on the basis of patronage and must make full use of their opportunities during their term in office because the next presidential administration will replace them. By the mid-1970s, as Sanders points out, PPM's operations had already lost an estimated 2.3 billion pesos (about $200 million by the former exchange rate).[35]

One of the chief criticisms of the federally organized fishing cooperatives is that they are politicized, which inhibits their essential economic function. The coops are organized into a National Federation of Cooperative Societies, which functions as a constituent organization of the PRI. In Yucatán, the PRI has used the coops as a base for political support among the population of the northern coast. The benefits of affiliation with the cooperative include subsidized financing, greater legal access to certain species than is available to independent fishermen, and participation in the health and insurance programs of the social-security system. Weighed against these benefits, coop members also perceive certain costs that directly or indirectly involve the loss of autonomy.[36] The Mexican fishing coops are not run on the cooperative principle; in practice, they are usually managed by political bureaucrats who may not even be fishermen. Significantly, nearly all the coop members interviewed by Murphy and Solís in the Yucatecan fishing village of San Felipe expressed some degree of mistrust for the state and federal officials who controlled the operation of their cooperatives.[37]

Finally, the Mexican government has failed to take effective measures against violations in peninsula waters to assure Mexican private investors that the potentially rich fishing grounds in the Gulf will not be overexploited by foreigners. As an example, failure of President López Portillo to apply sanctions against Cuba, the worst violator in Mexican waters, suggests that the maintenance of cordial relations with that Marxist regime took precedence over the interests of Yucatecan deep-water fishermen.[38]

In sum, social goals, principally employment creation, and political motives (PRI dominance and patronage) have vied with production-efficiency goals in the shaping of federal fishing policy. However, notwithstanding the rapid increase in the number of cooperative units since 1970 and the organization of a Yucatecan branch of PPM, private enterprises still accounted for about 80 percent of the state's fish catch in 1981.

CONCLUSIONS AND PROSPECTS

The growing economic dynamism of Yucatán in the recent past is the consequence of export diversification, regional market expansion, and import-substitution, especially in nontraditional agriculture. As table 21 shows, total agricultural sales in 1980 exceeded 5.1 billion pesos, of which crops contributed 42 percent and livestock production 58 percent. Significantly, gross income from henequen fiber contributed about one-half to crop sales, but only 21 percent of total agricultural sales. The cattle industry accounted for 23 percent of the gross income of the agricultural-pastoral sector—a share exceeding henequen fiber in importance. Poultry and eggs together contributed 940 million pesos, and their share in gross farm income approached that of henequen. Vegetables grown in Yucatán supplied less than half the requirements of the state's population in the mid-1960s; the balance needed to be purchased from other parts of Mexico. Currently, the state, because of its improved agricultural production capabilities, is much less dependent upon imports of vegetables, corn, beans, and fruits.

The acceleration of industrial diversification is largely a response to regional market expansion. Among the factors that have shaped this expanded market are (1) population growth; (2) greatly improved regional infrastructure, including highways and roads, telecommunications, and electric power; (3) the emergence of an urban middle class; and (4) the spectacular growth of tourism during the past decade. The city of Mérida has become the commercial and industrial center for the entire peninsula, including the neighboring states of Quintana Roo and Campeche. Furthermore, the market reach of numerous plants located in Mérida, including those producing steel products, vegetable oils, office equipment, and animal feeds, extends to the new oil-rich states of Chiapas and Tabasco.

Commercial fishing, of negligible importance two decades ago, has become the major source of employment and income for the numerous communities lying along Yucatán's northern coast. An estimated 16,500 persons are employed in fishing and related activities. Backwardly-linked activities include ice-making, and boat repair and construction; fish processing is the most important forwardly-linked activity.

In 1980 state income from tourism (1,774 million pesos) for the first time exceeded the sales of Cordemex (1,537 million pesos). The expenditures generated by foreign visitors in the state (762 million pesos) nearly matched the value of foreign exchange earned by the firm's export sales (782 million pesos). As has been noted, the state's capacity to serve visitors had increased notably since 1970, and its inhabitants also benefit economically from the expanding tourist trade in the beach resorts located in Quintana Roo: Cancún, Cozumél, and Isla Mujeres. Yucatán's premier growth industry has expanded employment by generating long-term, service-intensive jobs and short-term, construction-intensive jobs. Tourist expenditures have also opened a major new market for Yucatán's traditional artisan and craft industries.

Considering the limits of economic development based on regional market expansion, Yucatán's prospects for sustained industrial growth would be better served by an export-oriented strategy aimed at the United States similar to Mexico's Border Industrialization Program. Both the peninsula and the country's northern border zone contain a relatively abundant labor force and enjoy a favorable location vis-à-vis the U.S. market. The distance between Progreso and New Orleans is only 460 maritime miles, and other U.S. Gulf ports are also within easy reach of Yucatán. The success of such a labor-intensive *maquiladora* program would hinge in part on the Mexican government's willingness to permit U.S. and other foreign-based firms to invest in Yucatecan manufacturing as well as repair facilities and to remove tariffs and quotas on raw materials and components imported by the newly established, export-oriented *maquiladora* plants.

Since 1984 several factors have converged that point to improved prospects for establishing Yucatán as the "other *maquiladora* frontier."[39] First, the newly installed governor, Victor Cervera Pacheco, has announced his strong support for a *maquiladora* program in Yucatán.[40] Second, the Henequen Rationalization and Integral Development Program for Yucatán, initiated in May 1984, includes numerous federal research and infrastructure projects to build the state's industrial export capacity. Finally, the federal Southeastern Regional Program confers upon Mérida strategic importance as a new industrial growth pole. The Mérida-Progreso corridor offers the requisite physical facilities and support services for a *maquiladora* venture. Moreover, because of its cultural and educational amenities, Mérida would provide an attractive environment for the foreign managerial and technical personnel who are associated with the new industrial plants.

Yucatán's prospects for significantly diversifying its agricultural base was the theme of a series of articles that appeared in the *Diario de Yucatán* under the general title "A Vision of

Yucatán in the Year 2,000."[41] Written by Ing. Manuel Mier y Terán, former director of economic planning for the state, the articles are based in part on economic feasibility studies regarding Yucatán's agricultural potential that were conducted by Israeli experts. According to them, the state has an ample labor force and adequate ground water resources, which, if combined with fertilizer and proper soil management, could serve as the basis for a long-range agricultural export program.

For many years, as Mier y Terán points out, the southern and eastern markets of the United States have been supplied with fresh vegetables during the winter season not only by products originating in northern Mexico, but also from areas in the Caribbean. He asks whether Yucatán could replicate this experience and concludes in the affirmative. By the year 2000, he anticipates that the state could be exporting tens of thousands of tons each of citrus fruit and concentrate to the United States and Canada. Furthermore, he expects Yucatán to export more than 40,000 tons of vegetables, such as chile habañero, peppers, and eggplant, to the United States.

Cut flowers and ornamental plants, accordng to Mier y Terán, present additional alternatives for agricultural exports during the winter months to the United States. Because of the peninsula's proximity to United States Gulf ports, the state offers a considerable transportation cost advantage over the current suppliers of cut flowers and ornamental plants: Colombia, Panama, Costa Rica, Honduras, and Guatemala. Significantly, Colombia's export sales of fresh-cut flowers yielded $123 million in 1983.[42] Mier y Terán concludes that if his "vision" is realized by the year 2000, these new export-oriented agricultural activities would offer substantial rural employment in the henequen zone.

The ambivalent federal economic posture in Yucatán has been noted earlier in this volume. Direct investment in and management of the henequen industry by the Mexican government through Cordemex and Banrural have tended to freeze the state's historical monocrop structure. On the other hand, federal initiatives in economic overhead projects, including electric power, transportation, and irrigation systems, have stimulated Yucatán's recent diversification. The federal government's intrusive position in the Yucatecan economy is dramatically illustrated by the following figures (in millions of pesos) for 1980:[43]

Federal public investment		3,764
Cordemex operational budget		2,813
Henequen Trust Fund (managed by Banrural for the ejidos)		2,710
State budget, of which:		1,801
Federal "ordinary participation" (78.4%)	1,412	
State's own resources (21.6%)	389	

The federal investment of nearly 3.8 billion pesos, it should be noted, was in addition to the operational budgets of Cordemex and the Banrural's henequen activities, as well as the 1.4-billion-peso direct federal contribution through revenue-sharing to the state's budget. Of the federal investment outlay in 1980, about half was directed to the industrial sector (mainly through the Federal Electricity Commission and Pémex to expand the state's energy resources), 14 percent to agriculture, about 8 percent to fishing, and 7 percent to education and technology.

Significantly, the combined operational budget of Cordemex and the Banrural of 5.5 billion pesos was fourteen times the state government's budget from its own resources, a confirmation of the state government's anemic economic posture vis-à-vis the federal government in Yucatán. Can the paternalistic/dependency syndrome that has characterized the federal relationship with the state be replaced by a mature relationship, including a more important role for its political authorities?

President Miguel de la Madrid delivered a major policy address on Yucatán's economic future while visiting the state late in May 1984.[44] He said that the henequen problem in its economic and social dimensions can only be resolved in the broader context of Yucatán's integral development based on diversification. He affirmed that the state's growth should be designed and executed by Yucatecans. "We have experienced vicious situations involving paternalism, centralization, and domination by federal officials and the absence of responsibility by Yucatecans," he said, and promised that this situation will change. "Our system," he continued, "rests on the premise that the federal union is strong to the degree that its parts are strong." The focus on Yucatán's integral development, including the solution of the henequen problem, should in de la Madrid's view, be based on the fundamental principle that the Yucatecans take responsibility for the problems of their state, and that the federal government assist and back their efforts. In support of the state's economic diversification program, he pledged 55 billion pesos of federal funds for 1984.

As a practical manifestation of his position, the president announced his decision to place in the hands of Yucatán's governor the supervision of all henequen operations, including authority over the Henequen Trust Fund and Cordemex's board of directors. De la Madrid also declared that the governor would head the new organization created to carry out the Integral Development Program for Yucatán.

9

Conclusions

▲▲▲

During a visit to Yucatán in 1977, President José López Portillo commented that agrarian reform there had failed to live up to its revolutionary promises, for, though it corrected some injustices, it did so inefficiently. What had started as a redistribution of wealth had become a distribution of misery.[1] In light of the results of the investigation of Yucatán's henequen industry by the authors of this volume, López Portillo's statement seems to be a fair assessment of more than four decades of agrarian reform and state activism in Yucatán. Both agrarian reform in the henequen zone and the formation of Cordemex were undertaken in the name of the henequen workers. Yet, the economic status of this group has changed little during the last four decades, despite the tens of millions of dollars that the federal government has invested in the henequen zone.

Yucatán's henequen industry is a classic example of how paternalistic government intervention in an economic activity can retard rather than advance development. It is difficult to imagine that the economic welfare of the 200,000 residents of the henequen zone would have been any lower in the absence of government intervention. This is not to suggest that Mexican presidents after Cárdenas have consciously fostered the underdevelopment and marginalization of henequen workers and their families. In Yucatán, however, as in other parts of Mexico, the political objectives of the dominant party are perceived by the leadership to conflict with the creation of an economically independent peasantry. Economic independence may be a precondition for independent political organization. And, according to Pablo González Casanova,

> the pact demands that it (the marginal population) not be touched, that it not be organized by either the friends or, even less, the enemies of the government; that it be left the way it

is without organizations, without effective public rights, in a silent and supplicating attitude and utterly dependent upon the nation's leaders.[2]

The corruption-ridden and inefficient production structure in Yucatán's henequen zone is the outcome of more than four decades of manipulative, as opposed to participative, politics. What then are the prospects for positive change? The present political and economic power structure of the nation is not conducive to a rapid and meaningful political assimilation of its marginal rural population. Economic realities, however, may prove to be an effective wedge for productive change in the countryside. The stagnation of production in the agricultural sector since the mid-1960s is increasingly perceived as the most serious drag on Mexican growth. The billions of dollars poured into the countryside through the Mexican Food System Program (SAM) during the last three years of the López Portillo administration are concrete testimony to the central place that the resumption of adequate rates of growth of agricultural production occupies in any development strategy.

To increase governmental expenditures on the agricultural sector without stimulating meaningful change in production organization and land-tenure arrangements will probably not produce the desired results. Many critics of Mexican agricultural policy view an overhauling of the existing land-tenure system and government agricultural pricing policies as being crucial to the establishment of a modern and productive agricultural sector. A major conclusion of the authors' analysis of the henequen industry is that the rigidity of agrarian reform legislation is a central problem of Yucatán's henequen industry, as well as much of the rest of Mexican agriculture.

The ejidatario cannot legally transfer or mortgage his land. He, therefore, possesses neither the incentive nor the means to improve it. This has meant that almost 100 percent of the investment in improving agricultural land in Mexico has been made or financed by the federal government. The collective organization of production in the henequen zone has placed even more restrictions on the ejidatario. Because he does not possess the right to a specific identifiable parcel of land, he is obligated to abide by the production decisions of the collective. These decisions are made by the federal government through its control over production financing. The ejidatario's choice is a simple one. He must devote his land to henequen production or sacrifice his ejido rights. To enjoy the benefits of land reform is to devote one's working life to back-breaking, unskilled labor that does not even provide bare subsistence for one's family. The present system, in reality, is little different from the one that prevailed at the turn of the century. The campesino's dependence upon the federal government is no less debilitating than his ancestor's dependence on the hacendado.

The guaranteed wage, health insurance, and retirement benefits that have been extended to the henequen ejidatario raise the opportunity cost of leaving the ejido and, therefore, contribute to the immobility and underdevelopment of the henequen-zone population. Agrarian reform in Yucatán has restricted the economic alternatives of the ejidatario instead of expanding them.

The nationalization of Cordemex by the federal government further circumscribed his alternatives, for he is required to sell his fiber to the public cordage monopoly. The ejidatario, thus, possesses no control over the way his land is used nor over the destination of the product of his land and labor. His mobility is restricted by governmental subsidy and he, as part of the collective, is indebted to Banrural throughout his life. The fruits of his labor are appropriated and enjoyed by a few hundred federal employees and officials and a few thousand cordage workers who receive above-market wages. To view the structure of production today as substantially better than that of the plantation era is to have fallen victim to revolutionary rhetoric and to ignore reality.

Any solution to the problems involves expanding the economic alternatives of all participants in both the agricultural and industrial sectors of the henequen industry. This necessarily implies a reorientation of the federal government's role. The ejidatario should be allowed to sell, transfer, or mortgage his ejido right as well as to decide what he produces on his land and the destination of the product. Were this to be the case, land in the henequen zone would be put to its most productive use. Henequen would be produced if it were cost-effective, and by the most efficient producers. Past decisions to restrict shipments of raw fiber out of the state and out of the country have provided a disincentive to producers and have sustained the existence of the inefficient and reportedly corrupt government cordage monopoly.

Critics of greater economic freedom for the campesino argue

that, in the absence of government protection, the henequen worker would again fall under the domination of the large land-owner. These critics, who represent the official view, believe that the behavior of the Mexican campesino differs fundamentally from that of the city dweller or the agricultural capitalist. This view derives from the unwarranted perception that the campesino is incapable of making intelligent, rational judgments in the marketplace and must, therefore, be led by the government in his own best interest. To deny the henequen workers official protection from real economic forces would—in this view—subject them to the likelihood of mass starvation or cause them to rage uncontrollably throughout the state, undermining the political status quo.

The suppression of economic choice by the government has not only impacted adversely on the henequen-zone population, but also on the state as a whole. Subsidies to henequen workers have impeded the orderly shift of human resources to nonhenequen activities. It may be asked, where would large numbers of uneducated and unskilled workers go? Most federal diversification programs in the henequen zone have discouraged migration to urban areas because of the perceived inability of industries there to absorb the increased labor force productively. In the case of the henequen workers, however, staying in their fields deprives them of the opportunity to gain skills, to enjoy access to education, and to adjust to the rhythm of modern industrial activity.

Any realistic long-term economic solution also necessarily involves radical changes in both raw fiber and cordage production. World hard fiber market trends dictate that a substantial proportion of the resources employed in the cordage industry must be withdrawn and engaged in more productive economic activities. At current production levels, raw-fiber production in Yucatán can only support 20,000 to 30,000 full-time workers. The Mexican government's answer to underemployment in the henequen zone since the "cleansing of the rolls" (depuración) has been to foster and fund diversification programs, while maintaining employment stable in the henequen industry. The federal government has increased support for nonhenequen activities without withdrawing support from marginal and inefficient henequen production units.

This strategy suffers from several deficiencies. First, it provides no incentive for an increase in efficiency in henequen production.

Second, the diversification programs have been poorly planned and administered and, therefore, offer only limited prospects for any permanent change in productive employment in the henequen zone. Aside from the administrative and technical deficiencies, two other serious obstacles hamper the present diversification program. First, the ejidatarios have been dependent upon the federal government for so long that they consider themselves employees rather than clients of Banrural. This perception often stifles initiative and gives rise to antiproductive behavior on their part. It has not been uncommon, for example, for ejidatarios enrolled in a pork- or beef-raising program to sell the animal feed they are provided or to consume the breeding stock. Second, imperfections in the organization of local markets make it difficult for the individual campesino to sell his product at a profitable price. If he is a recipient of official bank credit and the bank markets his production, the situation improves little because he may have only a vague notion of his return. Isolated success stories in the countryside seem to suggest that the best way to stimulate diversified activities is to put the campesino directly in touch with the market rather than insulating him from it.

Ejidatarios should be weaned away from the present system rather than further tied to it. Diversification activities should be encouraged, but only to the extent they are economically feasible within the constraints of the market. Ejidatarios must not be transferred from one corruption-ridden and subsidized system to another. To ease the transition, the government should provide some form of subsidy to the campesino, but to him directly, and not under the pretense of production credit. If diversification is to succeed, the government must minimize restrictions and red tape on export industries. Both export-oriented agriculture and labor-intensive *maquila* (assembly plants), which have been successful on Mexico's northern border, offer promising opportunities and should be encouraged.

Governmental support of both fiber and cordage production, as well as of diversification activities, should be facilitative but not overtly interventionist. Federally directed, large-scale agricultural diversification projects—notably "Santa Rosa" and "Dzonot Carretero"—have been costly failures. As was shown in chapter 8, the federal government has facilitated Yucatán's economic diversification in the recent past through investment in its infrastructure, including highways and roads, electricity, telecommunications, irrigation, and a sheltered commercial-fishing port near Progreso. Compared with 1970, the state's current economic profile reflects a diminished dependency upon the henequen industry, both as a source of employment and of income. Tourism has emerged since 1980 as the preeminent source of state income, exceeding the sales of Cordemex. Although henequen-fiber production continues to engage (at least part time) about half the state's campesinos, the agricultural sector has achieved impressive diversification, particularly through the expansion of livestock production. Commercial fishing, of negligible importance two decades ago, has become the major source of employment and income for the numerous communities lying along the peninsula's northern coast.

Industrial diversification has accelerated since the mid-1970s, responding to growing demand for such items as cement, light steel products, shoes, animal feeds, marine products, building materials, and beverages. Newly organized, modern industrial enterprises have increasingly located in metropolitan Mérida, an urbanized regional center of more than 400,000 inhabitants, whose market reach for manufactured goods extends beyond Yucatán and the peninsula to the new oil-rich states of Tabasco and Chiapas.

The technology utilized in the production of raw henequen fiber has remained essentially unchanged for more than a century. Research that has been done suggests that more intensive plantings, the use of herbicides and fertilizers, and the partial mechanization of the leaf-harvesting function can lower costs and increase productivity.[3] Such changes, if widespread, could permit the industry to regain its competitive footing in the domestic and world markets, as well as provide those henequen workers that remained in the industry a higher standard of living. To argue that it is irrational to increase the mechanization of industry because labor is relatively abundant is specious. Conventional methods of performing field tasks inhibit the possibility for raising the incomes or skill levels of the population in the henequen zone.

During his official visit to Yucatán in May 1984, President de la Madrid announced his decision to place in the hands of the governor all henequen operations, including authority over Cordemex. His policy orientation toward the state responds in part to the exigencies of carrying out the austere IMF-mandated adjustment program, but it also reflects his own political philosophy that the nation's future is best served through broader economic decentralization.

After having achieved some initial success in its adjustment program, Mexico failed to meet inflation and public deficit targets for 1984. Consequently, the federal government signed its 1985 letter of intent with the IMF by agreeing to contain public spending further than originally planned and to exert stronger budgetary control over public enterprises. Furthermore, in February 1985 the president announced his government's decision to liquidate, consolidate, sell, or transfer a total of 236 parastatal entities as part of a process to concentrate federal efforts on high-priority and strategic activities.[4] Among those entities scheduled for liquidation is a long list of enterprises, including sugar mills, textile plants, food-products companies, and real-estate agencies. Among those to be sold are eight film companies in which the federal government holds a minority interest and a large number of tourist hotels. The seven public enterprises designed for transfer to state governments, including Cordemex, are those whose regional or local impact is strong.

The de la Madrid administration's policies toward public enterprises and the states mark a de facto trend reversal since the revolution. What is not at all clear is the posture of future Mexican presidents regarding the optimal public-private organizational mix and the proper federal-state relationship.

Based upon the past performance of Cordemex, a strong case can be made for returning Yucatán's cordage industry to private ownership or, as a second-best solution, greatly reducing official involvement in it. Unless the firm's management can be disassociated from the PRI-dominated political system—an unlikely possibility even under the aegis of the state government— no basis exists for assuming that a smaller-scale cordage manufacturing complex under public control would be better managed than the current large one.

From the perspective of four decades of losses and scandals, the henequen industry's future should meet the market test, both at home and abroad. A strategic withdrawal of government, both federal and state, from the industry would finally allow Yucatecans to put behind them the protracted "henequen malaise" and to seek new, more promising, economic horizons.

Notes

▲▲▲▲▲▲▲▲▲▲▲▲▲▲▲▲▲▲▲▲▲▲▲▲▲▲▲▲▲▲▲▲▲▲▲▲▲

Chapter 1

1. Nelson Reed, *The Caste War of Yucatán* (Stanford: Stanford University Press, 1964), p. 232.

2. El Colegio de Mexico, *Fuerza de trabajo y actividad económica por sectores*, pp. 45–60, cited in Laura Randall, *A Comparative Economic History of Latin America, 1500–1914*, vol. 1, *Mexico* (Ann Arbor, Mich.: University Microfilms International, 1977), p. 251, table 5–15.

3. The leaves, or *pencas*, of the henequen plant, which is indigenous to Yucatán, produce a natural fiber that is used to elaborate harvest twine, ropes and cables, sacks, and similar articles.

4. Ejidos can be formed by Mexican villages (*pueblo ejido*) or by the population of a former hacienda (*acasillado ejido*). Most ejido lands are worked individually rather than collectively. The henequen ejidos in Yucatán were organized into collective units to take advantage of the existing economies of scale in production. The Mexican ejido has antecedents in both Spain and preconquest Mexico. Eyler N. Simpson, *The Ejido: Mexico's Way Out* (Chapel Hill: University of North Carolina Press, 1937), pp. 11–14.

5. Roland E. P. Chardon, *Geographic Aspects of Plantation Agriculture in Yucatán*, NAS-NCR Publication 876 (Washington, D.C.: National Academy of Sciences-National Research Council, 1961).

6. Carlos Tappan de Arrigunaga, "Trade, Development, and Structural Change: The Future of Mexico's Henequen Industry" (Ph.D. dissertation, Texas A&M University, 1971).

7. Nathaniel C. Raymond, "The Impact of Land Reform in the Monocrop Region of Yucatán, Mexico" (Ph.D. dissertation, Brandeis University, 1971); Antonio Rodríguez, *El henequen: Una planta calumniada* (México, D.F.: Costa Amic, 1966); Malcolm

Shuman, "The Town Where Luck Fell: The Economics of Life in a Henequen Zone Pueblo," (Ph.D. dissertation, Tulane University, 1974).

8. For a review of the issues raised in recent studies by critics of Mexican economic policy, see Jeff Brannon, "Mexican Agriculture in the 1980s: A Review Essay," *South Eastern Latin Americanist* 27 (1): 19–22; and James W. Wessman, "The Agrarian Question in Mexico," *Latin American Research Review* 19 (2): 243–259.

9. Gustavo Esteva, *The Battle for Rural Mexico* (South Hadley, Mass.: Bergin and Garvey Publishers, 1983), p. 7.

10. Jorge Madrazo, "A Discussion of Constitutional Rights Regarding Property in Mexico," *The Mexican Forum* 3 (4): 18.

11. Esteva, *The Battle*, pp. 30, 50.

12. John Mogab, "The Mexican Experience in Peasant Agricultural Credit," *Development and Change* 15 (2) (1984): 205–207.

13. Esteva, *The Battle*, pp. 35–36.

14. A. V. Chayanov, *The Theory of Peasant Economy*, ed. Daniel Thorner, Basile Kerblay, and R. E. F. Smith (Homewood, Ill.: Richard D. Irwin, 1966).

15. Ibid., p. 6.

16. The following description of the behavior of the Mexican campesino leans heavily on Comisión Económica para la America Latina (CEPAL), *Economía campesina y agricultura empresarial* (México, D.F.: Siglo Veintiuno Editores, 1982), pp. 60–91, which represents the views of that segment of the Mexican historical materialists who are labeled as campesinistas.

17. Esteva, *The Battle*, p. 54.

18. For analyses of the debate between the campesinistas and descampesinistas, see Ann Lucas, "El debate sobre los campesinos y el capitalismo en México," *Comercio exterior* 32 (April 1982): 371–383; and CEPAL, *Economía campesina*, pp. 48–59.

19. Alejandro Shejtman, "El agro mexicano y sus interpretes," *Nexos* (March 1981): 37–47.

20. P. Lamartine Yates, *Mexico's Agricultural Dilemma* (Tucson: University of Arizona Press, 1981).

21. Robert H. Bates, using evidence from Africa, argues that the utopian natural community of the peasant probably never existed. Further, he hypothesizes that the organization of native rural society is as much a consequence of the state's efforts to establish political control over the population as it is an outcome of the

penetration of market forces. Bates, "Some Conventional Or-thodoxies in the Study of Agrarian Change," *World Politics* 36 (2): 234–254.

22. For a fairly representative sample of populist-campesinista policy prescriptions, see Rodolfo Stavenhagen, *Problemas étnicos y campesinos* (México, D. F.: Instituto Nacional Indigenista, 1979), pp. 138–141. Also see Esteva, *The Battle*, pp. 221–235; and CEPAL, *Economía campesina*, pp. 233–274.

23. Yates, *Mexico's Agricultural Dilemma*.

24. Arturo Warman, "Frente a la crisis ¿política agraria o po-lítica agrícola?" in Warman, *Ensayos sobre el campesinado en México* (Mexico, D.F.: Editorial Nueva Imagen, 1980), pp. 85–108.

25. See Roger D. Hansen, *The Politics of Mexican Development* (Baltimore: Johns Hopkins University Press, 1971). Also see Esteva, *The Battle*, pp. 73–93; Stavenhagen, *Problemas étnicos*, 102–143; and Mogab "The Mexican Experience."

26. Arturo Warman, "La colectivización en el campo: Una crítica," in Warman, *Ensayos sobre el campesinado*, pp. 61–83.

27. Rodolfo Stavenhagen, "Collective Agriculture and Capi-talism in Mexico: A Way Out or a Dead End?" *Latin American Perspectives* 2 (2): 146–163.

28. Peter Singelmann, "Rural Collectivization and Dependent Capitalism: The Mexican Collective Ejido," *Latin American Per-spectives* 5 (3): 39.

29. See David Barkin and Blanca Suárez, *El fin de la autosufi-ciencia* (México, D.F.: Editorial Nueva Imagen, 1982).

30. Arturo Warman, "Los campesinos y el estado," in Warman, *Ensayos sobre el campesinado*, pp. 142–144.

31. Esteva, *The Battle*, p. 89

32. Ibid., p. 143.

33. Warman, "Frente a la crisis," p. 91.

34. Robert Patch, "Apuntes acerca de los orígenes y las carac-terísticas de la hacienda henequenera en Yucatán," *Yucatán: His-toria y economía* 9 (September–October 1978): 12–15.

35. For an analysis and description of the characteristics of the traditional hacienda, see Sidney W. Mintz and Eric R. Wolf, "Haciendas and Plantations in Middle America and the Antilles," *Social and Economic Studies* 6 (September 1957): 380–412.

Chapter 2

1. Secretaría de Programación y Presupuesto, *X censo general de población y vivienda* (México, D.F., 1981).

2. Eugene M. Wilson, "Physical Geography of the Yucatán Peninsula," in *Yucatán, A World Apart,* ed. Edward H. Moseley and Edward D. Terry (University, Ala.: University of Alabama Press, 1980), p. 25.

3. Annual precipitation may vary as much as 30 percent from the long-term average. Ibid.

4. The peninsula is a porous limestone platform. At least 80 percent of the annual precipitation filters through the surface into natural reservoirs, which are today the major sources of fresh water for public consumption and irrigation in Yucatán. Until quite recently, *cenotes,* or natural wells, which formed in areas where the limestone had collapsed and exposed the water table, were the most dependable source of water in the region and a major determinant of settlement patterns. Nelson Reed, *The Caste War of Yucatán* (Stanford: Stanford University Press, 1964), pp. 35–41.

5. "La madera en Yucatán," *Diario de Yucatán,* 24 July 1977.

6. John L. Stephens, *Incidents of Travel in Central America, Chiapas, and Yucatán,* 2 vols. (New Brunswick, N.J.: Rutgers University Press, 1949); idem, *Incidents of Travel in Yucatán,* 2 vols. (Norman: University of Oklahoma Press, 1962).

7. Robert Redfield, *The Folk Culture of Yucatán* (Chicago: University of Illinois Press, 1941), p. 1.

8. In 1928 Dr. Eulogio Salazar Ramírez traveled from Acanceh, a village south of Mérida, to Mexico City, a distance of 1,700 kilometers, on horseback. This overland trip, which took forty-five days, was considered such an accomplishment that fiestas in his honor continued for three days after his arrival in the capital. "A 50 años de distancia, D. Eulogio Salazar relata su arriesgado viaje a caballo de Mérida a la Metropoli," *Diario de Yucatán,* 16 July 1978.

9. Gobierno del Estado de Yucatán, *Estudio económico de Yucatán y programa de trabajo* (Mérida, 1960), p. 411.

10. Gabriel Ferrer de Mendiolea, "Historia de las comunicaciones," in *Enciclopedia yucatanense,* vol. 3, ed. Carlos A. Echanove Trujillo (México, D.F.: Edición Oficial, 1946), pp. 597–598;

Keith Hartman, "The Henequen Empire in Yucatán, 1870–1910" (Master's thesis, University of Iowa, 1966), p. 51.

11. Sherburne F. Cook and Woodrow Borah, "The Population of Yucatán, 1517–1960," in Cook and Borah, *Essays in Population History: Mexico and the Caribbean*, 2 vols. (Berkeley: University of California Press, 1974), 1:76–77.

12. The hacienda was preceded by the *estancia* in Yucatán. The *estancia* was primarily an economic unit to which were assigned only a few resident workers (*peones acasillados*), whose main activity was the production of beef for local markets; the hacienda produced agricultural products as well as cattle and its resident population was much larger. Robert Patch, *La formación de estancias y haciendas en Yucatán durante la colonia* (Mérida: Ediciones de la Universidad de Yucatán, 1976), pp. 5, 37–38.

13. Arnold Strickon, "Hacienda and Plantation in Yucatán," *América Indígena* 21 (January 1965): 43–46.

14. Patch, *La formación de estancias y haciendas*, p. 38.

15. Sidney W. Mintz and Eric R. Wolf, "Haciendas and Plantations in Middle America and the Antilles," *Social and Economic Studies* 6 (September 1957): 386–388.

16. Strickon, "Hacienda and Plantation," pp. 47–48; Patch, *La formación de estancias y haciendas*, p. 31.

17. Gonzalo Cámara Zavala, "Historia de la industria henequenera hasta 1919," *Enciclopedia yucatanense*, vol. 3, ed. Carlos A. Echanove Trujillo (México, D.F.: Edición Oficial, 1946), p. 676.

18. Howard F. Cline, "The 'Aurora Yucateca' and the Spirit of Enterprise in Yucatán, 1821–1847," *The Hispanic American Historical Review* 27 (February 1947): 57.

19. Ferrer de Mendiolea, "Historia de las comunicaciones," p. 522.

20. José Ma. de Calzadilla et al., *Apuntaciones para las estadísticas de Yucatán del ano de 1814* (Mérida: J. D. Espinosa e Hijos, 1871; reprint ed. Mérida: Ediciones del Gobierno del Estado de Yucatán, 1977), p. 37.

21. Reed, *The Caste War*, p. 17.

22. Howard F. Cline, "The Sugar Episode in Yucatán: 1825–1850," *Inter-American Economic Affairs* I (March 1948): 79–80, 91.

23. Gilbert M. Joseph, *Revolution from Without* (Cambridge, Mass.: Cambridge University Press, 1982), p. 15.

24. Edward H. Moseley, "From Conquest to Independence:

Yucatán under Spanish Rule, 1521–1821," in *Yucatán, A World Apart*, pp. 106–107.
25. Cline, "The 'Aurora Yucateca,'" p. 32.
26. Idem, "The Sugar Episode," p. 79.
27. Idem, "The 'Aurora Yucateca,'" pp. 31–41.
28. Ibid., p. 59.
29. Cline, "The Sugar Episode," p. 91.
30. Ibid., p. 90.
31. Victor M. Suárez Molina, *La evolución económica de Yucatán*, vol. 2 (México, D.F.: La Universidad de Yucatán, 1977), p. 150.
32. Cline, "The Sugar Episode," p. 91; Idem, "The 'Aurora Yucateca,'" p. 57.
33. Strickon, "Hacienda and Plantation", p. 47.
34. Reed, *The Caste War*, p. 11. Also see Margarita Rosales González, "Etapas en el desarollo regional del Puuc, Yucatán," *Yucatán: Historia y economía* 18 (March–April 1980): 41–43.
35. Reed, *The Caste War*, p. 18.
36. Patch, *La formación de estancias y haciendas*, pp. 39–41.
37. Howard F. Cline, "The Henequen Episode in Yucatán," *Inter-American Economic Affairs* 2 (Autumn 1948): 37–38.
38. See Moisés González Navarro, *Raza y tierra: La Guerra de Castas y el henequen* (México, D.F.: El Colegio de México, 1970), for a good description of debt peonage in postindependence Yucatán.
39. Reed, *The Caste War*, p. 8; Cline, "The 'Aurora Yucateca,'" p. 59.
40. González Navarro, *Raza y tierra*, p. 180.
41. Roland E. P. Chardon, *Geographic Aspects of Plantation Agriculture in Yucatán*, NAS-NCR Publication 876 (Washington, D.C.: National Academy of Sciences-National Research Council, 1961), p. 23.
42. Reed, *The Caste War*, p. 85.
43. Victor M. Suárez Molina, *La evolución económica de Yucatán*, vol. 1 (México, D.F.: La Universidad de Yucatán, 1977), p. 219.
44. González Navarro, *Raza y tierra*, p. 182.
45. Cámara Zavala, "Historia de la industria henequenera," 3:681–682.
46. Suárez Molina, *La evolución económica*, 1:48–50.
47. Ibid., p. 49.

48. Renán Irigoyen, "¿Fué el auge del henequen producto de la Guerra de Castas?" in Irigoyen, *Ensayos henequeneros* (Mérida: Ediciones de Cordemex, 1975), p. 20.
49. González Navarro, *Raza y tierra*, p. 182.
50. Suárez Molina, *La evolución económica*, 1:137–144.
51. Irigoyen, "¿Fué el auge," pp. 5–44.

Chapter 3

1. Roland E. P. Chardon, *Geographic Aspects of Plantation Agriculture in Yucatán*, NAS-NRC Publication 876 (Washington, D.C.: National Academy of Sciences-National Research Council, 1961), p. 160.
2. Howard F. Cline, "The 'Aurora Yucateca' and the Spirit of Enterprise in Yucatán, 1821–1847," *The Hispanic American Historical Review* 27 (February 1947): 30–60.
3. Renán Irigoyen, "¿Fué el auge del henequen producto de la Guerra de Castas?" in Irigoyen, *Ensayos henequeneros* (Mérida: Ediciones de Cordemex, 1975), p. 25.
4. José Luis Sierra V., "Hacia una economía política de la hacienda henequenera: Primera parte, los hacendados," *Yucatán: Historia y economía* 17 (January–February 1980): 59.
5. Allen Wells, *Yucatán's Gilded Age: Haciendas, Henequen, and International Harvester, 1860–1915* (Albuquerque: University of New Mexico Press, forthcoming), chapter 5.
6. See Alejandra García Quintanilla, "Historia y etapas de la producción de una mercancia," *Yucatán: Historia y economía* 26 (July–August 1981): 3–22, for a discussion of the difficulties that hacendados encountered in trying to convert their haciendas to commercial henequen plantations in the capital-scarce environment of post-Caste War Yucatán.
7. Gilbert M. Joseph, *Revolution from Without* (Cambridge: Cambridge University Press, 1982), p. 29.
8. Thebaud Brothers was not a North American financial institution but a commercial house that borrowed from U.S. banks to establish credit facilities for Yucatecan planters through local export agents. See Raquel Barceló Quintal, "El desarollo de la banca y el henequen," *Yucatán: Historia y economía* 29 (January–February 1982): 4–5.
9. Chardon, *Geographic Aspects*, p. 31.

10. Keith Hartman, "The Henequen Empire in Yucatán, 1870–1910" (Master's thesis, University of Iowa, 1966), p. 51.

11. For an extensive discussion of the economics and politics of railroad building in late-nineteenth-century Yucatán, see Raquel Barceló Quintal, "El ferrocarril y la oligarquía hene-quenera," *Yucatán: Historia y economía* 26 (July–August 1981): 23–54; and Allen Wells, "Economic Growth and Regional Dispar-ity in Porfirian Yucatán: The Case of the Southeastern Railway Company," *South Eastern Latin Americanist* 22 (2): 1–16.

12. Joseph, *Revolution from Without*, p. 34.

13. Until the beginning of the nineteenth century, henequen fiber had only one competitor: abaca *(Musa textilis)* from the Philippines. Cultivation of sisal *(Agave sisalana)* was begun in earnest in Africa, Asia, and other parts of Latin America during the last decade of the nineteenth century. Although abaca and sisal are superior to henequen in some uses, the three hard fibers are competitive with one another in the production of binder twine.

14. Enrique Aznar Mendoza, "La industria henequenera desde 1919 hasta nuestros días," *Enciclopedia yucatanense*, vol. 3, ed. Carlos A. Enchanove Trujillo (México, D.F.: Edición Oficial, 1946), pp. 778–780.

15. Esther Iglesias, "Yucatán, monocultivo, oro verde, y deca-dencia henequenera: La región y dependencia del mercado nor-teamericano," (Paper presented at the *Primer encuentro sobre impactos regionales de las relaciones económicas México-Estados Unidos*, Guanajuato, Mexico, 1981), p. 6.

16. The *Ley Lerdo*, a law promulgated in 1856, prohibited religious foundations and civic communities from owning real property. The major purposes of the law were to destroy the economic power of the Roman Catholic Church in Mexico and to create a new class of small landowners. Díaz and his followers used this law to dispossess Mexico's Indians of their remaining communally held lands. Lesley Byrd Simpson, *Many Mexicos*, rev. 4th ed. (Berkeley: University of California Press, 1969), pp. 273, 293.

17. A. J. Graham Knox, "Henequen Haciendas, Maya Peones, and the Mexican Revolution Promises of 1910: Reform and Reac-tion in Yucatán, 1910–1940," *Caribbean Studies* 17 (April–July, 1977): 64.

18. Victor M. Suárez Molina, *La evolución económica de*

Yucatán, vol. 2 (México, D.F.: La Universidad de Yucatán, 1977), pp. 70–71.

19. Chardon, *Geographic Aspects*, p. 33.

20. Gilbert M. Joseph and Allen Wells, "Corporate Control of a Monocrop Economy: International Harvester and Yucatán's Henequen Industry during the Porfiriato," *Latin American Research Review* 17 (1): 77.

21. Salvador Rodríguez Losa, *La población de los municipios del estado de Yucatán* (Mérida: Ediciones del Gobierno del Estado de Yucatán, 1977).

22. David A. Franz, "Bullets and Bolshevists: A History of the Mexican Revolution and Reform in Yucatán, 1910–1924" (Ph.D. dissertation, University of New Mexico, 1973), p. 18.

23. Sierra V., "Hacia una economía política," p. 61.

24. Eric N. Baklanoff, "The Diversification Quest: A Monocrop Export Economy in Transition," in *Yucatán, A World Apart*, ed. Edward H. Moseley and Edward D. Terry (University, Ala.: University of Alabama Press, 1980), p. 209.

25. Joseph and Wells, "Corporate Control," p. 71.

26. Joseph, *Revolution from Without*, p. 59.

27. Joseph and Wells, "Corporate Control," pp. 84–85.

28. The essential arguments in the ongoing debate over International Harvester's involvement in Yucatán are presented in the following works: Joseph and Wells, "Corporate Control"; Joseph, *Revolution from Without*, chapter 2; Wells, *Yucatán's Gilded Age*, chapter 2; Thomas Benjamin, "International Harvester and the Henequen Marketing System in Yucatán, 1898–1915: A New Perspective," *Inter-American Economic Affairs* 31 (Winter 1977): 3–19. Also see Jeffery Brannon and Eric N. Baklanoff, "Corporate Control of a Monocrop Economy: A Comment"; Fred V. Carstensen and Diane Roazen-Parillo, "International Harvester, Molina y Compañia, and the Henequen Market: A Comment"; Gilbert M. Joseph and Allen Wells, "Collaboration and Informal Empire in Yucatán: The Case for Political Economy." All the above are found in *Latin American Research Review* 18 (3): 193–218.

29. See Benjamin, "International Harvester and the Henequen Marketing System, pp. 7–8, 17–18.

30. Reguladora had been created in 1912 to increase low prices through the valorization of raw fiber.

31. Aznar Mendoza, "La industria henequenera," pp. 778–780.

32. Joseph, *Revolution from Without*, p. 142.

33. Although sisal plantings in Java and Africa were made from Yucatecan henequen plants, different soil conditions and climatic factors give sisal an advantage over henequen in some uses. In addition, sisal has a shorter cycle from planting to first harvest, which makes its price elasticity somewhat greater than henequen's.

34. Aznar Mendoza, "La industria henequenera," p. 740.

35. Ibid., p. 765.

36. Ibid., pp. 778–780.

37. Moisés González Navarro, *Raza y tierra: La Guerra de Castas y el henequen* (México, D.F.: El Colegio de México, 1970), p. 254.

38. González Navarro, *Raza y tierra*, p. 180; Cline, "The 'Aurora Yucateca,'" p. 59.

39. Suárez Molina, *La evolución económica*, 1:147; idem, *La evolución económica*, 2:28.

40. See Douglass C. North, "Agriculture in Regional Economic Growth," *Journal of Farm Economics* 69 (1959): 943–951; and Douglass C. North, *The Economic Growth of the United States, 1790–1860* (New York: W. W. Norton and Co., 1966). A statement of the basic tenets of the staple theory as well as some evidence that supports its conclusions can be found in Melville Watkins, "A Staple Theory of Economic Growth," in *Readings in Economic Development*, ed. Walter L. Johnson and David R. Kamerschen (Cincinnati: Southwest Publishing Co., 1972), pp. 458–476.

41. Albert Hirschman, *The Strategy of Economic Development* (New Haven, Conn.: Yale University Press, 1958), pp. 106–110.

42. See William Alonso, "Industrial Location and Regional Policy in Economic Development," in *Regional Policy*, ed. John Friedmann and William Alonso (Cambridge, Mass.: MIT Press, 1975), pp. 64–96; and John Friedmann, *Regional Development Policy: A Case Study of Venezuela* (Cambridge, Mass.: MIT Press, 1966), pp. 14–16.

43. Chardon, *Geographic Aspects*, pp. 28–29.

44. Joseph, *Revolution from Without*, p. 63.

45. Hartman, "The Henequen Empire," p. 109.

46. Joseph, *Revolution from Without*, pp. 64, 167.

47. For a more detailed discussion of the evolution of the machine industry in Yucatán, see Eric N. Baklanoff and Jeffery

Brannon, "Forward and Backward Linkages in a Plantation Economy: Immigrant Entrepreneurship and Industrial Development in Yucatán, Mexico," *The Journal of Developing Areas* 19 (1) (October 1984): 83–94.

48. "Talleres mecánicos y de fundición de Mérida en el siglo XIX," *Diario de Yucatán*, 13 March 1977; Suárez Molina, *La evolución económica*, 1:268–271.

49. Baklanoff and Brannon, "Forward and Backward Linkages," p. 14.

50. An extensive discussion of the growth of local financial institutions is presented in Barceló Quintal, "El desarollo de la banca," pp. 3–24.

51. Joseph, *Revolution from Without*, p. 32.

52. See R. E. Baldwin, "Patterns of Development in Newly Settled Regions," *The Manchester School of Economic and Social Studies* 24 (May 1956): 161–179.

53. See Wells, *Yucatán's Gilded Age*, chapter 6, for a discussion of wages and living conditions on the henequen haciendas.

54. Suárez Molina, *La evolución económica*, 1:51.

55. See María Cáceres Menéndez and María Loret de Mola, *La migración libanesa a Yucatán* (Mérida: La Universidad de Yucatán, 1977); and Baklanoff and Brannon, "Forward and Backward Linkages."

56. See Allen Wells, "Family Elites in a Boom-and-Bust Economy: The Molinas and Peons of Porfirian Yucatán," *Hispanic American Historical Review* 62 (May 1982): 224–253.

57. Franz, "Bullets and Bolshevists," pp. 116–117.

58. Joseph, *Revolution from Without*, pp. 125–130.

59. Ibid., pp. 260–262.

60. Although Alvarado did not favor the large-scale expropriation of henequen properties, he apparently did feel that the small group of great hacendados had to be destroyed. Ibid., pp. 127–128.

61. Eyler N. Simpson, *The Ejido: Mexico's Way Out* (Chapel Hill: University of North Carolina Press, 1937), pp. 611, 625.

62. Nathaniel C. Raymond, "The Impact of Land Reform in the Monocrop Region of Yucatán, Mexico" (Ph.D. dissertation, Brandeis University, 1971), p. 7; Simpson, *The Ejido*, p. 607.

63. Raymond, "The Impact of Land Reform," p. 114.

64. The proposal contained the following provisions: (1) give each ejidatario eight hectares from public lands to be used for cultivation of henequen; (2) give ejidatarios collectively eight

haciendas complete with equipment for rasping and packing; and (3) give the ejidatarios collectively seven million pesos (from hacendados) to be used as working capital.

65. Antonio Rodríguez, *El henequen: Una planta calumniada* (México, D.F.: Costa Amic, 1966), p. 259.

66. Armour Research Foundation of Illinois Institute of Technology, *Technological Audit of Selected Mexican Industries with Industrial Research Recommendations* (Ann Arbor: Edward Brothers, 1946), p. 86; Jorge Tomás Vera Pren, "La industria henequenera en la perspectiva histórica," *Yucatán: Historia y economía* 35 (January–February 1983): 30.

67. Gonzalo Cámara Zavala, "Historia de la industria henequenera hasta 1919," *Enciclopedia yucatanense*, vol. 3, ed. Carlos A. Echanove Trujillo (México, D.F.: Edición Oficial, 1946), p. 760.

68. As stated in chapter 1, the Cárdenas administration organized more than 5,000 collective ejido production units between 1935 and 1940. Interestingly, he made mistakes similar to those made in Yucatán during the massive redistribution in La Laguna. In light of the organizational problems experienced in Yucatán and La Laguna, it could be surmised that the dismantling of the collective program nationwide after 1940 was at least partially attributable to the Cárdenas administration's own errors in the organizational phase, which made many of those ejidos expensive wards of the federal government. For the experience of La Laguna, see Rodolfo Stavenhagen, *Problemas étnicos y campesinos* (México, D.F.: Instituto Nacional Indigenista, 1979), pp. 115–122.

69. González Navarro, *Raza y tierra*, p. 275.

70. Rodríguez, *El henequen*, pp. 260, 267.

71. Output per hectare fell from 1,111 kilograms of fiber in 1937 to 806 kilograms the following year. Manuel Pasos Peniche, *Historia de la industria henequenera desde 1945 hasta nuestros días* (Mérida: Editorial "Zamna," 1974), pp. 53–54.

72. González Navarro, *Raza y tierra*, p. 259.

73. Aznar Mendoza, "La industria henequenera," 3:760–761.

74. Ibid., pp. 768–769.

75. Rodríguez, *El henequen*, pp. 280, 283.

Chapter 4

1. William P. Glade notes that "hacienda management (in Spanish America) was . . . noninnovative in character. Stable and limited markets, deficient transportation systems, the virtual absence of competition in input and output markets, the assured income and status position of the large landowners, and their ignorance of, and indifference to, productive processes were all forces which favored continuation of traditional and backward methods of organization and productive technique." Glade, *The Latin American Economies* (New York: Van Nostrand Reinhold, 1969), p. 129. Also see Sidney W. Mintz and Eric R. Wolf, "Haciendas and Plantations in Middle America and the Antilles," *Social and Economic Studies* 6 (September 1957): 380–412.

2. See Allen Wells, *Yucatán's Gilded Age: Haciendas, Henequen, and International Harvester, 1860–1915* (Albuquerque: University of New Mexico Press, forthcoming), chapter 6, for a discussion of real wages on the prereform haciendas.

3. A description and analysis of henequen cultivation is found in Jorge Tomás Vera Pren, "Labores agrícolas en las plantaciones henequeneras," *Yucatán: Historia y economía* 2 (July–August 1977): 32.

4. The Spanish-American War period provides a good example of the hacendados' investment psychology. The price of henequen fiber rose from $.0264 per pound in 1897 to a record price of $.0984 per pound in 1902 and remained above $.06 per pound until 1906. During this period of record prices, exports rose by only 25 percent because of the relative inelasticity of short-run supply (table 19). The high profits, however, stimulated the hacendados to bring unprecedented amounts of new land into cultivation between 1900 and 1905. So extensive were the new plantings that the hacendados were able to expand annual raw fiber output from 94,789 tons to 201,990 tons between 1910 and 1916 (table 1). Also see Thomas Benjamin, "International Harvester and the Henequen Marketing System in Yucatán, 1898–1915: A New Perspective," *Inter-American Economic Affairs* 31 (Winter 1977): 3–19.

5. Victor M. Suárez Molina, *La evolución económica de Yucatán*, vol. 1 (México, D.F.: La Universidad de Yucatán, 1977), pp. 151–153. Also see Wells, *Yucatán's Gilded Age*, chapter 5.

NOTES TO CHAPTER 4

6. Although fewer than three hundred ejidos were established in the henequen zone in 1937, legislation after 1955 allowed the formation of "economic" or "solidarity" groups of five or more ejidatarios, who were granted a semiautonomous status within the ejido. The fragmentation of Yucatán's ejidos had two basic objectives: (1) the government hoped that the creation of a large number of financially autonomous units would reduce the incidence of corruption; and (2) it was seen as a first step toward the long-term goal of assigning each ejidatario an individual parcel of land, i.e., to do away with the collective production of henequen. The change was also seen as a concession to politically influential members of the ejido who had been excluded from the administration of the ejido credit societies. Nathaniel C. Raymond, "The Impact of Land Reform in the Monocrop Region of Yucatán, Mexico" (Ph.D. dissertation, Brandeis University, 1971), p. 297. Jorge Tomás Vera Pren, "La industria henequenera en la perspectiva histórica," *Yucatán: Historia y economía* 35 (January–February 1983): 36.

7. For an interesting and perceptive analysis of the work of the Banco Nacional de Crédito Ejidal, Banrural's predecessor in the countryside, see John Mogab, "The Mexican Experience in Peasant Agricultural Credit," *Development and Change* 15 (2) (1984): 203–221.

8. Jorge Tomás Vera Pren, "Estructura de la industria henequenera en Yucatán," *Yucatán: Historia y economía* 36 (March–April 1983): 17.

9. Ibid., p. 22.

10. Salvador Rodríguez Losa, *La población de los municipios del estado de Yucatán* (Mérida: Ediciones del Gobierno del Estado, 1977).

11. Roland E. P. Chardon, *Geographic Aspects of Plantation Agriculture in Yucatán*, NAS-NCR Publications 876 (Washington, D.C.: National Academy of Sciences-National Research Council, 1961), p. 148.

12. The agricultural bank became the Banco de Crédito Rural Peninsular, S.A. (Banrural), in 1975. Before that date, it was known as the Banco Agrario de Yucatán, S.A. (Banco Agrario).

13. United Nations, Food and Agriculture Organization (FAO), *El henequen mexicano* (New York, 1968), p. 1.

14. Vera Pren, "Estructura de la industria henequenera," pp. 12, 17–20.

NOTES TO CHAPTER 4

15. Interview of Vincente Solís Aznar, at Mérida, Yucatán, by Brannon, on 6 June 1977.

16. A *mecate* is a twenty meter x twenty meter area, or one twenty-fifth of a hectare.

17. Carlos Tappan de Arrigunaga, "Trade, Development, and Structural Change: The Future of Mexico's Henequen Industry" (Ph.D. dissertation, Texas A&M University, 1971), p. 47.

18. "Desde hoy: más dinero para los parcelarios," *Diario de Yucatán*, 29 May 1977.

19. David A. Franz, "Bullets and Bolshevists: A History of the Mexican Revolution and Reform in Yucatán, 1910–1924" (Ph.D. dissertation, University of New Mexico, 1973), p. 295.

20. Raymond, "The Impact of Land Reform," p. 100.

21. Ibid.

22. Humberto Carranca Tomassi, *La industrialización del henequen en Yucatán* (México, D.F.: Banco de México, 1953), pp. 28–29, 98.

23. Ibid., p. 23.

24. Cordemex, *Henequen y sisal producción mundial* (Mérida: 1977).

25. Interview with Vincente Solís Aznar.

26. "Estado de la empresa cordelera," *Diario de Yucatán*, 16 January 1982.

27. Enzo R. Grilli, *The Future of Hard Fibers and Competition from Synthetics*, World Bank Occasional Staff Paper No. 19 (Baltimore: Johns Hopkins University Press, 1975), p. 91.

28. The recovery rate of Banco Agrario was far worse than that of the major lender to Mexico's ejidos. During the period 1952–70 the Banco Nacional de Crédito Ejidal had a repayment rate of almost 75 percent. Mogab, "The Mexican Experience," p. 214.

29. Laureano Cardos Ruz, *El drama de los Mayas* (México, D.F.: n.p., 1977), pp. 31–32.

30. Chardon, *Geographic Aspects*, p. 163.

31. FAO, *El henequen mexicano*.

32. "Sigue en declive la producción henequenera de nuestro estado," *Diario de Yucatán*, 23 November 1978.

33. One executive of Banrural, when asked why its officials supervised the ejido-owned processing facilities rather than the ejidatarios themselves, stated that the henequen workers were not "ready" to run them—four decades after land reform. Interview, at Mérida, Yucatán, by Brannon, in 1977.

34. Raymond, "The Impact of Land Reform," p. 162.

35. Marvin Alisky, "The Relations of the State of Yucatán and the Federal Government of Mexico, 1823–1977," in *Yucatán, A World Apart*, ed. Edward H. Moseley and Edward D. Terry (University, Ala.: University of Alabama Press, 1980), pp. 253–254.

36. The famous intersection in Mérida where the mansions of four former governors of Yucatán are located is popularly known as the "corner of the four thieves" because each governor was associated with either Henequeneros de Yucatán or the official bank. For more information on corruption in the henequen industry, see Raymond, "The Impact of Land Reform," pp. 158–162; Antonio Rodríguez, *El henequen: Una planta calumniada* (México, D.F.: Costa Amic, 1966), pp. 290–294; Malcolm Shuman, "The Town Where Luck Fell: The Economics of Life in a Henequen Zone Pueblo" (Ph.D. dissertation, Tulane University, 1974), pp. 122–125; and Thomas G. Sanders, *Henequen: The Structure of Agrarian Frustration*, American Universities Field Staff Report, North America Series 5, no. 3 (Hanover, N.H., July 1977).

37. Vera Pren, "Estructura de la industria henequenera," p. 19.

38. Before 1972 and the rigorous enforcement of a state law that prohibited such behavior, ejidatarios routinely knocked down the stone walls that surrounded ejido henequen fields to allow their cattle to feed on the plants. This activity alone was estimated to have caused an average of 10 million pesos damage annually. Rodríguez, *El henequen*, p. 288.

39. A discrepancy exists between the production figures published by Banrural and those of Cordemex for the year 1964. Banrural records indicate that ejido production was 66,483 tons, but Cordemex recorded 77,768 tons. If the Banrural figure is used, then smallholder production increased from 31,530 tons in 1956 to 64,785 tons in 1964, or by 33,255. Cordemex's records, on the other hand, would indicate an increase of only 21,969 tons between the two years. Because Banrural administers the ejidos and maintains their accounts, the official bank's records are the ones used in this study. See table 3; and Cordemex, *Henequen y sisal producción mundial*.

40. This figure was arrived at by using rough estimates of the output and the land in full production of pequeñas propiedades from 1962 through 1977. The Food and Agriculture Organization arrived at similar estimates in a 1968 study. FAO, *El henequen mexicano*. For prereform yields, see table 1.

41. Interview with Vincente Solís Aznar.

Chapter 5

1. Frederic L. Pryor, "Public Ownership: Some Quantitative Dimensions," in William G. Shepherd, ed., *Public Enterprise: Economic Analysis of Theory and Practice* (Lexington, Mass.: D. C. Heath and Co., 1976), p. 9.
2. Raúl Prebisch, "Towards a Theory of Change," *CEPAL Review* 10 (April 1980): 164.
3. Peter H. Smith, *Labyrinths of Power: Political Recruitment in Twentieth-Century Mexico* (Princeton, N.J.: Princeton University Press, 1979), p. 164.
4. *The Global Development Plan, 1980–1982: Synopsis* (México, D.F.: Ministry of Programming and Budget, 1980), p. 29.
5. Enrique Olivares Santana, "Productividad en el sector público," *El mercado de valores* 40 (November 1980): 1062.
6. *Loc. cit.*
7. Armour Research Foundation of Illinois Institute of Technology, *Technological Audit of Selected Mexican Industries with Industrial Research Recommendations* (Ann Arbor: Edward Brothers, 1946), p. 93; Jorge Tomás Vera Pren, "La industria henequenera en la perspectiva histórica," *Yucatán: Historia y economía* 35 (January–February 1983): 31.
8. Humberto Carranca Tomassi, *La industrialización del henequen en Yucatán* (México, D.F.: Banco de México, 1953), p. 151.
9. Ibid., p. 24.
10. Ibid., pp. 22–23, 33.
11. Henequen Industrial, S.A., one of the largest cordage enterprises, employed 118 persons during peak-demand periods. Owned by Ignacio Pedro Manzanilla, it financed its working capital needs through New Orleans banks. Wholesale distributors and grain cooperatives in the Midwest were the company's principal outlets in the United States. Interview of William Terry, North American Sales Manager, Henequen Industrial, S.A., from 1948 to 1956, at Point Clear, Ala., by Baklanoff, on November 16, 1980.
12. Carranca Tomassi, *La industrialización*, pp. 32, 37.
13. Ibid., pp. 33, 113–115.
14. Ibid., p. 59.
15. Carlos Tappan de Arrigunaga, "Trade, Development, and Structural Change: The Future of Mexico's Henequen Industry" (Ph.D. dissertation, Texas A&M University, 1971), pp. 85, 87.

16. Malcolm Shuman, "The Town Where Luck Fell: The Economics of Life in a Henequen Zone Pueblo" (Ph.D. dissertation, Tulane University, 1974), p. 37.

17. Carranca Tomassi, *La industrialización*, p. 151.

18. During some periods in 1951 and 1952, manufactured cordage products sold at prices that were substantially less than those being paid for raw sisal fiber from Brazil and Tanzania. Vera Pren attributes this phenomena to the reputation for low quality that Yucatecan producers acquired during World War II. Vera Pren, "La industria henequenera," pp. 33–34.

19. Ibid., pp. 32–37.

20. See F. M. Scherer, *Industrial Market Structure and Economic Performance* (Chicago: Rand McNally, 1971), p. 206.

21. For descriptions of the transactions between Cordemex and the government, see Antonio Rodríguez, *El henequen: Una planta calumniada* (México, D.F.: Costa Amic, 1966), pp. 311–319; and Vera Pren, "La industria henequenera," pp. 37–42.

22. Tappan de Arrigunaga, "Trade, Development, and Structural Change," p. 79; Manuel Pasos Peniche, *Historia de la industria henequenera desde 1945 hasta nuestros días* (Mérida: Editorial "Zamna," 1974), pp. 42–44.

23. Vera Pren, "La industria henequenera," pp. 39, 42.

24. Enzo R. Grilli, *The Future of Hard Fibers and Competition from Synthetics*, World Bank Occasional Staff Paper No. 19 (Baltimore: Johns Hopkins University Press, 1975), p. 52.

25. Carranca Tomassi, *La industrialización*, p. 99.

26. See Kenneth Arrow, "Vertical Integration and Communication," *The Bell Journal of Economics* 6 (Spring 1975): 173–183.

27. In the bilateral monopoly model, conflict arises over market price and quantity. Because both must be negotiated, the equilibrium solution is generally considered to be indeterminant. In a situation, however, where the monopsonist is purchasing inputs for further elaboration and resale, the quantity of raw material to be exchanged is determinant because there is a unique output of the finished product that will maximize the joint profits for the upstream and downstream firm. The transfer price of the input and, therefore, the distribution of profits between the two firms will subsequently be determined through bargaining. See C. E. Ferguson and J. P. Gould, *Microeconomic Theory*, 4th ed. (Homewood, Ill.: Richard D. Irwin, 1975), pp. 288–289; and Oscar E. Williamson, "The Vertical Integration of Production: Market

Failure Considerations," *American Economic Review* 61 (May 1971): 114–115.

28. Harvest-twine imports increased from 15 percent of U.S. domestic consumption in 1940 to 90 percent in 1970. Tappan de Arrigunaga, "Trade, Development, and Structural Change," p. 104.

29. Ibid., p. 83.

30. Ibid., pp. 83, 88.

31. Margaret Goodman, "The Effectiveness of the Mexican Revolution as an Agent of Change in the State of Yucatán, Mexico" (Ph.D. dissertation, Columbia University, 1970), pp. 103–104.

32. Tappan de Arrigunaga, "Trade, Development, and Structural Change," pp. 84–85.

33. Ibid., p. 86.

34. In 1980 cordage mill workers earned 175 percent of the minimum wage.

35. In 1976 some 85 percent of Mexico's henequen fiber was produced in Yucatán. Almost all the remainder was grown in the state of Tamaulipas. Cordemex, *Henequen y sisal producción mundial* (Mérida, 1977).

36. Cordemex's new desfibradoras have the capacity to process 250,000 leaves per eight-hour shift. Ejido and private desfibradoras, whose ages vary between forty and a hundred years, can process between 100,000 and 150,000 leaves in ten hours. For a comparison of the operating characteristics of the two types of processing facilities, see Jorge Tomás Vera Pren, "Estructura de la industria henequenera en Yucatán," *Yucatán: Historia y economía* 36 (March–April 1983): 15.

37. For information on Cordemex's diversification plans, see "Vendrá Cordemex 8 ton. de sapogeninas del henequen," *Diario de Yucatán*, 10 December 1977; and "Equiparán 4 desfibradoras para producir más forraje," *Diario de Yucatán*, 29 March 1978.

38. Cordemex, *Seis años de labores* (Mérida, 1976).

39. "Cordemex no tiene dinero para elevar los precios," *Diario de Yucatán*, 25 May 1982.

40. Cordemex, *Seis años de labores*.

41. See Frank Brandenburg, *The Making of Modern Mexico* (Englewood Cliffs, N.J.: Prentice-Hall, 1964), pp. 158–159, for a description of the "pecking order" among PRI and government functionaries.

42. Goodman, "The Effectiveness of the Mexican Revolution," p. 108.

43. Ibid., pp. 103–104.

44. The following description of trends in the world hard fiber market relies heavily on Grilli, *The Future of Hard Fibers,* pp. 11–81.

45. In his 1970 study, Tappan de Arrigunaga estimated United States demand for Mexican henequen baler twine. He found that both the own-price elasticity of henequen twine and the cross-price elasticity of henequen twine with respect to sisal to be well above unity at high confidence levels. Tappan de Arrigunaga, "Trade, Development, and Structural Change," pp. 111–113.

46. Ibid., pp. 75–77.

47. Grilli, *The Future of Hard Fibers,* p. 101.

48. Cordemex, *Seis años de labores.*

49. Between 1964 and 1975 Mexico's annual raw henequen fiber output varied between 137,185 tons and 149,960 tons. Producers in the Mexican states of Tamaulipas and Campeche accounted for the discrepancy between the nation's total production and that of Yucatán (table 3). Cordemex, *Henequen y sisal producción mundial.*

50. For a history of the cordage workers' movement in Yucatán, see Pedro Echeverría V., *Los cordeleros, 1933–1980* (Mérida: La Universidad de Yucatán, 1981).

51. Tappan de Arrigunaga, "Trade, Development, and Structural Change," p. 89.

52. Vera Pren, "Estructura de la industria henequenera," pp. 23, 32.

53. Iván Menéndez, "El estado y la zona henequenera de Yucatán, 1970–1976," *Comercio exterior* 27 (December 1977): 1513–1514.

54. Cordemex, *Seis años de labores.*

55. Cordemex, *Sesión del consejo de administración de Cordemex* (Mérida, May 1978).

56. Carranca Tomassi, *La industrialización,* p. 117.

57. Goodman, "The Effectiveness of the Mexican Revolution," p. 105.

58. Between 1965 and 1972, the average price of grade A Mexican raw henequen fiber landed in New York varied between $.101 per pound and $.08 per pound, or between 1.78 pesos per kilo and 1.41 pesos per kilo, assuming a 12.5 pesos to the dollar exchange

rate. Tappan de Arrigunaga, "Trade, Development, and Structural Change," p. 34.

59. Cordemex's purchase prices from 1965 through 1970 ranged from 1.90 pesos per kilogram for grade AA down to 1.10 pesos per kilogram for badly stained, low-grade fiber. Ibid., p. 57.

60. Banrural records show that total ejido production for those six years was 405,420,220 kilograms and receipts from the sale of ejido fiber were 428,100,470 pesos. The figure of 1.06 pesos per kilogram is admittedly only an approximation of the average price received per kilogram of fiber sold by the bank because ejido production is used as a proxy for total sales. Information on sales volume for the period, however, was not available. Banco de Crédito Rural Peninsular, *Resultados del cultivo del henequen para el período 1955–1974*, unpublished report (Mérida, 1976).

61. A spokesman for the pequeños propietarios stated in 1968 that the prices paid by Cordemex for raw fiber after 1964 had caused private producers to abandon some fields and cease completely their investment in new sowing. Echeverría V., *Los cordeleros*, p. 136.

62. Cordemex, *Informe anual de Cordemex* (Mérida, 1974).

Chapter 6

1. "Medidas para resolver el problema henequenero yucateco," *Diario de Yucatán*, 24 November 1977.

2. "Cuantiosas pérdidas de Cordemex en 1978," *Diario de Yucatán*, 31 July 1979.

3. Pedro Góngora Paz, "El desastre económico de Cordemex," *Diario de Yucatán*, 12 November 1979.

4. Carlos Tappan de Arrigunaga, "Trade, Development, and Structural Change: The Future of Mexico's Henequen Industry" (Ph.D. dissertation, Texas A&M University, 1971), p. 24.

5. Iván Menéndez, "Yucatán, la doble dependencia," *Comercio exterior* 28 (August 1978): 968.

6. Cordemex, *Informe anual de Cordemex* (Mérida, 1976).

7. United Nations, Food and Agriculture Organization (FAO), Committee on Commodity Problems, *Report of the Eleventh Session of the Intergovernmental Group on Hard Fibers* (New York, 1976), p. 4.

8. Cordemex, *Informe anual de Cordemex* (Mérida, 1977).

9. Cordemex, *Informe anual* (1976).

10. FAO, *Report of the Eleventh Session,* p. 6.

11. Marvin Alisky, "The Relations of the State of Yucatán and the Federal Government of Mexico, 1823–1977," in *Yucatán, A World Apart,* ed. Edward H. Moseley and Edward D. Terry (University, Ala.: University of Alabama Press, 1980), p. 255.

12. It is somewhat amazing that Mexico City allowed the election results to stand because, according to Roger D. Hansen, "While a degree of political pluralism is not anathema to the Revolutionary Coalition, there is a great deal of evidence to suggest that effective competition will still not be tolerated." In 1968, for example, the PAN won similar victories in Tijuana and Mexicali. The election results, however, were quickly annulled by the PRI-controlled state legislature of Baja California Norte. Hansen, *The Politics of Mexican Development* (Baltimore: Johns Hopkins University Press, 1971), p. 122.

13. "La trampa," *Diario de Yucatán,* 18 July 1979.

14. Agricultural bank subsidy payments to the ejidos totaled 331.3 million pesos from 1968 through 1970, which was an 83 percent increase over the previous three-year period (1965–1967). See table 4.

15. Luis Miguel Boyoli and Charles Richter, "El desarollo regional mexicano," *Comercio exterior* 26 (February 1976): 175–176.

16. For an account of the battle between Correa Racho and the state legislature from 1967 through 1969, see Alisky, "The Relations of the State of Yucatán," pp. 253–259.

17. Hansen, *The Politics of Mexican Development,* p. 123.

18. For Carlos Loret de Mola's own account of the election and his stormy tenure as governor of Yucatán, see Carlos Loret de Mola, *Confesiones de un gobernador* (México, D.F.: Editorial Grijalbo, 1979).

19. See Iván Menéndez, "El estado y la zona henequenera de Yucatán, 1970–1976," *Comercio exterior* 27 (December 1977): 1510–1516, for an analysis of the elements that threatened the political stability of the state during this period.

20. See Loret de Mola, *Confesiones,* for an interesting account of Luis Echeverría's numerous visits to Yucatán during his *sexenio,* or six-year term.

21. Gobierno del Estado de Yucatán, *El tercer informe del*

gobernador (Mérida, 1979); Secretaría de Programación y Presupuesto, Delegación en Yucatán, *La economía del estado de Yucatán en 1978* (Mérida, 1979), p. 1.

22. "Las finanzas estatales: Una historia de déficit," *Diario de Yucatán*, 21 November 1978.

23. "Mil 500 millones de pesos destinará el Banrural a la producción del henequen," *Diario de Yucatán*, 9 January 1979; SPP, *La economía del estado de Yucatán*, p. 6.

24. "Mas de un tercio de los ejidatarios inscritos hasta 1977 en el Banrural eran impostores y ya estan incluidos," *Diario de Yucatán*, 15 April 1978; "Mas de 20,000 fantasmas y muertos había en las nóminas ejidales del Banrural," *Diario de Yucatán*, 3 February 1978.

25. "La depuración en el Banco Rural Peninsular," *Diario de Yucatán*, 30 January 1978; Gobierno del Estado, *El tercer informe*.

26. Salvador Rodríguez Losa, *La población de los municipios del estado de Yucatán* (Mérida: Ediciones del Gobierno del Estado, 1977).

27. "Sigue en declive la producción henequenera de nuestro estado," *Diario de Yucatán*, 23 November 1978.

28. Cordemex, *Seis años de labores* (Mérida, 1976).

29. Ibid.

30. Ibid.

31. Menéndez, "El estado y la zona," pp. 1514–1515.

32. Ibid., p. 1513.

33. Cordemex, *Informe anual de Cordemex* (Mérida, 1974).

34. Cordemex, *Seis años de labores*.

35. Cordemex, *Sesión del consejo de administración de Cordemex* (Mérida, March 1980).

36. Ibid.

37. Cordemex, *Informe anual* (1977).

38. Cordemex, *Sesión del consejo*, May 1978.

39. Jorge Tomás Vera Pren, "Estructura de la industria henequenera en Yucatán," *Yucatán: Historia y economía* 36 (March–April 1983): 35.

Chapter 7

1. "Hay muchas y francas salidas—indica el Lic. José López Portillo," *Diario de Yucatán*, 20 November 1977.

2. James R. Fortson, "Civilismo en Yucatán: Alpuche," *Excelsior*, 18 June 1983.

3. "Mil campesinos de la zona de Motul llegan a Mérida a plantear sus problemas al banco," *Diario de Yucatán*, 13 January 1978.

4. Jorge Tomás Vera Pren, "Estructura de la industria henequenera en Yucatán," *Yucatán: Historia y economía* 36 (March–April 1983): 7.

5. "La reestructuración henequenera," *Diario de Yucatán*, 1 December 1978; "No debe desaparecer el cultivo del henequen," *Novedades de Yucatán*, 27 May 1982.

6. Commodity Research Bureau, Inc., *1982 Commodity Yearbook* (New York, 1982), p. 165.

7. "Descanso sostenido en las exportaciones de henequen," *Diario de Yucatán*, 10 April 1981.

8. The price of grade A East African sisal rose from $489.50 per ton in 1978 to $764.80 per ton in 1980 as a result of the impact of petroleum price increases on the price of synthetics during the period. The price subsequently fell to $596.67 in 1982. International Monetary Fund, *International Financial Statistics* 39 (9): 48–49.

9. "Estado de la empresa cordelera," *Diario de Yucatán*, 16 January 1982.

10. Vera Pren, "Estructura de la industria henequenera," p. 7.

11. Manuel Mier y Terán, "El henequen es un desafío," *Diario de Yucatán*, 4 April 1983.

12. Health-insurance payments to the Mexican Institute of Social Security are made from the proceeds of Banrural's credit advances to the ejidatarios. In 1982 henequen ejidatarios were authorized to receive retirement payments ranging from 3,500 pesos to 7,000 pesos after age sixty-five. Reportedly, some 11,000 ejidatarios were eligible to receive these payments. "Cuotas de hasta $7 mil mensuales recibirán unos 11 mil campesinos de la zona henequenera," *Novedades de Yucatán*, 11 May 1982.

13. "La suma acendía a 1969 millones," *Diario de Yucatán*, 1 December 1978.

14. "1,436 millones al Fideicomiso Henequenero," *Diario de Yucatán*, 16 November 1978; "Se vislumbra leve majoría en el producción del henequen ejidal," *Diario de Yucatán*, 17 July 1982.

15. "La producción agropecuaria de Yucatán llegó a ser 518,679 toneladas durante 1981," *Diario de Yucatán*, 17 July 1982.

16. Cordemex, *Sesión del consejo de administración de Cordemex*, (Mérida, September 1982).

17. "Cordemex usará una política comercial más agresiva para contrarrestar a Cuba y Haití," *Novedades de Yucatán*, 19 June 1982.

18. "Acusa la IP a Cordemex de desplazarlos del mercado," *El Fronterizo*, 29 August 1983.

19. Secretaría de Programación y Presupuesto, *La economía del estado de Yucatán en 1979* (Mérida, 1980).

20. Cordemex, *Informe anual* (1976); "Correos dejó de utilizar los sacos de henequen," *Novedades de Yucatán*, 22 August 1980.

21. "El gobernador presidirá el consejo de Cordemex," *Diario de Yucatán*, 30 May 1984.

22. Secretaría de Programación y Presupuesto, *La economía del estado de Yucatán en 1978* (Mérida, 1979), p. 20.

23. Cordemex, *Sesión del consejo*, May 1978.

24. Ibid., March 1980.

25. "Estado de la empresa cordelera," *Diario de Yucatán*.

26. "Planes de Cordemex: Una cuenca lechera en la zona henequenera," *Diario de Yucatán*, 8 February 1980; "Es probable que Cordemex administre la fábrica celulosa: Dr. Rioseco," *Diario de Yucatán*, 20 March 1980.

27. "Interesante projecto: 60 modulos de agroindustrias en las desfibradoras," *Diario de Yucatán*, 4 August 1981.

28. "Autoriza el presidente la planta de celulosa," *Diario de Yucatán*, 24 November 1979; "Los planes para encontrar nuevos usos al henequen," *Diario de Yucatán*, 23 November 1979.

29. "La planta de celulosa costará más de 3,500 millones de pesos," *Diario de Yucatán*, 10 January 1980.

30. "Que el Dr. Luna Kan propicia que el Banrural se encargue de Cordemex," *Novedades de Yucatán*, 28 October 1982.

31. Cordemex, *Sesión del consejo*, March 1980.

32. Secretaría de Agricultura y Recursos Hidráulicos, *Boletín informativo* (Mérida, March 1980); idem, *Boletín informativo* (Mérida, January 1981); Gobierno del Estado de Yucatán, *El sexto informe del gobernador* (Mérida, 1981); "Se han paralizado ya 45 desfibradoras privadas," *Diario de Yucatán*, 27 May 1982.

33. Vera Pren, "Estructura de la industria henequenera," pp. 21–25.

34. "Cordemex debe subordinarse al gobierno del estado: GAP," *Novedades de Yucatán*, 28 October 1982.

35. "Nueva empresa estatal manejará las desfibradoras de Cordemex," *Diario de Yucatán,* 1 May 1982.

36. "Presentan nuevo projecto para una fábrica de celulosa de henequen," *Diario de Yucatán,* 24 January 1982.

37. "A 50 por ciento de su capacidad labora la planta lechera Cordemex," *Novedades de Yucatán,* 29 July 1982.

38. "La obsesión del henequen ha terminado - el presidente," *Diario de Yucatán,* 30 May 1984.

Chapter 8

1. Secretaría de Programación y Presupuesto (SPP), *Sistema de cuentas nacionales de México: Producto interno bruto por entidad federativa, 1980* (México, D.F., 1982), p. 5, table 1.

2. SPP, *X censo general de población y vivienda, 1980: Estado de Yucatán,* vol. 2 (México, D.F., 1983), p. 87, table 9.

3. Gobierno del Estado de Yucatán, *Monografía de Yucatán, 1980* (Mérida, 1981), p. 271, table 1.

4. Victor M. Suárez Molina, *La evolución económica de Yucatán,* vol. 1 (México, D.F.: La Universidad de Yucatán, 1977), pp. 153–154.

5. Suárez Molina, *La evolución económica,* p. 51.

6. María Cáceres Menéndez and María Loret de Mola, *La migración libanesa a Yucatán* (Mérida: La Universidad de Yucatán, 1977).

7. "Talleres mecánicos y de fundición de Mérida en el siglo XIX," *Diario de Yucatán,* 13 March 1977, p. 3. Also see Eric N. Baklanoff and Jeffery Brannon, "Forward and Backward Linkages in a Plantation Economy: Immigrant Entrepreneurship and Industrial Development in Yucatán, Mexico," *The Journal of Developing Areas* 19 (1) (October 1984): 87–88.

8. Humberto Carranca Tomassi, *La industrialización del henequen en Yucatán* (México, D.F.: Banco de México, 1953), p. 59.

9. Gobierno de Yucatán, *VI informe de gobierno* (Mérida, 1982), appendix, n.p.

10. *Monografía de Yucatán 1980,* p. 15.

11. Ignacio Argaez and Carlos Montañez, *Yucatán: Las condiciones del desarrollo de la agricultura de subsistencia* (Mérida: Universidad de Yucatán, Facultad de Economía, 1975), pp. 8–9.

12. Loc. cit.

13. Gobierno del Estado de Yucatán, *Plan de desarrollo estatal 1982–88* (Mérida, 1982), p. 39.

14. "Santa Rosa: Nueva esperanza sobre las ruinas del fracaso," *Diario de Yucatán*, 23 June 1980.

15. Loc. cit.

16. "Dzonot Carretero 10 años después: Ruinas, pérdidas y tierra ociosa," *Diario de Yucatán*, 23 June 1980.

17. "'Yo rompí el mito'—dijó el Ing. Tinajero en 1976,"*Diario de Yucatán*, 23 June 1980.

18. *Plan de desarrollo estatal, 1982–88*, p. 58.

19. *VI informe de gobierno*, p. 33.

20. Silvia Terán and Christian Rasmussen, *Artesanías de Yucatán* (Mérida: Dirección General de Culturas Populares, 1981).

21. Terán and Rasmussen, *Artesanías de Yucatán*, pp. 15–20.

22. *VI informe de gobierno*, appendix, n.p.

23. *VI informe de gobierno*, appendix, n.p.

24. *IDB News* 2 (2) (January 1976).

25. Andreas S. Gerakis, "Economic Man: The Tourist," *The Fund and Bank Review* 3 (1) (March 1966), pp. 47–48.

26. *Plan de desarrollo estatal, 1982–88*, p. 64.

27. Rosemary Louise Lee, "The Tourist Industry in Yucatán: A Case Study in the Interaction between Class Structure and Economic Development," Ph.D. dissertation, University of California, Irvine, 1977 (Ann Arbor: Xerox University Microfilms, 1978).

28. SPP, *Yucatán: Informe económico, 1980* (Mérida, 1981), p. 132.

29. *Plan de desarrollo estatal, 1982–88*, p. 53.

30. *Plan de desarrollo estatal, 1982–88*, p. 48.

31. *Yucatán: Informe económico, 1980*, pp. 107, 109.

32. For background on Yucatán's fishing industry, including its problems, see Jeffery Brannon, "Federal Policy and Regional Economic Development in Mexico: The Case of Yucatán's Fishing Industry." *South Eastern Latin Americanist* 23 (3) (December 1979), pp. 1–11; and "La pesca en Yucatán," *Diario de Yucatán*, 20 May 1978, p. 4.

33. Manuel Mier y Terán, "La pesca en Yucatán," part 2, p. 1, in Gobierno del Estado de Yucatán, *Monografía de Yucatán, 1975* (Mérida, 1975).

34. Thomas G. Sanders, *The Fishing Industry in Mexico*,

American Universities Field Staff Report, North America Series 5, no. 9 (Hanover, N.H., September 1977), p. 4.

35. Sanders, *The Fishing Industry in Mexico*, p. 5.

36. Michael D. Murphy and Carlos Solís, "Cooperation and Rivalry in Coastal Yucatán: Implications for the Expansion of a Fishing Industry," *Yucatán: Historia y economía* (in press).

37. Murphy and Solís, "Cooperation and Rivalry in Coastal Yucatán."

38. Brannon, "Federal Policy and Regional Economic Development in Mexico," p. 7.

39. "Yucatán: La otra frontera maquiladora," *Expansión*, 21 November 1984, pp. 47–55.

40. "Victor Cervera, gobernador de Yucatán: Bienvenida la industria," *Expansión*, 21 November 1984, pp. 62–64.

41. Manuel Mier y Terán, "Visión de Yucatán en el año 2000," *Diario de Yucatán*, 1983: January 10, January 16, January 23, February 28, March 28, April 3, April 4, April 11, April 26.

42. *Colombia Today* 19 (4) (1984), n.p.

43. *Yucatán: Informe económico*, 1980, pp. 70–76.

44. "Los yucatecos, con recursos para forjar su propio destino," *Diario de Yucatán*, 30 May 1984, pp. 6-C and 7-C.

Chapter 9

1. "Hay ahora muchas y francas salidas—indica el Lic. José López Portillo," *Diario de Yucatán*, 20 November 1977.

2. Pablo González Casanova, *Democracy in Mexico* (London: Oxford University Press, 1970), p. 134.

3. See Manuel Mier y Terán, "El henequen, nueva esperanza," *Diario de Yucatán*, 11 April 1983; and idem, "Solución definitiva," *Diario de Yucatán*, 26 April 1983.

4. "Reestructuración del sector paraestatal," *Excelsior*, 4 March 1985, p. 13-A.

Bibliography

BOOKS, DISSERTATIONS, AND MONOGRAPHS

Argaez, Ignacio, and Carlos Montañez. *Yucatán: Las condiciones del desarrollo de la agricultura de subsistencia.* Mérida: Universidad de Yucatán, Facultad de Economía, 1975.

Armour Research Foundation of Illinois Institute of Technology. *Technological Audit of Selected Mexican Industries with Industrial Research Recommendations.* Ann Arbor, Mich.: Edward Brothers, 1946.

Barkin, David, and Blanca Suárez. *El fin de la autosuficiencia.* México, D.F.: Editorial Nueva Imagen, 1982.

Brandenburg, Frank. *The Making of Modern Mexico.* Englewood Cliffs, N.J.: Prentice-Hall, 1964.

Cáceres Menéndez, María, and María Loret de Mola. *La migración libanesa a Yucatán.* Mérida: La Universidad de Yucatán, 1977.

Cardos Ruz, Laureano. *El drama de los Mayas.* México, D.F.: n.p., 1977.

Carranca Tomassi, Humberto. *La industrialización del henequen en Yucatán.* México, D.F.: Banco de México, 1953.

Chardon, Roland E. P. *Geographic Aspects of Plantation Agriculture in Yucatán.* NAS-NRC Publication 876. Washington, D.C.: National Academy of Sciences-National Research Council, 1961.

Chayanov, A. V. *The Theory of Peasant Economy.* Edited by Daniel Thorner, Basile Kerblay, and R. E. F. Smith. Homewood, Ill.: Richard D. Irwin, 1966.

Comisión Económica para la América Latina (CEPAL). *Economía campesina y agricultura empresarial.* México, D.F.: Siglo Veintiuno Editores, 1982.

Commodity Research Bureau, Inc. *1982 Commodity Yearbook.* New York, 1982.

Cook, Sherburne F., and Woodrow Borah. *Essays in Population History: Mexico and the Caribbean.* 2 vols. Berkeley: University of California Press, 1974.

De Calzadilla, José Ma., Policarpo Antonio de Echanove, Pedro Bolio Torresillas, and José Miguel Zunzanauar. *Apuntaciones para las estadísticas de Yucatán del año de 1814.* Mérida: J. D. Espinosa e Hijos, 1871; reprint ed., Mérida: Ediciones del Gobierno del Estado, 1977.

Echeverría V., Pedro. *Los cordeleros, 1933–1980.* Mérida: La Universidad de Yucatán, 1981.

El Colegio de México. *Fuerza de trabajo y actividad económica por sectores.* Cited in Laura Randall. *A Comparative Economic History of Latin America, 1500–1914.* Vol. 1, *Mexico.* Ann Arbor: University Microfilms International, 1977.

Esteva, Gustavo. *The Battle for Rural Mexico.* South Hadley, Mass.: Bergin and Garvey Publishers, 1983.

Ferguson, C. E., and J. P. Gould. *Microeconomic Theory.* 4th ed. Homewood, Ill.: Richard D. Irwin, 1975.

Franz, David A. "Bullets and Bolshevists: A History of the Mexican Revolution and Reform in Yucatán, 1910–1924." Ph.D. dissertation, University of New Mexico, 1973.

Friedmann, John. *Regional Development Policy: A Case Study of Venezuela.* Cambridge, Mass.: MIT Press, 1966.

Glade, William P. *The Latin American Economies.* New York: Van Nostrand Reinhold, 1969.

González Casanova, Pablo. *Democracy in Mexico.* London: Oxford University Press, 1970.

González Navarro, Moisés. *Raza y tierra: La Guerra de Castas y el henequen.* México, D.F.: El Colegio de México, 1970.

Goodman, Margaret. "The Effectiveness of the Mexican Revolution as an Agent of Change in the State of Yucatán, Mexico." Ph.D. dissertation, Columbia University, 1970.

Grilli, Enzo R. *The Future of Hard Fibers and Competition from Synthetics.* World Bank Occasional Staff Paper No. 19. Baltimore: Johns Hopkins University Press, 1975.

Hansen, Roger D. *The Politics of Mexican Development.* Baltimore: Johns Hopkins University Press, 1971.

Hartman, Keith. "The Henequen Empire in Yucatán, 1870–1910." Master's thesis, University of Iowa, 1966.

Hirschman, Albert. *The Strategy of Economic Development.* New Haven, Conn.: Yale University Press, 1958.

Irigoyen, Renán. *Ensayos henequeneros*. Mérida: Ediciones de Cordemex, 1975.

Joseph, Gilbert M. *Revolution from Without*. Cambridge: Cambridge University Press, 1982.

Lee, Rosemary Louise. "The Tourist Industry in Yucatán: A Case Study in the Interaction between Class Structure and Economic Development." Ph.D. dissertation, University of California, Irvine, 1977. Ann Arbor: Xerox University Microfilms, 1978.

Loret de Mola, Carlos. *Confesiones de un gobernador*. México, D.F.: Editorial Grijalbo, 1979.

Marentes Miranda, Tomás. *Notas sobre agricultura, ganadería, e industrias de transformación en Yucatán*. Anexo No. 6. México, D.F.: Costa Amic, 1951, pp. 97–101.

North, Douglass C. *The Economic Growth of the United States, 1790–1860*. New York: W. W. Norton and Co., 1966.

Pasos Peniche, Manuel. *La intervención estatal en la industria henequenera*. Mérida: n.p., 1951.

———. *Historia de la industria henequenera desde 1945 hasta nuestros días*. Mérida: Editorial "Zamna," 1974.

Patch, Robert. *La formación de estancias y haciendas en Yucatán durante la colonia*. Mérida: Ediciones de la Universidad de Yucatán, 1976.

Pozen, Robert, C. *Legal Choices for State Enterprise in the Third World*. New York: New York University Press, 1976.

Raymond, Nathaniel C. "The Impact of Land Reform in the Monocrop Region of Yucatán, Mexico." Ph.D. dissertation, Brandeis University, 1971.

Redfield, Robert. *The Folk Culture of Yucatán*. Chicago: University of Illinois Press, 1941.

Reed, Nelson. *The Caste War of Yucatán*. Stanford: Stanford University Press, 1964.

Rodríguez, Antonio. *El henequen: Una planta calumniada*. México, D.F.: Costa Amic, 1966.

Rodríguez Losa, Salvador. *La población de los municipios del estado de Yucatán*. Mérida: Ediciones del Gobierno del Estado, 1977.

Sanders, Thomas G. *The Fishing Industry in Mexico*. American Universities Field Staff Report, North America Series 5, no. 9. Hanover, N.H., September 1977.

———. *Henequen: The Structure of Agrarian Frustration*. American Universities Field Staff Report, North America Series 5, no. 3. Hanover, N.H., July 1977.

Scherer, F. M. *Industrial Market Structure and Economic Performance.* Chicago: Rand McNally, 1971.

Shuman, Malcolm. "The Town Where Luck Fell: The Economics of Life in a Henequen Zone Pueblo." Ph. D. dissertation, Tulane University, 1974.

Simpson, Eyler N. *The Ejido: Mexico's Way Out.* Chapel Hill: University of North Carolina Press, 1937.

Simpson, Lesley Byrd. *Many Mexicos.* Rev. 4th ed. Berkeley: University of California Press, 1969.

Smith, Peter H. *Labyrinths of Power: Political Recruitment in Twentieth-Century Mexico.* Princeton, N.J.: Princeton University Press, 1979.

Stavenhagen, Rodolfo. *Problemas étnicos y campesinos.* México, D.F.: Instituto Nacional Indigenista, 1979.

Stephens, John L. *Incidents of Travel in Central America, Chiapas, and Yucatán.* 2 vols. New Brunswick, N.J.: Rutgers University Press, 1949.

―――. *Incidents of Travel in Yucatán.* 2 vols. Norman: University of Oklahoma Press, 1962.

Suárez Molina, Victor M. *La evolución económica de Yucatán.* 2 vols. México, D.F.: La Universidad de Yucatán, 1977.

Tappan de Arrigunaga, Carlos. "Trade, Development and Structural Change: The Future of Mexico's Henequen Industry." Ph.D. dissertation, Texas A&M University, 1971.

Terán, Silvia, and Christian Rasmussen. *Artesanías de Yucatán.* Mérida: Dirección General de Culturas Populares, 1981.

Wells, Allen. *Yucatán's Gilded Age: Haciendas, Henequen, and International Harvester, 1860–1915.* Albuquerque: University of New Mexico Press, forthcoming.

Yates, P. Lamartine. *Mexico's Agricultural Dilemma.* Tucson: University of Arizona Press, 1981.

ARTICLES

Alisky, Marvin. "The Relations of the State of Yucatán and the Federal Government of Mexico, 1823–1977," pp. 245–263. In *Yucatán, A World Apart.* Edited by Edward H. Moseley and Edward D. Terry. University, Ala.: University of Alabama Press, 1980.

Alonso, William. "Industrial Location and Regional Policy in Economic Development." In *Regional Policy,* pp. 64–96. Edited by John Friedmann and William Alonso. Cambridge, Mass.: MIT Press, 1975.

Arrow, Kenneth. "Vertical Integration and Communication." *The Bell Journal of Economics* 6 (Spring 1975): 173–183.

Aznar Mendoza, Enrique. "La industria henequenera desde 1919 hasta nuestros días." In *Enciclopedia yucatanense.* Vol. 3, pp. 727–787. Edited by Carlos A. Echanove Trujillo. México, D.F.: Edición Oficial, 1946.

Baklanoff, Eric N. "The Diversification Quest: A Monocrop Export Economy in Transition." In *Yucatán, A World Apart,* pp. 202–244. Edited by Edward H. Moseley and Edward D. Terry. University, Ala.: University of Alabama Press, 1980.

Baklanoff, Eric N., and Jeffery Brannon. "Forward and Backward Linkages in a Plantation Economy: Immigrant Entrepreneurship and Industrial Development in Yucatán, Mexico." *The Journal of Developing Areas* 19 (1) (October 1984): 83–94.

Baldwin, R. E. "Patterns of Development in Newly Settled Regions." *The Manchester School of Economic and Social Studies* 24 (May 1956): 161–179.

Barceló Quintal, Raquel. "El ferrocarril y la oligarquía henequenera." *Yucatán: Historia y economía* 26 (July–August 1981): 27–54.

———. "El desarollo de la banca y el henequen." *Yucatán: Historia y economía* 29 (January–February 1982): 3–24.

Bates, Robert H. "Some Conventional Orthodoxies in the Study of Agrarian Change." *World Politics* 36 (2): 234–254.

Benjamin, Thomas. "International Harvester and the Henequen Marketing System in Yucatán, 1898–1915: A New Perspective." *Inter-American Economic Affairs* 31 (Winter 1977): 3–19.

Boyoli, Luis Miguel, and Charles Richter. "El desarollo regional mexicano." *Comercio exterior* 26 (February 1976): 172–180.

Brannon, Jeffery. "Federal Policy and Regional Economic Development in Mexico: The Case of Yucatán's Fishing Industry." *South Eastern Latin Americanist* 23 (3) (December 1979): 1–11.

———. "Mexican Agriculture in the 1980s: A Review Essay." *South Eastern Latin Americanist* 27 (1) (June 1983): 19–22.

Brannon, Jeffery, and Eric N. Baklanoff. "Corporate Control of a Monocrop Economy: A Comment." *Latin American Research Review* 18 (3): 193–196.

Cámara Zavala, Gonzalo. "Historia de la industria henequenera hasta 1919." In *Enciclopedia yucatanense.* Vol. 3, pp. 657–725. Edited by Carlos A. Echanove Trujillo. México, D.F.: Edición Oficial, 1946.

Carstensen, Fred V., and Diane Roazen-Parillo. "International Harvester, Molina y Compañía, and the Henequen Market: A Comment." *Latin American Research Review* 18 (3): 197–203.

Cline, Howard F. "The 'Aurora Yucateca' and the Spirit of Enterprise in Yucatán, 1821–1847." *The Hispanic American Historical Review* 27 (February 1947): 30–60.

———. "The Sugar Episode in Yucatán, 1825–1850." *Inter-American Economic Affairs* 1 (March 1948): 79–100.

———. "The Henequen Episode in Yucatán." *Inter-American Economic Affairs* 2 (Autumn 1948): 30–51.

Ferrer de Mendiolea, Gabriel. "Historia de las comunicaciones." In *Enciclopedia yucatanense.* Vol. 3, pp. 507–626. Edited by Carlos A. Echanove Trujillo. México, D.F.: Edición Oficial, 1946.

Fortson, James R. "Civilismo en Yucatán: Alpuche." *Excelsior.* June 18, 1983.

García Quintanilla, Alejandra. "Historia y etapas de la producción de una mercancia." *Yucatán: Historia y economía* 26 (July–August 1981): 3–22.

Gerakis, Andreas S. "Economic Man: The Tourist." *The Fund and Bank Review* 3 (1) (March 1966): 47–58.

Iglesias, Esther. "Yucatán, monocultivo, oro verde, y decadencia henequenera: La región y dependencia del mercado norteamericano." Paper presented at the *Primer encuentro sobre impactos regionales de las relaciones económicas México-Estados Unidos,* Guanajuato, Mexico, 1981.

International Monetary Fund. *International Financial Statistics* 39 (9).

Inter-American Development Bank. *IDB News* 2 (January 1976).

Joseph, Gilbert M., and Allen Wells. "Corporate Control of a Monocrop Economy: International Harvester and Yucatán's Henequen Industry during the Porfiriato." *Latin American Research Review* 17 (1): 69–99.

_____. "Collaboration and Informal Empire in Yucatán: The Case for Political Economy." *Latin American Research Review* 18 (3): 204–218.

Knox, A. J. Graham. "Henequen Haciendas, Maya Peones, and the Mexican Revolution Promises of 1910: Reform and Reaction in Yucatán, 1910–1940." *Caribbean Studies* 17 (April–July 1977): 55–82.

Lucas, Ann. "El debate sobre los campesinos y el capitalismo en México." *Comercio exterior* 32 (April 1982): 371–383.

Madrazo, Jorge. "A Discussion of Constitutional Rights Regarding Property in Mexico." *The Mexican Forum* 3 (4): 15–19.

Menéndez, Iván. "El estado y la zona henequenera de Yucatán, 1970–1976." *Comercio exterior* 27 (December 1977): 1510–1516.

_____. "Yucatán, la doble dependencia." *Comercio exterior* 28 (August 1978): 960–968.

Mier y Terán, Manuel. "El henequen es un desafío." *Diario de Yucatán.* April 4, 1983.

_____. "El henequen, nueva esperanza." *Diario de Yucatán.* April 11, 1983.

_____. "Solución definitiva." *Diario de Yucatán.* April 26, 1983.

_____. "Visión de Yucatán en el año 2000." *Diario de Yucatán.* 1983: January 10, January 16, January 23, February 28, March 28, April 3, April 4, April 11, April 26.

Mintz, Sidney W., and Eric R. Wolf. "Haciendas and Plantations in Middle America and the Antilles." *Social and Economic Studies* 6 (September 1957): 380–412.

Mogab, John. "The Mexican Experience in Peasant Agricultural Credit." *Development and Change* 15 (2) (1984): 203–221.

Moseley, Edward H. "From Conquest to Independence: Yucatán under Spanish Rule, 1521–1821." In *Yucatán, A World Apart,* pp. 83–121. Edited by Edward H. Moseley and Edward D. Terry, University, Ala.: University of Alabama Press, 1980.

Murphy, Michael D., and Carlos Solís. "Cooperation and Rivalry in Coastal Yucatán: Implications for the Expansion of a Fishing Industry." *Yucatán: Historia y economía* (in press.)

Nacional Financiera. *El mercado de valores.* February 1, 1982.

North, Douglass C. "Agriculture in Regional Economic Growth." *Journal of Farm Economics* 69 (1959): 943–951.

_____. "Location Theory and Regional Economic Growth." In *Regional Economics,* pp. 26–49. Edited by David L. McKee,

Robert D. Dean, and William H. Leahy. New York: The Free Press, 1970.

Olivares Santana, Enrique. "Productividad en el sector público." *El mercado de valores* 40 (November 1980).

Patch, Robert. "Apuntes acerca de los orígenes y las características de la hacienda henequenera en Yucatán." *Yucatán: Historia y economía* 9 (September–October 1978): 3–15.

Paz, Pedro Góngora. "El desastre económico de Cordemex." *Diario de Yucatán*. November 12, 1979.

————. "La pesca en Yucatán." *Diario de Yucatán*. May 20, 1978: 4.

Prebisch, Raúl. "Towards a Theory of Change." *CEPAL Review* 10 (April 1980): 155–208.

Pryor, Frederic L. "Public Ownership: Some Quantitative Dimensions." In *Public Enterprise: Economic Analysis of Theory and Practice*, pp. 7–28. Edited by William G. Shepherd. Lexington, Mass.: D. C. Heath and Co., 1976.

Rosales González, Margarita. "Etapas en el desarollo regional del Puuc, Yucatán." *Yucatán: Historia y economía* 18 (March–April 1980): 41–53.

Shejtman, Alejandro. "El agro mexicano y sus interpretes." *Nexos* (March 1981): 37–47.

Sierra V., José Luis. "Hacia una economía política de la hacienda henequenera: Primera parte, los hacendados." *Yucatán: Historia y economía* 17 (January–February 1980): 57–63.

Singelmann, Peter. "Rural Collectivization and Dependent Capitalism: The Mexican Collective Ejido." *Latin American Perspectives* 5 (3): 38–61.

Stavenhagen, Rodolfo. "Collective Agriculture and Capitalism in Mexico: A Way Out or a Dead End?" *Latin American Perspectives* 2 (2): 146–163.

Strickon, Arnold. "Hacienda and Plantation in Yucatán." *América indígena* 21 (January 1965): 35–63.

Vera Pren, Jorge Tomás. "Labores agrícolas en las plantaciones henequeneras." *Yucatán: Historia y economía* 2 (July–August 1977): 32–53.

————. "La industria henequenera en la perspectiva histórica." *Yucatán: Historia y economía* 35 (January–February 1983): 21–42.

————. "Estructura de la industria henequenera en Yucatán." *Yucatán: Historia y economía* 36 (March–April 1983): 3–37.

"Victor Cervera, gobernador de Yucatán: Bienvenida la industria." *Expansión*, November 21, 1984: 62–64.

Warman, Arturo. "Frente a la crisis ¿política agraria o política agrícola?" In Warman, *Ensayos sobre el campesinado en México.* México, D.F.: Editorial Nueva Imagen, 1980, pp. 85–108.

————. "La colectivización en el campo: Una crítica." In Warman, *Ensayos sobre el campesinado en México.* México, D.F.: Editorial Nueva Imagen, 1980, pp. 61–83.

————. "Los campesinos y el estado." In Warman, *Ensayos sobre el campesinado en México.* México, D.F.: Editorial Nueva Imagen, 1980, pp. 133–147.

Watkins, Melville. "A Staple Theory of Economic Growth." In *Readings in Economic Development,* pp. 458–476. Edited by Walter L. Johnson and David R. Kamerschen. Cincinnati: Southwest Publishing Co., 1972.

Wells, Allen. "Economic Growth and Regional Disparity in Porfirian Yucatán: The Case of the Southeastern Railway Company." *South Eastern Latin Americanist* 22 (2): 1–16.

————. "Family Elites in a Boom-and-Bust Economy: The Molinas and Peons of Porfirian Yucatán." *Hispanic American Historical Review* 62 (May 1982): 224–253.

Wessman, James W. "The Agrarian Question in Mexico." *Latin American Research Review* 19 (2): 243–259.

Williamson, Oscar E. "The Vertical Integration of Production: Market Failure Considerations." *American Economic Review* 61 (May 1971): 112–123.

Wilson, Eugene M. "Physical Geography of the Yucatán Peninsula." In *Yucatán, A World Apart,* pp. 5–40. Edited by Edward H. Moseley and Edward D. Terry. University, Ala.: University of Alabama Press, 1980.

"Yucatán: La otra frontera maquiladora." *Expansión.* November 21, 1984: 47–55.

"Los yucatecos, con recursos para forjar su propio destino." *Diario de Yucatán.* May 30, 1984: 6-C and 7-C.

GOVERNMENT PUBLICATIONS

Banco de Crédito Rural Peninsular. *Resultados del cultivo del henequen para el período 1955–1974.* Unpublished report. Mérida, 1976.

Banco Nacional de México (Banamex). *Review of the Economic*

Situation of Mexico, Special Document: Mexican Statistical Data. México, D.F.: Banamex, 1983.

Gobierno del Estado de Yucatán. *Estudio económico de Yucatán y programa de trabajo.* Mérida, 1960.

————. *El segundo informe del gobernador.* Mérida, 1978.

————. *El tercer informe del gobernador.* Mérida, 1979.

————. *El sexto informe del gobernador.* Mérida, 1982.

————. *Monografía del estado de Yucatán, 1978.* Mérida, 1978.

————. *Monografía de Yucatán, 1980.* Mérida, 1981.

————. *Plan de desarrollo estatal, 1982–1988.* Mérida, 1982.

Ministry of Programming and Budget. *The Global Development Plan, 1980–1982: Synopsis.* México, D.F.: Ministry of Planning and Budget, 1980.

Poder Ejecutivo Federal. *Plan nacional de desarollo, 1983–1988.* México, D.F.: Poder Ejecutivo Federal, 1983.

Secretaría de Agricultura y Ganadería, Agencia General en Mérida, Yucatán. *Henequen 1901 a 1973.* Mérida, 1974.

Secretaría de Agricultura y Recursos Hidráulicos, Representación en Yucatán. *Yucatán en cifras, 20 años de estadísticas agropecuarias.* Mérida, 1978.

Secretaría de Agricultura y Recursos Hidráulicos. *Boletín informativo* (No. 6). Mérida, March 1980.

————. *Boletín informativo.* Mérida, January 1981.

Secretaría de la Presidencia Naciones Unidas. *Información básica para la planificación regional industrial: Industria de transformación datos básicos de 1960.* México, D.F., 1975.

Secretaría de Programación y Presupuesto, Delegación en Yucatán. *La economía del estado de Yucatán en 1978.* Mérida, 1979.

Secretaría de Programación y Presupuesto. *X censo general de población y vivienda.* México, D.F., 1981.

————. *La economía del estado de Yucatán en 1979.* Mérida, 1980.

————. *Yucatán: Informe económico, 1980.* Mérida, 1981.

————. *X censo general de población y vivienda, 1980: Vol. 2, Estado de Yucatán.* México, D.F., 1983.

————. *Sistema de cuentas nacionales de México: Producto interno bruto por entidad federativa, 1980.* México, D.F., 1982.

United Nations, Food and Agriculture Organization, *El henequen mexicano.* New York, 1968.

United Nations, Food and Agriculture Organization, Committee on Commodity Problems. *Report of the Eleventh Session of the Intergovernmental Group on Hard Fibers.* New York, 1976.

MISCELLANEOUS

Cordemex. *Henequen y sisal producción mundial.* Mérida, 1977.
_____. *Informe anual de Cordemex.* Mérida, 1974; 1976; 1977.
_____. *Seis años de labores.* Mérida, 1976.
_____. *Sesión del consejo de administración de Cordemex.* Mérida, January 1978; May 1978; March 1980; September 1982.
Diario de Yucatán (Mérida).
El Excelsior (México, D.F.).
El Fronterizo (Ciudad Juárez).
Novedades de Yucatán (Mérida).

Index